In this era when so much concern has arisen about Indigenous health, Brian McCoy is to be congratulated for his thoughtful and illuminating exploration of the ways in which Western Desert men themselves understand and engage with health and well-being. I read this book with great interest for its ethnographic sensitivity and depth of engagement. McCoy's consideration of the discourse of kanyirninpa — or 'holding' — and its centrality in the development of male personhood contributes significantly both to our basic knowledge of these communities and also to the ways in which historical events have affected the inter- and intra-generational relationships in which men's lives are organized and expressed.

Fred Myers
Silver Professor of Anthropology, New York University

I was incredibly moved when I read *Holding Men: Kanyirninpa and the health of Aboriginal men.* It is rare for an academic work to so sensitively and poignantly capture the social realities for Aboriginal men growing up in contemporary desert communities. An intellectual work of considerable compassion, it grows from many decades of living and working in remote Australia and presents us with the intellectual apparatus to understand the dimension of the inter-generational processes which have the potential to both enable Aboriginal men to realize their potential as well as reproduce the social dislocation that is so fundamental to Aboriginal disadvantage. Petrol sniffing, Australian Rules football and imprisonment continue to impact the lives of desert men. Each one discloses the power, fragility and potential of kanyirninpa. Kanyirninpa is a concept that encapsulates both cultural authority and nurturing. It provides an insight into the ways in which Aboriginal men can be 'held' and strengthened through their journey to adulthood.

Ian Anderson
Professor of Indigenous Health, The University of Melbourne

Holding Men

Kanyirninpa and the health of Aboriginal men

Brian F McCoy

Aboriginal
Studies
Press

First published in 2008
by Aboriginal Studies Press

Aboriginal Studies Press
is the publishing arm of the
Australian Institute of Aboriginal
and Torres Strait Islander Studies
GPO Box 553, Canberra, ACT 2601
Phone: (61 2) 6246 1183
Fax: (61 2) 6261 4288
Email: asp@aiatsis.gov.au
Web: www.aiatsis.gov.au/aboriginal_studies_press

National Library of Australia
Cataloguing-In-Publication data:

Author: McCoy, Brian Francis
Title: Holding Men: Kanyirninpa and the health of Aboriginal
men / author, Brian F. McCoy.
Publisher: Canberra: Aboriginal Studies Press, 2008.
ISBN: 9780855756581 (pbk.)

Notes: Includes index.
Bibliography.

Subjects: Aboriginal Australians—Health and hygiene—Western Australia
—Kimberley. Young men—Health and hygiene—Western Australia—
Kimberley. Aboriginal Australians—Western Australia—Kimberley. Social
life and customs, interpersonal relations—Western Australia—Kimberley.
Aboriginal Australians—Western Australia—Kimberley. Ethnic identity.
Petrol sniffing—Western Australia. Men—Health and hygiene—Western
Australia. Prisoners, Aboriginal Australian—Western Australia. Australian
football.

Dewey Number: 362.849915

Index compiled by Michael Harrington
Printed in Australia by Ligare Pty Ltd

Contents

Illustrations

Figures

Illustrations (colour plates between pages 110–111)

Acknowledgments

There is no word in the Kukatja language that easily translates the English word 'acknowledge'. *Maninypuwa*, has been translated as 'praise' or 'give thanks' and is possibly closest to the English word 'respect'. When saying at the beginning of this book: *Maninypunginparnatjananya Puntu Wirrimanutjanu, Malarntjanu, Kururrungkutjanu kamu Yaka Yakatjanu*, I wish to do more than simply acknowledge the desert people of the four Kimberley communities of Wirrimanu, Malarn, Kururrungku and Yaka Yaka. I owe much to those whose lives and stories lie at the heart of this book. They have enriched my life enormously over the years as they have lived and expressed those values and relationships expressed by *kanyirninpa*. I would particularly like to pay respect and give thanks to them.

I would like also to acknowledge and also thank the agencies that work in the Kutjungka region for their co-operation and hospitality over many years. In particular, the Palyalatju Maparnpa Aboriginal Corporation Health Committee, the Kutjungka Catholic Parish, the Wirrumanu Adult Education Centre, the Wirrimanu, Malarn, Kururrungku and Yaka Yaka Community Offices and Councils, the Luurnpa, Kururrungku and John Pujajangka-Piyirn Schools, and Warlayirti Artists.

I am particularly grateful to those who have mentored and guided me in the process of research. In particular, I acknowledge Professor Ian Anderson, Dr Kim Humphery, Associate Professor Marilys Guillemin, Associate Professor Martha McIntyre and those associated with the Centre for Health and Society and Onemda VicHealth Koori Health Unit at The University of Melbourne.

In addition, I was fortunate to have received the advice of a number of Aboriginal people outside the desert region who guided me through that time of research. They included Associate Professor Jacinta Elston, Pat Dodson, Mark Saunders, Sharijn King and Gregory Phillips.

I am grateful to the National Health and Medical Research Council (NHMRC) and the Australian Institute for Aboriginal and Torres Strait Islander Studies (AIATSIS) who provided me with scholarships to support my fieldwork. I am grateful to the Cooperative Research Centre for Aboriginal Health (CRCAH) who accepted my work as in-kind and have supported the transfer and dissemination of its findings. I am particularly grateful to Rhonda Black, Gabby Lhuede and Janet Hutchinson at Aboriginal Studies Press for guiding this work through to publication.

I wish also to acknowledge my family in Melbourne who have been constant, generous and faithful supporters of my efforts as well as my Jesuit family and the Newman College extension of it.

However, none of this book would have been possible without the many Aboriginal and Torres Strait Islander people who have patiently loved and taught me over the years. They, like the desert people, have taught me the depth and power of what it means to be held and what it might mean for older men to hold and look after those who follow.

This book is dedicated to the many Aboriginal and Torres Strait Islander men and women who have befriended me over the years, and to the many we have lost, too young and far too early.

Note regarding quotations and paintings

Extracts from a number of interviews and conversations conducted in the Kutjungka region between 2001–04 are quoted in this book. They are presented as (R) being myself and (A), (B) and (C) as the person(s) speaking. Sometimes, as in the beginning of some chapters or during chapters, direct quotes are offered. Unless specifically referenced all such quotations come from interviews and conversations during this same period of time.

For reasons that are further explained in the Introduction, those who are speaking are not identified. However, full copies of the original work and interviews can be found in the archives at the Australian Institute of Aboriginal and Torres Strait Islander Studies (AIATSIS) in Canberra.

Also, a number of paintings were offered as part of this work and some of them are reproduced here. The artists' names have been mentioned only when permission to do so was granted. Similarly, with the names of anyone deceased.

Note on orthography and word usage

There are some terms that are used in this book that may be spelt or understood differently in other sources or places. They will be explained in greater detail in the following chapters. At this point, however, some initial explanation of the terms used throughout this work is necessary.

The region that includes the four communities mentioned I refer to as the Kutjungka region. These four communities have been variously known by different names, sometimes with different spellings: Wirrumanu or Wirrimanu (previously known as Balgo, Balgo Mission, Balgo Hills), Mulan or Malarn or Malan (Lake Gregory), Kururrungku (Billiluna or Mindibungu) and Yaka Yaka or Yagga Yagga. I have sought advice from people within the region regarding the most appropriate spellings and will follow the orthography used for the Kukatja language. I refer to Wirrimanu, Malarn, Kururrungku and Yaka Yaka.

When I am using Kukatja words, or words from another Aboriginal language, for the first time in each chapter I will place a brief English translation in brackets (see glossary for further information).

Specifically, I will use the word *Puntu* to refer to the Aboriginal people of this desert region, similar to the use of Anangu in Pitjantjatjara. I will use the word *wati* (initiated man) to refer to men who are considered as adult. I will use the words 'Aboriginal' or 'Indigenous' when I am referring to Aboriginal and Torres Strait Islander people who live outside this particular region. I will use the word *kartiya* to refer to non-Aboriginal people.

Due to the importance of the Kukatja word and concept *kanyirninpa* within this book, I will provide the appropriate English words when they are being used to translate this particular meaning of *kanyirninpa*, such as 'hold', 'held' and 'holding'.

There are some words I will use that can possess several meanings, depending on their context, such as the English words 'family', 'community' and 'law'.

The word *walytja*, translated from Kukatja as 'one's own, relatives', I will use to refer to *Puntu* who are closely related through kinship. In English the word 'family' can be used to translate *walytja* but in this book use of the word *walytja* refers to kindred, a much broader social inter-connectedness and relatedness than is usually meant by the English word family (see glossary).

When I use the word 'community' I am referring to one of the four geographical and identifiable localities within the region: Wirrimanu, Malarn, Kururrungku and Yaka Yaka.

The English word 'law' can refer to both the principles and regulations of the Australian legal system and also *Puntu* law, the principles and regulations that have been handed down from the ancestral *tjukurrpa* and which determine social and religious behaviour. When using the word in this latter meaning I will refer to it as the Law.

Glossary

The majority of the following words are Kukatja and come from *A Basic Kukatja to English Dictionary* (1993), edited by Hilaire Valiquette and based on earlier linguistic work by Fr Anthony R. Peile. In some cases, alternative spellings, additional words and contemporary meanings are offered.

kantjilyi	bush raisins
kanyila	to have; keep; hold; give birth to; have (young); wear
kartiya	a non-Aboriginal person; also the white colour of bands or stripes on a reptile
kipara	bush turkey; Australian bustard
kukurr(pa)	evil spirit
kumpupatja	bush tomato
kumunytjayi	used instead of a taboo name (the actual name or a word close to the name of the person who has died)
kurlarta	long spear
kurnta	1) shame; sense of shame; 2) respectful; 3) embarrassed; 4) shy; coy; 5) uneasy (ref. cattle)
kurrun(pa)	1) spirit; 2) life principle; life-essence
kurta	brother; any male, same skin
kutjarra	1) two; 2) counting number two
kutjungka	of the same kind, and 1) at the one time; 2) for the last time

lalka or larlka	1) dry; 2) healthy; 3) past menopause
luurn(pa)	red-backed kingfisher (*halcyon pyrrhopygia*)
mama	father; father's brother
mamangku	your father; used in reference to a priest
mamu	1) evil spirit; 2) devil (in Christian religion)
maparn(pa)	traditional doctor; healer
marlpa	1) companion; 2) friend
marlurlu	novice; boy who has been initiated; * boy who is to be initiated; who brings others to his initiation
marnti	boy
marra	1) catch; get; 2) handle; grasp; 3) deal with; 4) make do; 5) take, bring; 6) give birth to
mawuntu	white ochre, rock or powder
milpiny(pa)	1) fingernail; toenail; 2) hoof; 3) claw of an animal
mimi	1) sick; 2) incapacitated by illness; 3) having a wound; 4) having pain; 5) reddening of the skin from fire or sun; 6) dead or unconscious; drunk; 7) sick, diseased; 8) inoperative
mirri	1) very sick person; 2) corpse; 3) an unconscious person or animal; 4) person who is exhausted or drunk; 5) sick; 6) beyond repair (ref. vehicle)
muntuny(pa)	children's python
murrungkurr	tree spirit
murtu	red ochre; see pilytji
ngalula	1) chase; 2) catch; 3) hold on tightly
ngampurr(pa)	1) caution; careful; 2) care; concern
ngampurrmarra	care for, take care of: see ngampurr and marra
ngarpu	Walmajarri: father; used as a term for God
ngawitji	husband's brother or wife's sister
ngawu	1) bad; evil; 2) not functioning normally on account of sickness, cold, injury or pain; 3) poisonous

ngawurna	I am getting sick
ngurra	1) camp; 2) country; 3) one's place
nyamu	1) finished; ended; 2) stop; 3) already
nyangu-la	they saw (nyawa = see, look at, watch)
nyurnu	1) sick; 2) slightly sick
palya	1) good, correct, beautiful; 2) healthy; 3) happy
palyalarni	make me well
palyalatju maparn(pa)	good health for all
panytji	wife's brother
parnku	cousin
patarla	skirt
pilali, pirlarli or pularli	* name given to the brothers and sisters of the tjamparti by the family of the one who has been initiated; also name given by the tjamparti to the family of the marlurlu
pilytji	red ochre; see murtu
puntu	1) human being; 2) Aboriginal person; 3) male; 4) adult male; 5) wife's brother; 6) a young unmarried man or a boy who has left school; 7) familiar term of address among young men. * can refer to a young man who has been through the first stage of initiation but is not yet a wati
punturringu	[he] became a man
pura	bush tomato
tali	sandhill
tilitja	* related to the deceased or initiate as kurta, tjurtu and parnku; they ensure the ceremonies are conducted properly
tingari	dreamtime hero(es)
tjamparti	promised bride. * those who perform the initiation on the marlurlu
tjamu	father's father

tjanu	from (postposition)
tjapu tjapu	1) ball; 2) football
tjarrampari	perenty goanna
tjarrtjurra or tjaatjurra	* women's healing
tjiitju	Jesus
tjirlpi	old man
tjitji or tjiitji	child; baby; offspring (male or female)
tjukurr(pa) (+ tjukurrta)	1) dreaming; 2) dreamtime (the ancestral or origin period of present-day society, landscape, customs etc.)
tjurni	1) stomach; 2) abdomen; 3) uterus; 4) the ovary of reptiles and birds; 5) arch of the foot, instep; 6) middle section of a trunk; 7) seat of the emotions
tjurta	sister; any female, same skin
tutju	1) female (human and non-human); 2) woman; girl
walytja	1) one's own; 2) relatives; 3) sense of identity with, relatedness to other people; 4) each other; 5) one; only
wati	initiated male, adult man
watirringu	[he] became a full man
wayirnuwatji, wayinwatji (+ wayirntatji)	chain-possessing, policeman
wikarrutja	* group of men who accompany the marlurlu
wiya	no
yalpurru	* those who are initiated together; in recent times to name those who share the same birthday; term used more by men
yalta	1) cold; 2) healthy; 3) better; well; 4) happy
yangka	* isn't that so? Often used at the end of a sentence

yarnangu, (+ yanangu)	1) body; 2) somebody; anybody; group of people; 3) stem, trunk of plant; 4) body of cloud; 5) flesh; 6) meat, flesh of fruit
yarnangurringu	* [that person] became an adult
yarnangurriwa	* literally, 'body-person-becoming'; a person who is growing into adulthood, both physically and socially
yipi	mother; mother's sister
yirrkapiri or yirrkapirri	* related to the deceased or initiate as the principal mourners; nyupa (spouse), yipi, mama, kamuru (uncle), pimirri (aunt). They are not actively involved in organising the ceremonies.
yumari	wife's mother
yurrka	spinifex
yuwayi	yes

The euphonic suffix '- pa' is often added to words ending in a consonant, e.g. tjukurrpa, maparnpa, kurrunpa.

* refers to words that are used today within the Kutjungka region but not found in *A Basic Kukatja to English Dictionary.*

+ refers to words found in William McGregor, *Handbook of Kimberley Languages, Volume 2, Word Lists*, Australian Institute of Aboriginal and Torres Strait Islander Studies, Canberra, 1992; some words are spelt differently from Valiquette and Peile.

Abbreviations

ABC	Australian Broadcasting Commission
ABS	Australian Bureau of Statistics
AFL	Australian Football League
AIATSIS	Australian Institute of Aboriginal and Torres Strait Islander Studies
ALS	Aboriginal Legal Service
ATSIC	Aboriginal and Torres Strait Islander Council
CDEP	Community Development Employment Programme (or Project)
CEO	Catholic Education Office
DIA	Department of Indigenous Affairs (Western Australia)
HDWA	Department of Health, Western Australia
IAD	Institute for Aboriginal Development
ISMA	Institute of Sisters of Mercy Australia
KAMSC	Kimberley Aboriginal Medical Service Council
KPHU	Kimberley Public Health Unit
MCHS	Mercy Community Health Service
NHMRC	National Health and Medical Research Council
PMACHC	Palyalatju Maparnpa Aboriginal Corporation Health Committee
PTSD	Post traumatic stress disorder
RCIADIC	Royal Commission into Aboriginal Deaths in Custody
RFDS	Royal Flying Doctor Service

Abbreviations

SROWA   State Records Office of Western Australia
STD   Sexually Transmitted Disease
STI   Sexually Transmitted Infection
WA   Western Australia
WMC   Well Men's Checks

Introduction

We were sitting together in a remote Kimberley community, five of us, watching people as they went in and out of the local store: an old man, his wife, her sister, the couple's eldest daughter and myself. They had been talking about the old days and how things had changed.

The daughter took up the conversation: in her view young people no longer had respect for older people. Women were now stronger as men were often in prison and the authority of older men was no longer evident. No longer were they considered the head of the family household. No longer did young people listen to them.

I was sitting on the red desert earth listening to her as she and the others spoke. It was a warm winter's day and the family was content to talk as people moved around them and did their shopping. She stressed the importance of young people needing to have 'respect' for older people and the serious responsibilities older people had to look after those that lived with them. 'They would be held to account,' she said, 'for what the young people did': if the young person did something wrong the adult person could get punished and get sick. This was because the older person was considered as 'holding' the younger person. They were responsible for them.

As she talked I noticed that partially embedded in the ground in front of me was a marble, a small, round object of play that a child had left. I lifted it up, felt its texture and weight, and pondered its place within the palm of my hand. I started to wonder what the daughter meant by this English word 'holding', how it seemed to include elements of care and responsibility, and what it might mean for the health of young Aboriginal men.

It was that moment, when I sat outside the community store, held the marble in my hand and listened as people spoke, that my understanding of Aboriginal people and their culture shifted significantly. As I came to explore more fully the contemporary desert meaning of the Kukatja word 'kanyirninpa', often translated into English by the word 'holding', I began to take a very different approach to Aboriginal health.

This book is focused on the stories and experiences of desert men who live in a remote part of Western Australia. While the poor health of Aboriginal people has been well documented, we actually know little about Aboriginal men and how they perceive well-being and illness. We also know little about those deeper values that have sustained, and continue to sustain, desert people's health.

The Kutjungka region is situated in the south-east region of the Kimberley. It lies on the north-eastern edge of the Great Sandy Desert and on the western edge of the Tanami Desert. The largely unsealed Tanami Road, sometimes called a 'track', links the region with Halls Creek in the north and Alice Springs in the south-east, a total distance of approximately 1000 kilometres. This connecting road between Western Australia and the Northern Territory provides a corridor of movement between the Aboriginal communities of the region as well as a bridge to other Aboriginal communities in Western Australia and the Northern Territory. The region exists as an important 'gateway' for Aboriginal culture and kartiya tourists between Western Australia and the Northern Territory. This book has arisen out of a long-term relationship that I have shared with the people of this region, a relationship of more than thirty years. It was from this relationship, and from relationships with other Aboriginal people, that my interest and motivation to explore men's health arose.

In 1973 I first arrived in the Kimberley as a lay missionary for the Catholic Diocese of Broome. I was a Jesuit seminarian at the time and had just completed an undergraduate degree at Melbourne University. The bishop had invited myself and another Jesuit colleague to work at Balgo Mission to administer the boys'

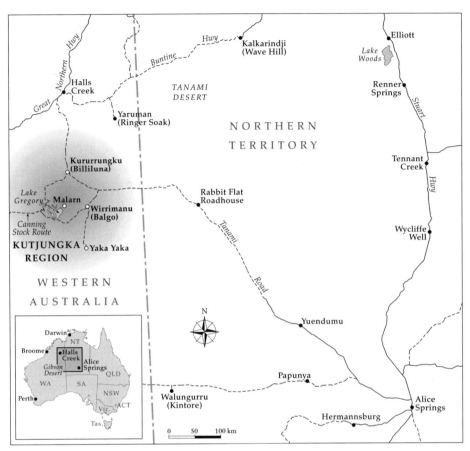

The Kutjungka region within Western Australia

dormitory. At that time, more than forty boys, aged from 5 to 15 years, lived together full-time in a corrugated iron building within the Mission. I spent one year in the community and then returned to Melbourne to continue my training. I revisited the region over the following years and accompanied some of the men to the 'hand-over' of Uluru to Anangu in 1985. In 1990 I also conducted research with some of the men as part of the Western Australian component of the Royal Commission into Aboriginal Deaths in Custody. Finally, in 1992 I was asked to return to the region in a formal church capacity as parish priest. While much had changed since 1973, and the community had been handed over to Puntu control in 1984, I followed a tradition of more than five decades of Catholic church involvement in this region. I arrived in the Kutjungka region in late 1992 and stayed there until April 2000.

In the more than seven years that I lived in the Kutjungka region in the 1990s I found myself being increasingly drawn into the culture of the people and issues around men's lives and health. Prison, court, petrol sniffing, music, football and hunting formed an increasing part of the realities I had to deal with, and issues that most interested me. I discovered, as I had with other Aboriginal men, great friendship, energy and humour in being with them. Between 1992–2000 I shared in around a hundred funerals, a number of them involving tragic and premature deaths of men and women. During this same period of time there was an increasing involvement by myself, and some other kartiyas, in the ceremonies around cultural 'sorry business' (Koning et al. 2000).

Puntu use these ceremonies in response to a person's death and they can take several weeks. Often the family of the deceased move out of their house to a 'sorry camp' where they refrain from eating certain foods and participate in ritual 'sorry meetings'. At these meetings, where white ochre (mawuntu) is put on the face and upper body of mourners, people express their grief and sorrow in very public, formal and demonstrative ways. The kartiya, and wider church acceptance of these rituals, led to significant changes in the ways in which Westernised Catholic funerals were formally conducted.

Learning to live more closely with the Puntu of the region, and beginning to see more of life through their eyes and experiences, led to a significant moment when the older men took me into their ceremonial Law. This only occurred after some years of living in the region, and was principally influenced by several strong and trusting relationships I had formed with men during that time.

My entry into the world of men's secret and sacred 'business' invited me into a new and deeper relationship with the people, especially the men. And while this book does not reveal any of the elements of this men's business, it acknowledges the trust and generosity of men, many older and some younger, who have taken, watched and guided me in their Law. My experience of men's Law has affected the writing of this book. One of my closest Aboriginal friends and advisors once commented about kartiyas who enter the Law, 'you trust him more than you trust other kartiya cause you know he's been there, he's seen it and he's not telling anyone'. My experience of Puntu trust has formed an important part of the motivation, process and method in my attempts to understand men's lives and health more deeply. It has influenced the ethical process and a desire that the work I do be accessible, accountable and beneficial.

Apart from the Kutjungka region I have lived and worked with other Aboriginal people in Victoria, Western Australia, North Queensland and the Northern Territory since the late 1960s. However, I decided to approach the Puntu of the Kutjungka region to research with the men for this work. Not only had I known the desert people over a long period of time but in those years we had shared much. The opportunities that arose from such a long and sustaining relationship offered the possibility of research that could be beneficial to them and, hopefully, other Aboriginal men. However, my own particular history with Puntu raised a number of ethical issues around the appropriateness of my doing health research in this particular location.

I was a kartiya, male and had been involved with Puntu in a church capacity. Apart from my gender and cultural background, was it possible to put aside a church role and perform health research? Some kartiyas did not believe so. They maintained that it was not appropriate to change roles from being a priest to being a health researcher and that my return would cause 'confusion' among the people. There was also a further ethical issue in relation to the regional health service, as I had worked as a volunteer St John Ambulance First Aid Instructor and Ambulance Officer during my years in the desert. I was asked whether, as a health researcher, I would be available to assist either the church or health agencies while I was doing this research. My initial response was to avoid carefully any blurring of roles. I sought the advice of the Palyalatju Maparnpa Aboriginal Corporation Health Committee (PMACHC), the regional Aboriginal health organisation. PMACHC had been incorporated in 1995 through the assistance of the Mercy Community Health Service (MCHS) who, at that time, held the WA State Government contract to provide clinic services within the Kutjungka region. PMACHC was established with the goal of becoming a community-based Aboriginal health service.

I also sought the advice of Aboriginal people outside the region who had been involved in health and research issues. They pointed out to me that my history suggested that research could be done but only within the context of contemporary desert life and the relationships I had formed with Puntu over the years. In the Kutjungka region Puntu had little choice over the services that were available to them, and I would need to work with some flexibility if church or health needs arose and local Puntu sought my assistance. And this was finally agreed. Ironically, it proved to be the area of health and not church business that would claim attention while I was doing research. Twice during my fieldwork, nurses absented themselves from Wirrimanu itself, and on one occasion from the region, and Puntu, particularly health workers, sought assistance from me during those times.

Puntu appeared to be less concerned with my change of role than kartiyas, some of whom seemed more concerned about my new relationship with the people than the proposed research. As three of my field trips coincided with the summer and men's ceremony time it was easier to move and identify with the men during those times. There were occasions when Puntu acknowledged a difference in my new role. On one occasion a community chairperson suggested that when visiting their community I reside somewhere within the community and not use school accommodation, as I had done in the past. To him it was important that I be seen as working with the whole community and not within the context of the school and its association with the Catholic church (all schools in the region are conducted by the Catholic Education Office). In another community the chairperson advised me to use the accommodation that was close to the school but available to all visitors. I was also advised to base myself at Wirrimanu as it was the largest of the communities and was perceived by some to have 'more problems' with its young people than the smaller communities. A number of women were very supportive of my work. They often expressed concern for the well-being of their young men and were pleased that I was returning to work with them. The older men were particularly glad when I attended Law ceremonies, and the younger men were happy that I had a vehicle in which they could go hunting, or which could be used to take them to other communities for family visits, football or for Law.

As I performed the research I took notice of how people addressed me. Sometimes I was called the more traditional mamangku, 'your father', as the English word 'father' had become kumunytjayi some years previously.[1] More often, I found myself being called by my designated kinship name, tjangala, or the relationship Puntu had with those who were tjangala (see Appendix, p. 226). Hence, I could be called panytji (brother-in-law), kurta (brother), parnku (cousin) and other relational names. The flexibility and creativity of people in relation to how they positioned themselves to me was well exemplified by a Nakamarra, one of my many kinship 'mothers-in-law'. She was my yumari, a relationship that would usually invite my avoidance, being her 'son-in-law'.

After I had gone through men's Law she came to me and said that because I had become a wati, I deserved greater respect. When her father died some years before, a wise and knowledgeable old man whom I called tjamu (grandfather), the family actively drew me for the first time into the rituals around sorry business. Now, through ceremonial Law, I had entered even more fully into her family and culture (her sister's son, my panytji, had looked after me when I first went into men's Law and was one of my closest friends and cultural mentors). Her comment about deserving further respect did not mean, as I was wondering, that we would have less contact or conversation. In fact, she maintained, this change in respect towards me ensured that we could continue to meet and talk. She had discussed this with the old men who had confirmed this, she reassured me. Such flexibility not only challenged my notions of 'fixed' kinship behaviour but reinforced the value Puntu placed on long-term relationships.

Eric Kolig, who performed research among the Walmajarri, once noted what it was like to be a male, and European, researcher:

> Even though I was supposed to act and behave like all Djangala (sic) men, and work with them, I was generously permitted to move fairly freely among other groups and to observe them closely. Here my being a European gave me an advantage that would have been denied to an Aboriginal of my age, sex, social status, and subsection affiliation. (Kolig 1981, p. xi)

Kolig's ability to 'move freely', he suggested, arose because he was European. He was not subject to the same demands or restrictions of age, gender and kinship. That was only partly applicable in my situation. I had for some years encountered Puntu when they were sick, their family was in the clinic, or they were awaiting evacuation to hospital by the Royal Flying Doctor Service (RFDS). I had witnessed deaths within communities, ritual payback, and been part of the preparation and memorial of an earlier massacre (Purrkuji) (Howard & Luby, 1999). I had shared in sporting carnivals, hunting trips, marriages, birthday celebrations and many other occasions when people gathered and enjoyed each other's company. I had come to learn a lot about Puntu and they also had come to know a lot about me. They had significantly shaped our relationship. My ability to move rather freely among men, but also among a number of women, had developed as a consequence of many formal and informal shared occasions over several decades.

Fred Myers performed research among the Pintupi in the early 1970s and admitted his difficulty in obtaining information from women:

> Although I had intended to study women as thoroughly as men, in my initial fieldwork I was unable to do so. In the Pintupi view, men do not socialize alone with women, except with their wives and mothers. Therefore, I talked with women only in the presence of their male relatives and this unfortunately did not allow me to collect data from them in any systematic or extensive way. In subsequent field trips, when I was accompanied by my wife, it was possible for me to spend much more time with women. The imbalance of my work was partially rectified, but I would certainly hesitate to regard it as definitive on Pintupi women's point of view. (Myers 1986, p. 298)

The gendered and separate worlds of the Pintupi in the 1970s, and that of the Kutjungka region in the 1990s and more recently, possess some similarities. A man does not generally socialise with a woman, especially if either of them is married or they share a more formal kinship relationship. However, because of the reasons mentioned previously, I have found myself able to move freely among a number of women. My kinship cousins (parnku), mothers (yipi), wife's sisters (ngawitji) and others have often sat with me, sometimes with other women, to talk about community or other issues. My sisters (tjurtu) have also been very supportive. While the relationship between sisters and brothers (kurta) becomes more formal as they become adults, a number of tjurtu have been both valuable friends and advisors. My involvement in the lives of the men has assisted in providing the trust and communication that a number of women have afforded me. While clearly remaining a kartiya I have found that the relationships Puntu have afforded me over the years have significantly shifted me from within my own culture to live and move far more easily within theirs.

The freedom I have experienced to move around the four different communities, and share in ceremonies and other activities, did not preclude the fact that people had come to know me as a priest who exercised power within a particular church tradition. The Catholic church was among the first group of kartiyas who encountered the desert peoples of the south-east Kimberley in the 1930s leading to the formation of Balgo Mission. The desert people's first encounter with me was through the dormitory system that was in a process of transition in 1973 and which I helped to administer. The effects of modernity upon desert people cannot be easily separated from a relatively recent mission history, or from particular aspects of it, such as the dormitory system. Nor can it be separated from the missionaries who held power over the lives of people for more than four decades.

When I first came to Balgo Mission in 1973, Fr Ray Hevern, priest and superintendent at that time, held substantial power over the lives of all who lived there. He administered and managed a community of Puntu in a most remote part of Australia. He was not expected to learn any of the local languages or understand the culture. His authority gave him control over the health, rations, work and movement of all who lived there. He could have people removed from the community, just as he could prevent people entering it. He employed almost all kartiya staff and was responsible for the wages given to Puntu. In addition, he was also the minister who performed regular church ceremonies, including marriages and funerals. The priest, at that time, held enormous social, economic, religious and political power.

In this book I cannot avoid the context of my own church and health-related activities, especially in this region in the 1990s. Nor can I deny my church background and Jesuit training. It is not my intention to discuss in detail the missiology of either the Catholic church or the other Christian churches that have had significant influence in this region. Nor is it my intention to examine the Catholic church influence and presence in the parish, schools and health service. However, I do want to examine how the early mission was established and how particular mission values and emphases influenced the health of later generations of Puntu. In this context I am aware I am presenting critical reflections of past church policies and behaviour — policies and behaviour that have affected my own work, attitudes and relationships with Puntu. Thus, this work includes, to some extent, a level of self criticism and consideration of my own past attitudes and practices.

When I took up a role as health researcher my power, compared with my role as parish priest, diminished significantly. My research depended on the availability of people, their disposition at a particular time and the information they chose to give or not to give. Over the years I had become more aware of the ways in which Puntu, subtly and skilfully, indicated their desire to postpone, avoid or decline requests. In addition, my place of accommodation was always uncertain and required negotiation on each field trip. I needed to gather research within the parameters of sorry business, Law ceremonies and sporting carnivals, each of which focused individual and communal energies at particular times. Clearly, as a researcher, I was in a very different social position than I had been previously. I was dependent on whether men wanted to talk and in what context. Without denying that I continued to exercise power as a kartiya researcher, the change in my social position was significant. Not only did it enable Puntu to shape further the reciprocal nature of our relationship, but it also provided opportunities for Puntu to share their concerns and beliefs about health and many other matters, when and as they preferred.

I visited the desert in June 2001 to get permission from PMACHC to perform research and to explore with them a wide range of ethical issues and research methods. While clear guidelines for conducting research within Indigenous communities became increasingly available (VicHealth 2000; VicHealth 2001; AIATSIS 2002; NHMRC 2003), developing the research within this desert region offered its own challenges. PMACHC had formally existed since 1994 but this was the first occasion that a kartiya had sought permission from them to do research. It was also the first time that collaborative research involving a researcher and themselves had been proposed. Despite receiving their approval, I was unable to work closely with them as government funding for PMACHC was suspended at the end of 2001. In 2002 a consultancy firm reviewed PMACHC and recommended that government funding recommence, and in late 2003, as my research was coming to an end, a new coordinator was appointed.

Despite the suspension of PMACHC I returned late in 2001 to begin research. I came to this study concerned about the status of Aboriginal men's health, wondering if theories of trauma might help illuminate the underlying causes of their precarious health and the high number of premature deaths.

Since the mid-1990s a number of Aboriginal leaders, researchers and others have used the term trauma to describe and explain Aboriginal historical and present experience. Pat Swan and Beverley Raphael's "*Ways Forward*": *National Consultancy Report on Aboriginal and Torres Strait Islander Mental Health* identified 'trauma and grief' as 'one of the significant and frequent problems identified by Aboriginal people' (Swan & Raphael 1995, p. 41). This trauma and grief, they suggested,

> relates to the history of invasion, the ongoing impact of colonisation, loss of land and culture, high rates of premature mortality, high levels of incarceration, high levels of family separations, particularly those consequent upon the forced separation of children and parents, and also Aboriginal Deaths in Custody. Domestic violence, sexual and physical abuse, and a whole range of other traumas also contribute. Sexual assault is considered to be very frequent and traumatic. (p. 41)

A link between the trauma of history and present experience was made by *Bringing Them Home* where this report referred to 'the trauma of forcible separation' (National Inquiry 1997, p. 212). The report linked the experience of trauma to that of 'profound disadvantages…including exclusion and control, racism and poverty which would have acted as severe stresses compounding grief and trauma' (p. 214).

Bain Attwood has argued that the Aboriginal experience of colonisation 'can and should be called a holocaust given the scale of loss and the trauma that has been suffered' (Attwood 2000, p. 258). Ernest Hunter has quoted Noel Pearson in identifying and distinguishing two types of trauma afflicting Aboriginal communities: the first as personal and immediate, the second as something that people have inherited (Hunter 2001). He has also argued that Aboriginal experiences of suicide, unemployment, violence, adult and juvenile arrest and many other events, 'may be seen as the psychosocial sequelae of traumatisation' (Hunter 1998, p. 10).

However, within the discipline of psychology, the concept of trauma has only occasionally been used in relation to Aboriginal experience. Pat Dudgeon et al.'s *Working with Indigenous Australians: A Handbook for Psychologists* rarely refers to trauma and does not mention post-traumatic stress disorder (PTSD) (Dudgeon et al. 2000). While acknowledging 'a story of invasion, genocide, misunderstanding, oppression, marginalisation and displacement', they do not describe or interpret the Aboriginal experience in either trauma or PTSD terms (Dudgeon & Pickett 2000, p. 83). The Australian Psychological Society's 2003 publication *Guidelines for the Provision of Psychological Services for and the Conduct of Psychological Research with Aboriginal and Torres Strait Islander People of Australia* does not use the word trauma at all (Australian Psychological Society 2003). Hence psychologists, while acknowledging the range and enormity of highly stressful events in Aboriginal people's lives, largely do not use trauma as a concept to describe or understand Aboriginal experience across generations or within generations.

In 2002 Judy Atkinson's *Trauma Trails, Recreating Song Lines: The Transgenerational Effects of Trauma in Indigenous Australia* explored the 'links between the child, adolescent and adult experiences of violence' (Atkinson 2002, p. 146). She proposed a distinction between intergenerational and transgenerational trauma: the former referring to what has been passed from one generation to the next, the latter referring to what has been transmitted across generations.

Despite some areas of psychological research where the concept of trauma has not been consistently or universally adopted, in less than a decade various and quite powerful perspectives of trauma, as it might apply within an Aboriginal context, have been proposed. They have included the trauma of a colonised history, the trauma of separation, trauma related to loss and grief, and ongoing events that add to trauma that has already been experienced. Trauma has been used to cover a wide field of personal suffering and communal experience. Analogous to a genetically inherited condition, trauma has also been understood as being handed down from one generation to the next. In many representations, narratives and discourses trauma has become a metaphor for what Noel Pearson has described as 'the sheer psychological toll which the Settlement pillar of White Australia has had on a people for most of Australia's colonial history' (Pearson 1995, p. 21).

The word 'trauma' comes from the Greek for 'wound' and can be traced back to the writings of Greek historians, such as Herodotus, around 500 BC. While the word referred principally to the physical wound a soldier might receive in battle, it also had other meanings such as the damage done to ships, defeat in war and an indictment for wounding when one had intended murder. It was not until late in the nineteenth century that a wider understanding of trauma was accepted. What Judith Herman has described as 'episodic amnesia', namely discourses involving the psychological phenomena of trauma, have only appeared in the past 150 years. Hysteria associated with women, shell shock (combat neurosis), and sexual and domestic violence were later, after the Vietnam War, followed by post-traumatic stress disorder (PTSD). In 1980, PTSD was included in the American Association's Diagnostic and Statistical Manual of Mental Disorders (DSM-III).

Not only have a number of Aboriginal researchers used the concept of trauma to describe Aboriginal experiences, but theories around trauma have seemed to provide helpful constructs to explain the effects of colonial experience. However, in the process of the research I intentionally put these theories aside, preferring to hear how men understood and constructed their own notions about well-being and the ways in which they understood the Western medical concept of 'health'. I wanted to hear how they envisioned the ideal of young men growing into adult men and how they enacted such ideals within a contemporary community and desert existence. Their beliefs, concerns and hopes for their health, and those of the younger generation of men, have been largely unknown, especially to Western health providers. However, near the end of this book

I return to the construct of trauma and explore its applicability in the light of what I learned. As I listened to Puntu talk about men's health, and as the concept of kanyirninpa emerged, I was able to bring my understanding of this back to Puntu for their comment, confirmation and correction. I was able to compare and contrast their use and understanding of this concept with a similar use and understanding offered by Myers among the Pintupi in the 1970s and Ralph Folds in 2001. My four research trips varied from one to three months in duration and were spread over more than two years.

In seeking to be more attentive to what men believed and experienced, I needed a flexible and open research method that enabled their voice to be heard. Hence, while interviews provided the initial and primary source of data, the provision of paintings by men provided an alternative and important form of expression. Returning for a number of field trips also enabled men to revisit their earlier interviews and paintings and confirm, add to or correct what they had earlier said or what I had previously understood. Some of the young petrol sniffers also took photos and, while they are not included in this book, they provided another form of expression that served to sharpen and strengthen the voice of young and old within the region.

While I speak and understand some Kukatja, the majority of my interviews were conducted in English. Most of my informants chose to speak in English and only one chose to speak for most of their interview in Kukatja. Usually, people spoke in English interspersed with some Kukatja. As English has become the language of communication with kartiyas, both within the region and elsewhere, it has also become the language that is used with other Puntu who do not speak Kukatja. Obviously, speaking in English offered many advantages for myself as a researcher, but it also offered an insight into how people understood English words and concepts when translating key Kukatja ideas. This proved particularly helpful when others repeated similar ideas in later interviews.

Individual and group interviews allowed people to speak privately, as some wished, or in small groups. I lived and moved around the four communities. I attended football games and funerals. I accompanied the men to ceremonial Law and participated in sorry business. I visited homes, camped and hunted. Sitting outside the store or community office, travelling between communities and camping at night were often the best times when men sat and talked. 'Telling stories' was the way in which many conversations were shared.

In all, individual and group interviews involved more than fifty men, from teenagers to the very old, with some of these men being interviewed on more than one occasion. As boys can enter initiation in their early teenage years, some of these 'men' were quite young. I also interviewed desert women, kartiya women and kartiya men.

I have avoided, as much as possible, identifying those who are speaking. While Puntu were happy to speak and offer personal views, they generally did not see themselves as speaking with authority where others also had the right to speak. Puntu would often emphasise that they were only speaking for themselves. They did not like to be identified as the authors of criticism involving others. In a very recent past the Puntu of this region have often been depicted in very negative ways, especially by the media, and they continue to be sensitive as to how they are perceived by others, kartiya and Aboriginal.

There are also some very personal and sensitive issues that Puntu prefer to discuss among walytja (family) and not with kartiyas. Some of these evoke kurnta (shame); they can cause tensions between families and reinforce the negative judgments that Puntu know kartiyas make of them. As there are very few areas of Puntu life that do not come under the scrutiny of kartiyas, it is not surprising when some issues are restrained from being made public. The deaths by suicide of three young men between August 2002 and September 2003 remain particularly sensitive issues. This work attempts to respect such sensitivities.

In this book I will further explore kanyirninpa or holding within desert society today. This word and symbol expresses a number of important values for desert people, values that have allowed their society to be reproduced in very particular ways over many generations. As a way of historically situating this concept of kanyirninpa, I will return to the first encounters between Puntu and kartiyas in this region of WA and the formal establishment of Balgo Mission in 1942. I want to show how the values of early contact and later mission life impacted on Puntu life, particularly through the use of rations, labour and dormitories. I then look more closely at the ways in which Puntu understand health and sickness. Puntu models of wellness and illness reflect an understanding of health that locates the physical body within a relational, social and spiritual context. In this context, kanyirninpa expresses an ideal form of palya, healthy relationships within an active, functioning, social body. These relationships particularly apply to the development of the male body, both physically and socially, as the marnti (boy) becomes a wati (man). It is this development that reveals the particular male aspect of kanyirninpa, where men assume important holding relationships with young men as, and after, they are initiated. These holding relationships express both the possibilities and the difficulties by which young men seek to become adult men today.

I then situate this male experience of kanyirninpa within three key social spaces for men: petrol sniffing, Australian Rules football and prison. From the perspective of kanyirninpa these socially significant spaces can offer men both healthy outcomes and unhealthy risks. Each context provides a different perspective of the lives of young men and the ways in which particular aspects of holding can be noted by their absence or presence.

Finally, I return to the question of trauma, asking whether Puntu experience can be better understood as traumatic. What I find is that the disclosure of kanyirninpa has revealed a particular perspective of Aboriginal experience that can be described as both intergenerational and intragenerational trauma. The Aboriginal male body can be understood as both wounded and resilient. The male practice of kanyirninpa discloses a wound that has been inscribed on the male social body but it also reveals possible ways to attend to that that wounding.

1

Kanyirninpa and 'Holding'

If you hold that person, that person will return that respect to you.

That day, when I first picked up the marble and considered the Puntu use of the Kukatja word 'kanyirninpa', translated by the English word 'holding', proved the beginning of many further reflections and discussions. Not only did I discover that Puntu use the word kanyirninpa in many different contexts, I realised as well that they perceive it as key to understanding walytja (family) and relationships (see Appendix, p. 226). Kanyirninpa is deeply embedded in desert life and values. Puntu also believe its absence helps to explain some of the social problems currently being experienced by young men. Myers discussed the concept of kanyirninpa in his work with the Pintupi in the early 1970s (Myers 1986). Folds developed his ideas further (Folds 2001) and Bob Randall discusses the concept in his book *Songman* (2003). However, no one has explored how holding related to the growth and health of young Aboriginal men, particularly within the contexts of contemporary and rapidly changing social worlds.

Kanyirninpa is the present tense of the Kukatja verb kanyila (imperative form). It has been translated into English as, '1) have; keep; hold; 2) give birth to; have (young); 3) wear (clothing)' (Valiquette 1993, p. 18). It can be used in a variety of contexts and with different meanings. 'Where's my car?' 'Nyarralu kanyirninpa', 'he has it over there'. Puntu will use kanyirninpa when describing something they possess or are wearing: 'kurlarta kanyirninpa', 'I am holding a spear' or 'kanyirninparnatju patarlarnatju', 'I am wearing a skirt'. Or, they will use it in reference to giving birth, such as the title of the Christmas carol, 'Marylu kanyirnu Tjiitju', 'Mary gave birth to Jesus'. The polysemic use of kanyirninpa is reflected in other desert languages such as Pitjantjatjara/Yakunytjatjara and Pintupi/Luritja. Not surprisingly, the translation of kanyirninpa into English provides its own range of polysemic variations around the English words, 'have', 'keep' and 'hold'. For example, in English there are 49 separate meanings associated with the word *have*, 48 for the word *keep*, and 55 for the word *hold* (*Macquarie dictionary* 2001).

In this book I am focusing on a particular cultural context and meaning of kanyirninpa, that of holding. Not only is this a rich and complex word within contemporary desert culture, but its use needs to be separated carefully from the use of kanyirninpa in other contexts, and the use of other Kukatja words that suggest holding. For example, the image of the hand holding a marble, with which I began this book, presents one aspect of holding. When Puntu say they are 'holding onto their culture' they will use the same word but mean something quite different. In the former case holding suggests support and nurturance; in the latter case it indicates firm control or possession. As a Puntu made the distinction: one might grab hold of one's culture but with people, 'you don't grab them, you care for them'. I am using the word kanyirninpa in the latter and very specific sense.

In his ethnographic work Myers identified the cultural significance of the Pintupi word kanyininpa. As with the Kukatja kanyirninpa, Myers identified a wide use of kanyininpa within Pintupi language and its association not only with various types of physical possession but also with the moral order (Myers 1982, p. 83). He suggested that kanyininpa existed as a 'dominant symbol' within Pintupi culture (p. 83).[1] Hence, when a child was held against its mother's breast, 'kanyinu yampungka', Myers argued that this invoked a double and inter-related effect. It evoked the 'image of security, protection and nourishment' (p. 83). It also, in reference to Victor Turner's understanding of symbols, invoked with it 'an ideological or social referent to the relationship between the generations' (p. 83). What Myers translated as, 'looking after', 'nurturance', 'holding', referred to a primary and highly significant way in which the Pintupi understood and reproduced their society across generations (Myers 1980, p. 312; 1982, p. 81).

Myers understood kanyininpa as a key cultural value that countered or resolved two other cultural values in Pintupi life, relatedness and autonomy (Myers 1986, p. 22). A strong and healthy Pintupi society needed to constrain the extremes of individual autonomy and social relatedness or egalitarianism. When older people took care of those who were younger they provided this counter or balance. Kanyininpa described a very particular expression of social reciprocity or exchange. While recognising different domains of kanyininpa, such as expressed in parental nurturance and the authority of the older men, Myers maintained that kanyininpa essentially derived from those ritual occasions when older men mediated the authority of the tjurrkupa at ceremony time (1980, p. 313). The authority of the older people also nurtured because it protected and cared for Pintupi society at that critical ceremonial moment when it experienced being renewed and reproduced. The nurturance of the older people was authoritative in that their instructions and directions arose from a cosmic imperative (p. 313). As a result, the older people ensured Pintupi life and culture would be maintained as each generation cared for and directed the generations that followed. Kanyininpa provided a critically important social context for young people to experience autonomy with responsibility, nurturance with authority. The values that linked walytja (family), ngurra (land) and tjukurrpa (dreaming) were deeply reinforced as older people inducted a younger generation into a cosmic and meaningful world. Pintupi society promoted individual autonomy, attentive care for members of one's walytja and respect for the authority of elders. Kanyininpa ensured that this society would be reproduced from one generation to the next.

While Myers acknowledged that holding was expressed shortly after birth (as the mother fed her baby at the breast), he did not

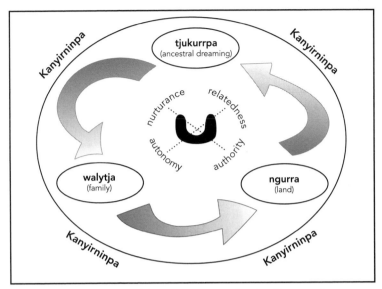

Kanyirninpa is represented here as encompassing key Puntu values and relationships found in walytja, ngurra and tjukurrpa. These are continually dynamic and inter-relating. Kanyirninpa balances the tensions of Puntu (∪) expression along key pathways: authority with nuturance, relatedness with autonomy.

explore how holding developed from childhood. Nor did he examine how holding might apply to young men outside the context of ceremonial Law and within the changing Aboriginal social world of the 1970s. It is also important to understand how Puntu men and women understand kanyirninpa. Gender voices offer distinctive, commensurate views, about the experience of holding which significantly changes when 'boys' become 'men'.

Some thirty years after Myer's work, kanyirninpa continues to exercise an important part of desert energy within the Kutjungka region. Kanyirninpa applies not just to men at the time of Law but to everyone. It includes people of all ages and both genders. Shortly after birth the mother can be seen to hold her child. She cares for her newborn child, 'yipilingku tjitji kanyirninpa'. She is nurturing, looking after, feeding and protecting her child. She, together with the child's father, is responsible for the child's safety, health and welfare. While the father also helps, particularly if the child is a son, the mother is seen to take primary responsibility. Parents, and in particular the mother, will be severely criticised if they do not take the responsibility to care for their children.

Kanyirninpa is expressed in a number of interconnected ways. It includes nurturance but it also involves older people taking responsibility and offering protection for those they hold. This relationship between generations is named as 'respect'. Kanyirninpa is also expressed in relationships that involve teaching and learning where older people help young people 'grow up the right way'. While some elements within kanyirninpa remain constant over one's lifetime, others assume different cultural expressions as those who are held grow older and in turn hold others.

One English word that is often used to describe the expression of kanyirninpa is nurture or nurturance, where nurture means, 'to feed, nourish, or support during the stages of growth, as children or young' (*Macquarie dictionary* 2001). Providing food was, and continues to be, a key element of the holding relationship. Recorded stories of pre-mission experience reinforce the priority which hunting and gathering had in daily life. Intimate knowledge of land and seasons provided adults with the challenges and demands of survival. An essential ingredient of that existence was the sharing of food. The provision of food also assumed a priority in many early first-contact experiences.

Today, families supplement regular trips to the local community store with occasional hunting forays. And while the source and nature of food has significantly changed, the priority of daily hunting and gathering has not. Not only has the store become a daily meeting place, but it has also become the place where daily transactions over food are negotiated. The young depend upon such daily negotiations and can be especially vulnerable if there is a lack of food, money or someone to provide for them. If the store remains closed, if older people are waiting for their cheques, or money has been spent on gambling or alcohol, the young can go hungry. It is significant that when men talk about imprisonment they often mention the provision and regularity of meals.

There is an important link between daily shopping and the expression of sharing among walytja. One young mother, married with children, strongly believed that Puntu needed to shop — or hunt — every day. People needed to take only what they needed and then to share it. To take more would be greedy. In her opinion it was important that people 'hunt for the day, share for the day', as the sharing of food strengthened relationships. In fact, she commented, if people did not share food others would not like them.

Within the kanyirninpa relationship the provision of food exercises an important and regular ingredient. It confirms, in daily and practical ways, that younger people are being held and older people care for them; it also confirms the gift of food as a powerful symbol of that relationship. From the time of birth Puntu babies come to learn that their need for food, and the obligations of older walytja to provide that for them, are closely and intimately connected.

Folds has drawn on Myers' concept of holding to explain the Pintupi's contemporary response and adaptability to the pressures provided by living in Australian society. According to Folds, the

> Pintupi have developed their own patron-client explanation of their relationship with the state, traced by Myers to the hierarchical relationships that dominated traditional life, in which 'the capability of seniors to "look after" dependents in a material sense was the moral basis of their authority'. (Folds 2001, p. 42, citing Myers 1980, p. 313)

The missionaries who fed the Pintupi at their first encounters, Folds argued, initiated this 'patron-client' relationship. The Pintupi believed they were being held, that Pastor Allbrecht was initiating a similar relationship to that of a holding relationship. This meant that the missionaries would continue to look after them. Over years, this was translated into contemporary society where the Pintupi sought to be supported, in a similar fashion, by the various 'provisions' of government.[2]

While Folds may be criticised for over-emphasising the resilience of the Pintupi against the Australian state, he has presented an important connection between holding and nurturance, kanyirninpa and being fed (Folds 2001, p. 12).³ As I have already mentioned, the provision of food was not only a high priority for survival in the desert but it was also a high priority for those who held, or were seen to hold, others. While the context of being fed has changed with community stores, and the presence of a monetary economy, young people today recognise they are held or being 'grown up' by those willing to feed them or assist them to obtain food. Hence, sharing access with an adult's keycard can be one contemporary way by which a holding relationship is expressed.

Desert men today cannot replicate the way their fathers and grandfathers hunted. They cannot support or provide for their families in the ways of the past. Later I will discuss how rations and food became part of mission policy, not only to separate children from their families but also to pressure adults to settle at the mission. It is important to note that the provision of rations not only cut across the ability of men and women to nurture their children, but it also served to fracture a more pervasive holding relationship across generations.

As kanyirninpa arises out of a particular and personal relationship between a person holding and a younger person being held, it reveals a particular context and significance for the English word 'respect'. While kanyirninpa usually refers to those who have taken the primary responsibility to feed, clothe, house and protect others when they were young, it can also be used to describe those who have played some part in a person's 'growing up'. In the desert, some Puntu have experienced a number of different people who have looked after them. They will, thereby, refer to the person who has held them, even for a short period of time, as one who 'grew them up'.

The relationship between the one who holds and the one who is held is recognised through life, even when people become adult and no longer see themselves as being held. This relationship is often publicly acknowledged at important times in a person's life, such as at funerals where mourners will refer to the deceased whom they grew up or who grew them up. This phrase 'growing up' is an important descriptor; it enables older people to publicly assert they have provided for younger people. In return, it allows younger people to acknowledge the abiding affection and respect they have for older people. In this way an older generation is acknowledged to have earned authority over the younger, and the younger generation acknowledge an obligation to listen to and follow their elders. Respect describes the relationship that emerges from an experience of kanyirninpa, and that binds and supports generations, even after young people have grown up and no longer see themselves as being held.

There is no Kukatja word that simply translates the English word 'respect'. Nor does the English word accurately convey, as kanyirninpa indicates, that blending of authority and nurturance that exists between younger and older generations. And nor does it clearly express how such a relationship depends on simple and practical expressions of care. Hence, when trying to explain the English word 'respect', a Puntu used the phrase 'body language'. She wanted to stress the importance of the practical, physical and relational expressions that lay within this notion of 'respect'. As she put it:

> There is no one word for the word 'respect' in Aboriginal languages but it is shown by body language. That is, you don't see people talking about it but showing it by what they do, that is by caring, sharing and helping others. Kartiyas talk too much and people [Puntu] say they [kartiyas] talk and then there is no action. Aboriginal people talk with their bodies, such as in sorry time and showing love for one another.

In her description, respect, as found within kanyirninpa, reveals social behaviour within desert society. Relationship values are demonstrated through physical and practical expression. While respect can be given to all those who are older, and especially to those who exercise authority in the Law, it is to those who have provided care, held and have grown up someone that the term respect is most often personally directed.

There is a young man, now in his early forties, who was in the boys' dormitory when I first lived at Balgo in 1973. He was a young boy then, around eight years old. Now, some 35 years later, he often introduces me to others as 'the one who grew me up'. As a young boy he had been removed from living with his family on Sturt Creek Station to live in the dormitory at Balgo. I only looked after him for a year but he continues to acknowledge publicly the significance of my role in his early life.

In the course of this research one father described how he had come to grow up two young children. His example has been repeated many times and in different communities.

> I got two I'm growing up from my family side. There's one boy and one girl. They're brother and sister. Their parents were getting carried away with grog and everything. That's why we had to look after them. They had to move...I had those kids for long time, from when they was seven years old, I think, and another one was only five years old. One's probably thirteen and fifteen now. They got a lot of respect for me and I got a lot of respect for them.

However, kanyirninpa is more than nurturance and authority. As older people 'grow up' younger people they protect and take responsibility for those under their care. There are times when this aspect of holding is particularly evident, as when a young person gets into trouble, either with Puntu or kartiya law. When this happens one might hear the question asked, 'nganalu kanyirninpa?' 'Whose holding that person, who is responsible for them?'. Those who hold that person are expected to stand up or speak for them. This can result in the older person accepting physical punishment for the behaviour of the one they hold. Such responsibility for another's behaviour can also apply if someone is living in another's house and does something wrong. 'Oh yeah,' said one mother, 'you are responsible for them. If that person is younger than you and you are older, you'll be responsible for that person'.

Puntu can describe kanyirninpa as a very high ideal of desert life. As one mother of four young children expressed it, 'kanyila means holding them, giving them, not for yourself but for growing them up'. She is a young mother, active in community and family affairs, who has recently taken into her care a young male teenager who was not being looked after by his mother. She was not concerned that social security money was being paid to someone else and not her.

She was happy to take him in and look after him. Holding those who were young, and those who needed to be held, meant much more to her than receiving social security money.

In a similar way her husband acknowledged how important the experience of holding had been for him. Until he got married he had moved around with older men and regularly got drunk and arrested. He remembered: 'Once I used to be a wild man in town, drinking and wasting money, being locked up. Looking at my father, they were all drinking and his brothers. I wanted to have a drink too'.

When his first daughter was born he found that 'growing up' his daughter motivated him against going to town and drinking. In his words, 'I had to look after the kid'. He was then 23 years old and faced with the responsibility of holding someone for the first time. He looked back on those early days: 'I don't want my kids to see me drunk and if they see that they'll feel not good and cry all around'. The responsibility he felt at that time for his daughter, at that time his first child, caused him radically to change his behaviour. Growing her up was more important to him than drinking. Some fourteen years, and four children later, it continues to be so.

In this family both parents have expended much of their energies on caring for their own and other children. They take their holding responsibilities seriously. However, they see holding as a reciprocal relationship where they have experienced their children supporting and encouraging them as parents. They are both abstainers from alcohol and they describe their commitment as part of the relationship they want to have with their children, as much as the relationship their children want with them. Describing her relationship with her children and this reciprocal nature of holding, the following exchange occurred:

> A: They help me and support me.
> R: The kids help you and support you?
> A: Mm.
> R: So you're not just looking after them?
> A: They are looking after me as well.
> R: Even the little ones?
> A: Mm.

In this holding relationship the parents experience affection and attention from their children in return for the care they provide. They are also conscious of their children's more recent efforts to encourage them to stop gambling and smoking. This reciprocated care from their children encourages them as parents and reinforces the holding relationship. The children are not holding their parents but they are acknowledging the care received from them. Puntu name this as 'respect'.

Later, in relation to her children getting older, this same mother would say, 'They'll respect you back, as they grow up. They won't just leave you'. The respect that is associated with kanyirninpa reinforces a lifelong reciprocity of care and attention between different generations. It promises that as people get older their children, and those they have grown up, will look after them. Unfortunately, as I explore in Chapter 2, prior to 1984 and the handover of community control, missionaries did not understand or appreciate the critical relationship between Puntu generations whereby the provision of care and nurturance was linked with that of authority and respect.

Puntu recognise that their manner of 'growing up' children seriously differs from that of kartiyas. They can believe that when kartiya children leave home or move away, as when they get older, kartiyas do not care for their children. One Puntu compared their system of holding with that of kartiyas:

> I think it's totally different to kartiyas how we hold onto someone. Kartiyas hold onto their children, or their grandchildren, until they're 18, 21, then they're out of their care and they're on their own. But Aboriginal people will look after each other for life.

As I will explain further, the Puntu ideal of holding does not always guarantee that Puntu will be cared for or looked after during their lives. Nor does the kartiya practice, where young people can leave home, necessarily imply that family members do not or will not care for each other. However, there are important differences between Puntu and kartiya child-rearing practices. Puntu come to know at a very early age the wide range of adults whom they can expect to care for them and hold them, as well as other Puntu with whom they can sleep, play and socialise.

By watching over younger siblings, especially when they are away from the gaze and protection of adults, children are encouraged to care for and protect those younger than themselves. At a very early age children learn about this aspect of holding. The young are not to be left alone or without someone to watch over them. As one mother described it: 'When kids are young they learn to take responsibility of their younger brothers and sisters — by helping to feed them, share things with them, play with them and keep them out of trouble'.

This growth of a child into attentive relatedness expresses more than 'the child has freedom, the adult has responsibility', as Hamilton described the child-rearing practices of the Anbarra people in Arnhem Land (Hamilton 1981, p. 113). Here in desert society, children are encouraged to consider those younger than themselves and learn the constant demands and watchfulness of relatedness. This does not mean that children are faced with the same pressures of responsibility as adults. At an early age they lead a relatively free and unrestricted life. However, while they are learning about family and kinship relationships, they are also learning about the reciprocal demands and expectations of relatedness in walytja.

Teaching, or showing young people how to live, is also an important aspect of this 'growing up'. Puntu can show great interest in kartiyas who introduce them to their families and homes and reveal to them knowledge of a wider kartiya world. What anthropologists Ronald and Catherine Berndt witnessed in 1970 continues to have some relevance: 'It is fairly obvious, especially with the girls, that their interest is centred largely on the mission and the world beyond it: the pastoral stations, Hall's Creek township, and the coastal towns of Broome, Derby, and Wyndham' (Berndt R & C 1970, p. 66). Puntu are interested in learning more about particular aspects of kartiya society beyond that of their immediate experience. Young men are also interested in other Puntu taking them on trips, showing them new things and revealing to them knowledge about the work they do. It is not uncommon for young men to accompany an older man as he grades a road, works in the stockcamp or picks up the community rubbish. Sometimes, these activities arise from the desire for company and to avoid boredom. However, they can also express a holding relationship. As in the earlier example of the family who were looking after a young teenager, this young man is seen to follow and work with the older man who is now 'growing him up'. Whether it be working around the community, on the grader or doing stockwork, his desire is to accompany and work with this older man. While this form of learning can appear very different from the more formal teaching processes of kartiya education and that of ceremonial experience, it reveals the importance and place of intergenerational accompaniment and learning within a holding context.

Some years ago, when visiting friends in an Aboriginal community in the Northern Territory, a mother asked me if I would take one of her teenage sons with me when I left. He had been getting into trouble with the police and even his own family was having difficulties controlling his behaviour. They were concerned about him being arrested and going to jail. It's only been in recent years that I have realised something of her perspective and what she was asking of me. I had known the family for a number of years and, in their kinship way, I was perceived as an older brother to the young man. It was reasonable for me to take him away for a while and 'grow him up'. It was understandable that his mother might ask me.

There is in Kukatja another word that expresses 'looking after', a word that can also be used to describe holding. 'Ngampurrmarra' has been translated into English as 'care for, take care of', and derives from two words, 'ngampurr' (careful, care, concern) and 'marra' (catch, get, make) (Valiquette 1993, p. 133). 'Ngampurrmaninpa' (present tense) can be used to demonstrate and describe a wide range of the nurturance aspects of kanyirninpa. Hence, when a person is offering another a place to sleep or something to eat, they are expressing care and affection that constitutes an active ngampurrmaninpa. However, it is important to make the distinction that, while kanyirninpa involves expressions of ngampurrmaninpa, the reverse does not necessarily apply. Hence, ngampurrmaninpa can be present without an experience of kanyirninpa, although both can be translated into English by use of the word holding.

The distinction between kanyirninpa and ngampurrmaninpa discloses an important transition for young people in desert life. People continue to experience being held (kanyirninpa) until as adults they recognise that they are no longer in need of being held, or as young adults they recognise that they are ready to take responsibility for their own lives and begin to hold others. As one adult described it, this stage occurs when a young man recognises that he is ready to 'put his foot down'. He believes he is ready to step out and take responsibility as an adult. In some cases the person will announce that they are no longer in need of being held. In other cases it will be apparent. While going through Law for a boy, and having a baby for a girl, continue to be occasions when young people are recognised as becoming adult, this does not necessarily preclude the experience of their being held, especially when they are young and continue to live at home. Sometimes, holding ceases for young people when they are in their early twenties. Sometimes, it comes when they establish a more permanent relationship and are perceived by others to be 'married'. Sometimes, however, young adults can find it difficult to 'put their foot down' and take responsibility for their own lives. One young man of 25 told how he was brought up by his mother, even after he had gone through the Law. His father had died when he was very young, and it took him until his late teenage years to make contact with his father's brothers and spend time living with them. For those early teenage years, he said, his mother held him and looked after him. Only recently has he acquired a female partner. Now he sees himself as ready to 'step out'. No longer does he see himself as being held by his mother or her generation.

However, because of the ongoing demands of walytja and rela-tedness, Puntu will continue be cared for (ngampurrmaninpa) even when they are no longer being held (kanyirninpa). When a young man grows up and moves away from being held by his mother or father, or their sisters or brothers, they will continue to care for him even though they are no longer holding him. 'Kanyirnmarna', 'I was holding him', said one woman describing her relationship with her grown up son, but now 'ngampurrmaninparna', 'I am looking after him'. She especially keeps looking after him by giving him money, food and cigarettes, but she is no longer holding him.

During 2003 one of the Wirrimanu church leaders painted a banner for the church with all the names of the petrol sniffers on it. This banner was hung behind a statue of Our Lady at the back of the church. The banner read, 'Mother Mary Bless All Our Childrens [sic]'. I later asked this church leader about the banner and the relationship she saw between Mary and the sniffers. She said that she imagined Mary kanyirninpa the children in her lap, but ngampurrmaninpa the older ones. She distinguished between the older and younger children by recognising that Mary could only kanyirninpa those who were young. Mary could take them and 'hold them in her lap'. She would pay very close attention to their lives. Those who were older were different: some of the young boys had been through Law and one young girl had a young baby. They required ngampurrmaninpa. But both groups needed Mary's care and help.

To test further the distinction between kanyirninpa and ngampurrmaninpa I asked a number of Puntu to imagine a situation where a stranger had taken their children away, had locked them up but continued to look after them. If those who had taken the children away were feeding and caring for them would that be kanyirninpa, ngampurrmaninpa or both? The answer was ngampurrmaninpa, not kanyirninpa, and the reason given was that kanyirninpa involved a 'proper looking after'. It was not sufficient simply to care for or feed others, one had to bring them up 'the right way'. Kanyirninpa involved the transmission and teaching of appropriate cultural behaviour. It assumed a moral responsibility for another.

During my last field trip in 2004 a father expressed his concern to me about his young teenage son who had gone off with an older man to town. The father did not feel he could stop his son, who had been through the Law, but he was angry at the older man. He was concerned the older man would not properly look after his son.

His son might be given money, food, alcohol and somewhere to stay, but he might not be protected and properly looked after. For the father, kanyirninpa meant that the older man needed to watch over the young man and bring him back home safely. Providing ngampurrmaninpa was not sufficient.

The different manifestations of holding and care that Puntu express for one another need to be understood in the contexts of relationships and what is available as nurturance. As a person becomes older, care for another will be expressed in gifts of money, cars, cigarettes, clothes, audio or video tapes. People also show their care for others by spending time with them, telling them stories, playing cards and inviting them to go hunting with them. It is not sufficient to claim either a holding or a caring relationship. One must show that one has made an effort to care for, or look after the other, through valued manifestations. The relational is expressed through the physical and material. One family struggled with their son who was petrol sniffing: 'We used to talk with him, you know, we used to talk with him, talk with him.' They tried various ways to stop him sniffing: 'Yeah, there were a few just slaps, but not with big sticks, and more talk, talk, talk, telling him, you know, but there was a lot of praying for him too. I used to pray for him, pray, pray.' His brother-in-law also promised him a car if he would stop sniffing. Holding requires time, effort and generosity, but also an exploration as to the most appropriate expression of nurturance for a person at a particular time.

When Puntu experience being held they also experience the power, strength and security of those who hold them. Nurturance is but one important element. For example, Puntu can see the land itself as caring for them, ngampurrmaninpa, by its provision of food and water. One adult described how the land holds and how 'we can go and look for that spot where there's always fresh water'. She was talking of a spring that always provided water, even during the hot summer months. Puntu referred to such places as sources of 'living water' because the water came from within the earth and was always available. To her, the land always nurtured and looked after the people, ngampurrmaninpa. However, she also said that the land could be described as kanyirninpa because it provided much more than the local store. It was a repository of sacred knowledge and power. It held the people by providing important cosmic meanings as well as the material means necessary for Puntu life.

This understanding of the land as both holding and nurturing provides an understanding as to why many adults believe in the power of the land to heal their young. Whether in relation to petrol sniffing, alternatives to imprisonment, learning about culture, respecting the old people, or simply growing up 'strong', the land is perceived as an important resource of strength and healing. Not only do Puntu believe the land has sustained their ancestors in the past but it also is capable of healing and holding their young people in the present. Today, many Puntu, particularly at Wirrimanu, do not live on their ancestral lands. But they still believe that having a relationship with the land will continue to provide the strength and nurturance that is needed for the health of their young people. Again, as with other holding relationships, their respect for the land that holds them is reciprocated by the ways in which they care for the land. They perform their ceremonies and burn off the old grass, and in return the land gives them food and 'living water'.

However, when taken outside the usual parameters of kanyirninpa, the provision of nurturance can prove problematic. When Puntu have entered kartiya domains, such as community councils, and sought the use of their vehicles, the experience of kanyirninpa, as Myers has explained, has often proved difficult and created conflict (Myers 1986, p. 262; Myers 1998, p. 63). Authority that Puntu expected to be generous and nurturing has not always matched communal (that is, wider than immediate walytja), government and funding expectations. However, it is possible to see where key aspects of kanyirninpa can be expressed in contemporary life, such as within one of the region's schools.

There are currently three schools in the Kutjungka region. All come under the umbrella of the Western Australian Catholic Education Office (CEO) and hence the jurisdiction of the local bishop, as well as a regional office in Broome. The schools differ, however, in size and history. Two of them, Malarn and Kururrungku, were established in 1979 and the Luurnpa school took over from the WA State Government school in 1984. The Yaka Yaka school, when it was operating, came under the umbrella of the Luurnpa school at Wirrimanu. While each struggles with regular attendance of children, continuity of staff, and the training and employment of Puntu teachers, the Kururrungku Catholic School has in recent years received a number of awards for school achievement.[4] One explanation that can be offered for this is that the school provided a contemporary, culturally appropriate and meaningful holding context for the children and also for the local, community teachers.

Sr Janet Lowe was the principal at the Kururrungku school for ten years, from 1993 until 2002. She had previously taught at the Luurnpa school for five years. She then took a break and returned to take up the job of principal at Kururrungku. Two of the Puntu staff had previously been taught by Lowe at Luurnpa. They returned to live at Kururrungku and work at the school. Others from the community joined as teaching assistants and some of them later became community teachers.

Before describing some of the dynamics that appear to have operated in this school it needs to be pointed out that Lowe, a kartiya, was not expected to express the responsibilities that are associated with being a member of Puntu walytja. She did not come under the same kinship demands of relatedness as would a local Puntu. In many ways, while she respected the authority of the local council, she did not immerse herself deeply in the culture or life of the local community. Her efforts and energies were based primarily around the school and its interests. In addition, Lowe was a religious sister (Mercy) and the Sisters of Mercy had provided a principal for the school since its inception. She had taught previously at the Luurnpa school and had experience in other forms of Aboriginal education. In essence, she was not Puntu but, according to the ways I have described desert values around nurturance and authority, she had gained their 'respect'.

Teaching is an important element of the kanyirninpa relationship where older generations induct younger people into knowledge that is culturally and ritually important. Myers identified this key aspect of holding at that moment when older men revealed the sacred to young men at Law time. However, teaching extends beyond the ceremonial Law experience. Part of the responsibility of holding another is that the older person teaches and shows younger people what they need to learn and do. Much of this teaching is informal and arises within the context of the relationship that older and younger people share.

When Kururrungku was established as an Aboriginal community in 1979, it drew together Puntu who had been living on the station (Billiluna), on other cattle stations, in nearby towns and at Balgo Mission. Not only did people come from different community backgrounds, but also from different Christian faiths and different mission backgrounds. Unlike the other communities of the region, Kururrungku in the 1990s had members of four different church or 'belief' groups (AOG [Assembly of God], UAM [United Aborigines Mission or People's church], Catholic and Bah'ai). Most of the Puntu at Balgo, Malarn and Yaka Yaka, through a shared history of living at Balgo Mission, were predominantly associated with the Catholic church. Shortly after Lowe had become principal, religious tensions emerged in light of the school being a Catholic school. (It came under the auspices of the Western Australian CEO.) Some of those who lived at Kururrungku, and were not Catholic, were concerned that some of the Catholic students were receiving favoured treatment. There was evidence in the early 1990s that the Kururrungku school was having particular difficulties in achieving harmony within the community, and good educational outcomes, compared with the other schools of the region.

The school, however, did achieve, according to national and Western Australian state educational indicators, significant steps in literacy and numeracy. Attendance rates also significantly increased. The quality of the staff, Puntu and kartiya, was obviously an important factor as were Lowe's experience, leadership and educational skills. That she had worked in the region previously, stayed as principal at Kururrungku for ten years, and encouraged other kartiya teachers to stay longer than they first intended, were also important factors.

There is also evidence that a form of holding existed within the school: Lowe had taught some of her staff. A positive 'growing up' relationship across generations had been established. Through this relationship she was able to invite others from the community to become teaching assistants and, in later years, qualified community teachers. These also included men, so that there were both female and male Puntu teachers active within the school. The three different generations of principal, teachers and children also reinforced the experience that older generations held and looked after the one that followed. As principal she looked after the teachers, who in turn looked after the children. Not only had the principal taught some of the staff but she continued to 'look after' them. For example, she gave them permission to access school vehicles, under certain conditions, on weekends.[5]

Lowe also introduced a morning tea, and later a breakfast, program. The morning tea program, organised by Lowe and school adult staff with the support of parents, enabled all children to obtain something to eat early in the day through the school canteen. The program worked on a credit system where adult members of the family provided the necessary finance, and the school staff monitored the provision of food. Not only could the children purchase morning tea but many of the Puntu staff as well. The program also provided a safety net so that those who had run out of credit could receive something to eat until the next payment. As many of the children, and also community staff, often came to school without having had breakfast, it provided them with a meal at the beginning of the day. It also removed the need for them to leave the school and visit the store (which opened in the morning after school began).

Kururrungku school provided a social context where children were fed and taught by an older generation of adults who were, in turn, 'looked after' by the principal. The school nurtured all who attended. According to one of the community teachers it was also a 'safe place'. Children who were experiencing difficulties at home, or whose parents were drinking or away in town, found the school to be somewhere they could attend and where older people cared for them. Over the decade of Lowe's principalship the parents of the children increased their support for the school and the attendance rates of the students rose accordingly.

The example of the Kururrungku school demonstrates some of the pervasive, complex and subtle aspects of holding where Puntu access social structures that kartiyas construct and control. It is not to suggest that holding simply explains the school's success or the high rate of attendance. However, the generations of principal, teachers and students encouraged not only an experience of ngampurrmaninpa but also one of kanyirninpa. Older people were given authority, not simply by their employment by the CEO, but by the ways they ensured that those who were younger experienced the school as nurturing and a place of learning. Most importantly, the parents of the children recognised that the school was growing up their children 'the right way'. Their support for the school enhanced the authority of the community and kartiya staff who worked there. It supported a notion that the school was safely and appropriately holding their children.

While, as the above example illustrates, kanyirninpa and ngampurrmaninpa can share much in common, there are occasions when the provision of care and nurturance without the presence of kanyirninpa can prove dangerous and life-threatening. One of the reasons for this, as Myers explained, is that holding keeps two values of desert life in careful balance: relatedness and autonomy. On those occasions when an older generation is not able to hold a younger one, providing it with care within the wider ambit of its authority, there can be the danger of extremes of relatedness or autonomy. The following example of alcohol use is one such case.

After a particular Law ceremony was concluded at Yaruman (Ringers Soak) in January 2002, most of the men who had attended from the Kutjungka region chose to return home via the closest town, Halls Creek. I had my own vehicle and the men who were with me also wanted to have a drink at the town's pub before heading home. Clearly, they wished to relax after the journey and ceremony; the trip to Yaruman had initially proved difficult and physically tiring due to the extremes of summer heat and rains, and some vehicles had got bogged. On their return journey some of the men wanted to impress upon the residents of the town that 'Balgo rules', referring to the men's ceremonies they had just completed and the pilytji (red ochre) they still wore proudly on their bodies. They wanted to impress upon the residents of the town that they were men of the Law, unlike a number of the Aboriginal residents of the town. It was also hot and men were thirsty and wanted to relax.

As men first gathered outside the hotel to drink, the conversations were open, warm and affectionate. Men would initially sit with close relations and friends but the large drinking space enabled them to move beyond the restrictions of kinship and gender. There were some women present but the majority of drinkers were male. I was made to feel welcome as men drank in groups inside the pub (after first buying the mandatory pair of thongs to put on their otherwise bare feet) and later outside the pub in an open space across the road. As the amount of drinking increased, and some of the men got drunk, the conversations occasionally strayed into the delicate area of 'secret men's business', which only that morning had been completed. Some of the conversations became louder and behaviour occasionally became aggressive. It took me several hours to leave the town as some of my travelling companions wanted to stay and drink for as long as possible. (One of the drinkers even offered to put me up at the hotel for the night so that they could continue drinking, arguing that we could all return the following day.) By the time we managed to leave all those who were with me were quite drunk, but this did not prevent them from having a very animated conversation all the way home. It was a time when they claimed, reinforced and reminded me of their affection and the close relationships we shared. It was a memorable trip because many of the things said to me in that car that night have rarely been repeated in other, more sober contexts. Alcohol not only allowed very strong and personal feelings to be expressed, but it also allowed their feelings towards me to be expressed. Fortunately, we left town before the fighting occurred later that night. Police were called to provide constraint and authority in what they described afterwards as 'a disturbance that got out of control'.

In many ways the men acted like kartiya men. They had shared a powerful, group experience. The weather was hot and the men were thirsty and tired. In this case the desire for relaxation and storytelling reinforced the close companionship that had recently been experienced at Law. However, with the provision of alcohol and the desire for nurturance there were no constraints on the men's behaviour. The social controls they had experienced during the ceremony were totally absent. There were no older men to direct, control and protect those who were younger (many of the older men do not drink). There was no religious, spiritual or cosmic experience. The pub provided the alcohol and a social context for drinking, but in a relatively short period of time the influence of the alcohol become manifest. As the amount of drinking increased, and more of the 'fuck you' type of statements were heard, the lack of social constraint on individual behaviour became more apparent and the dangers of unfettered, autonomous behaviour more likely.

Much has been written and researched about Aboriginal alcohol consumption. Within the particular focus of kanyirninpa the following comments can be offered. Clearly, elements of nurturance would appear to be present as men share alcohol as well as each other's company. Desert men often talk about the enjoyment of drinking, especially the sharing of stories and humour. However, these same men largely do not consume alcohol within a holding context. There is often no distinction between older and younger generations of drinkers, nor is it presumed that older people will provide drinks for younger ones. There is also no clear guidance or protection for those who drink. In addition, those who provide the alcohol are rarely, if ever, held responsible for the behaviour of those who drink, and those who drink can later use alcohol as an excuse for their behaviour. Without constraint, drinkers can easily become highly autonomous, seeking to express their emotions and opinions, while behaving outside the usual constraints. Whereas in Law the social boundaries around kinship and gender are clearly defined, in drinking such boundaries are less clear. An antinomy is revealed: the desire and high value placed on male sociality opposes the respect and restraint that men usually demonstrate with one another. While drinking enacts positive social relationships, it also heightens individuality, tension and violence. While men might sit around showing the outward signs of the Law on their bodies, the social construction of body and space becomes very different. It can also be very dangerous.

A year later, in 2003, in very similar circumstances and also after a Law ceremony at Yaruman, a man who had been sitting and drinking with his relatives and friends killed his sister-in-law while drunk. It is difficult to describe the immense pain and suffering this caused. Not only was this violent incident so unexpected, but it brought much hurt to the members of both families and a long prison sentence to the man involved.

This final example, where men gathered after a Law ceremony to drink at the Halls Creek hotel, discloses some of the key and contemporary aspects of kanyirninpa. The sociality that was offered by a Law ceremony brought a company of men together, a company linking the importance and interconnectedness of walytja, ngurra and tjukurrpa. Older men held the younger as important cosmic meanings were celebrated between themselves, across the land and upon human bodies. The authority of the older men held the young within appropriate boundaries of autonomy and relatedness as social behaviour was mandated by the tjukurrpa and through the older men as intermediaries. When the ceremonies were completed, men continued to seek the sociality they had previously enjoyed, but without the presence of elders and the context of ceremony. Alcohol provided moments of humour and positive relationship but it also led to the surfacing of tensions and anger that until then had been restrained. While kanyirninpa provided a key value for all in desert society, when Puntu gathered to drink alcohol, authority was diminished, respect became compromised and people's health and lives were put at risk.

The social expression of kanyirninpa reveals key elements of important values that lie deeply embedded within desert society. These values are acknowledged by 'respect' and the designation of 'growing up' that describes Puntu relationships that bridge gen-erations. Kanyirninpa needs, however, to be distinguished from ngampurrmaninpa. The moral responsibilities and authority associated with kanyirninpa provide more than the nurturance offered by ngampurrmaninpa. A kartiya domain, such as a school, can promote the values of kanyirninpa and find Puntu support for its goals of education. However, in other kartiya domains, such as the drinking space around a hotel, important values around sociality and kanyirninpa can find opposition from those that alcohol and drinking encourage. In these cases, men face serious risks to their health and an antinomy of those key values that kanyirninpa and desert society promote.

In the following chapter I will focus on the early history of this region and show how colonial and mission contact gathered desert people into artificial geographical communities. As the Puntu world changed and people became sedentary, Balgo Mission became a new 'home' to many. Rations, labour and the dormitory system attempted to socialise Puntu into a kartiya controlled and dominated world. This greatly influenced the ability of Puntu to exercise, express and experience the values found within kanyirninpa.

2
The Shaping of History

*We did not know what the Aborigines thought
about it all. We would never have dreamed of
asking them.*   (Willey 1971, p. 52)

In the preceding chapter I looked at kanyirninpa as a deeply
embedded value within the lives of Puntu who today live in the
Kutjungka region. I will now examine the history of this region to
identify key factors that have impacted on Puntu ability to sustain
the value of kanyirninpa. These factors include early kartiya-Puntu
relations in the south-east Kimberley and some of the particular
ways in which Balgo Mission was established. In this chapter I am
not attempting to present a full history of the region nor a detailed
analysis of mission life. Instead, I want to show that not only have
the behaviours and powers of kartiyas had a significant influence on
Puntu life, but they have also worked to seriously undermine and
restrict the capacity of Puntu to socially reproduce themselves. The
transmission of kanyirninpa across generations has been seriously
undermined and wounded, and this has serious implications for the
health of all Puntu.

While there is currently no detailed and written tradition relating to this part of the Kimberley, Puntu oral tradition has been
published in the past decade. This includes, *Minya Manpangu
Marnu Yapajangka: Stories from our childhood* (Mulan Storytellers,
1999), *Yarrtji: Six women's stories from the Great Sandy Desert* (Peter
& Lofts, 1997), *Footprints Across Our Land: Short stories by senior*

Western Desert women (Crugnale, 1995) and *The Telling of Stories: A spiritual journey of Kimberley Aboriginal people* (Bibby, 1997). These are principally stories by women. The history of Balgo Mission has been told, as part of the history of the Kimberley Catholic church, in works such as *From Patrons to Partners* (Zucker, 2005), *Nothing is Wasted in the Household of God* (Nailon, 2000), *A Hard Road* (Byrne, 1989) and *The Rock and the Sand* (Durack, 1969). However, not only are Aboriginal voices particularly lacking in these histories, but also their stories and reflections regarding contact with kartiyas that now extends for almost seventy years.

Those whose research significantly focused on this Kimberley region — and are of particular relevance to the theme of this book — were the anthropologists Ronald and Catherine Berndt, who began fieldwork at Balgo in 1957, and Anthony Peile, Pallottine priest and linguist, who lived at Balgo from 1973 until his death in 1989.[1] His posthumous work, *Body and Soul: An Aboriginal View* (edited by Peter Bindon) ranges widely over Kukatja understandings of the human body and ethno-fauna and flora (1997). Valiquette edited Peile's work in the Kukatja language which led to the publication of the first Kukatja dictionary in 1993. These authors have provided important cultural and historical insights into this desert region, especially over the past five decades.[2]

The four communities of this desert region have been, and still are, known by different names: The largest — and oldest — community has been known by several names including Balgo, Balgo Hills and Balgo Mission.[3] It was re-sited in early 1965 to its present location. Sometimes in this book, in order to distinguish the pre-1965 or post-1965 sites, I will use the terms 'old Balgo' or 'new Balgo'. Today, it is more often known by its Aboriginal name of Wirrimanu. Wirrimanu refers to the track caused by the kingfisher (luurn) in the tjukurrpa, or time of ancestral dreaming.[4] About 50 kilometres to the west of Wirrimanu is Malarn (also known as Lake Gregory). Malarn is the Walmajarri word for a gum tree (*Eucalyptus microtheca*). Kururrungku (also known as Mindibungu or Billiluna) lies some 120 kilometres north of Wirrimanu and is the Walmajarri name for a small wallaby.[5] It describes a wallaby tjukurrpa of that particular place. Yaka Yaka, approximately 100 kilometres south of Wirrimanu, means 'quiet'.[6] Wirrimanu, Malarn, Kururrungku and Yaka Yaka each have small outstation communities where very few people permanently live and only small numbers occasionally visit. Malarn and Kururrunkgu were, for some years, cattle stations comprising the Billiluna Pastoral Lease. The Western Australian Government (Aboriginal Lands Trust) acquired them in 1979. People moved to live in these communities from Wirrimanu and also from Billiluna, Sturt Creek and Gordon Downs, where they had been living as station families, and part of the pastoral industry, for many years. Some came from Halls Creek or from further afield in the Kimberley or Northern Territory. Yaka Yaka was established as an outstation, south of Wirrimanu, resulting in large part from Scott Cane's 1989 report, *Return to the Desert*, which looked at the value and possibility of establishing several outstation communities from Wirrimanu. People moved to live there perma-nently in 1991.[7] However, between 2002–04 a number of people moved away to live elsewhere, mainly to Wirrimanu. This community finally closed in 2005.

The 2006 Census indicated that there were approximately 719 people resident in the Kutjungka region: 460 at Wirrimanu (Balgo), 115 at Malarn (Mulan) and 144 at Kururrungku (Mindibungu) (ABS 2006). This revealed a reduction of nearly 200 people since the 2001 Census (ABS 2002).[8] In the 2001 Census, Yaka Yaka was still existing (76 people), but between 2001 and 2006 the greatest reduction in numbers was at Malarn (from 168 to 115) and Kururrungku (from 213 to 144). The numbers at Wirrimanu increased (from 448 to 460), largely influenced by the movement of people after Yaka Yaka closed down. Of this total population of 719, approximately 87 were kartiya, similar to their number in 2001 (84) but an increase in percentage from 9 per cent to 12 per cent. Most of these were staff employed in the communities, especially in the community offices, schools, health clinics and stores that are present in each of the three communities. The Catholic Parish, The Balgo Multifunctional Police Post, Kapululangu Women's Centre, Palaylatju Maparnpa Health and the Warlayirti Artists and Culture

Centre are all based at Wirrimanu. There are also a small number of kartiya men and women married to Puntu.

A brief look at the different languages spoken by people in the south-east Kimberley region today reveals some of the complexities of this region and the past movements of people. While Kukatja has become the lingua franca of the region it is not the first or only language. Walmajarri, Jaru and Kriol are the preferred first languages for a significant minority. A smaller number of people have some familiarity with Ngarti and Wangkatjungka, the languages of their parents or grandparents, but which they rarely speak today. Also, Warlpiri people, especially from Lajamanu and Yuendumu, have married people from the four communities and now live in the region.

While Kukatja became the dominant language of those who lived at old Balgo, it has now become the preferred language for the majority of those who live at Wirrimanu. Many people at Malarn, and a small number at Kururrungku, also speak it.[9] As I spent many years resident in Wirrimanu, and because many in the region continue to speak it, I have used the Kukatja language predominantly in this book. While English is understood and spoken by all people of the region, with varying degrees of competence and confidence, it is not the language of birth for most. The majority of people in the Kutjungka region understand at least one Aboriginal language and they usually speak it in preference to English. While there may be different interpretations as to the precise linguistic and cultural boundaries of the above groups, anthropologists accept that they form part of Western Desert culture (Berndt R 1972, p. 181). This great variety of language and history within the region is reflected in the many and various connections people have with others in the Kimberley and the Northern Territory. Consequently, while they express many linguistic differences, Puntu share many similar patterns of social and ritual life.

While the south-east Kimberley was one of the last parts of the Australian continent to be colonised, significant kartiya influences began to shape the landscape in the late 1880s. The first kartiya explorer into this area was likely to have been AC Gregory in 1856, who followed Sturt Creek southwards and to the Lake that now bears his name. In April 1873, Colonel PE Warburton travelled west from Alice Springs to Roebourne, but could not find the salt lake previously encountered by Gregory. Some four months after leaving Alice Springs, his track took him some 20–30 kilometres south of the lake. His exploring party captured a young Aboriginal woman so that she might lead them to water. She was tied to a tree but managed to escape during the night. Not surprisingly, Warburton records, 'the blacks all avoided us as though we had been plague-stricken' (Warburton 1968, p. 206). In 1896 DW Carnegie travelled from the Western Australian goldfields to Halls Creek and back. He also came to realise that without help from the desert people to find water he could not survive. He felt justified, 'having to a small extent used rough treatment to some natives so caught' (Carnegie 1989, p. 133). The capture and chaining of desert people to suit the purposes of kartiyas in such a harsh physical environment became rationalised, established and justified.

The exploration of Alexander Forrest in 1879 led to the gradual opening up of land in the east Kimberley to outsiders. Between 1881 and 1886 most of the land in the north-east Kimberley was taken up by speculators, miners and pastoralists. Cattle were brought into the region in 1884 and this particularly affected the hunting and gathering patterns of Aboriginal people. Gold was found in Halls Creek in 1885, leading to a gold rush the following year. Not only did Aboriginal people have increasingly restricted access to their traditional lands, food and water supplies, but they also suffered a range of sanctions when they killed cattle for food. There are records of widespread massacres, mainly from 1884 until 1894 (Clement 1989; Ross 1989; Ross & Bray 1989). This colonial contact formed the basis of an Aboriginal oral tradition that remembered violence, sexual exploitation of women and survival.

The discovery of gold in Halls Creek brought a significant shift of attention to the south-east Kimberley. By September 1886 the population of this small town had risen to 2000. When gold was found in Coolgardie in 1892, cattle stations in the Kimberley sought to have their cattle moved south to feed the large numbers of miners. Alfred Canning, in 1906, was financed to check the possibilities of a stock route linking Halls Creek in the north with Wiluna in the south. The expedition proved successful but signalled new and further violent relationships with the Aboriginal people along that route.

In 1922 a group representing the Locke Oil Prospecting Syndicate was travelling up the Canning Stock Route. Near Well 37 John McLernon, a member of that party, was killed. It was early September. Around the same time Joseph Condren and Timothy O'Sullivan were shot at Billiluna Station.[10] Their deaths, and the kartiya response to them, disclose much about kartiya and Puntu relationships during that era. The police reaction, the pursuit of the alleged offender Banjo and allegations that other Puntu were killed around that time reveal the fears and violence of many kartiya in those times. Four police parties, more than thirty men, set out to track Banjo. They came from Halls Creek, Fitzroy Crossing, Turkey Creek and the Northern Territory. While the party from Halls Creek tracked, found and eventually shot Banjo, the police party from Fitzroy Crossing allegedly killed a number of Puntu at Kalputitjarra, who were found to be in possession of some of the stolen guns (Bohemia & McGregor 1995). Matt Savage was to later note, 'his [Banjo's] fate was a lesson to any other black with similar ideas' (Willey 1971, p. 52).

In 1997 an older Puntu woman recounted her version of what happened at Billiluna in 1922. Her understanding was that the two men were killed because of their interest in Banjo's wife.

> That girl — Napanangka — she bin married to that Tjangala. That kartiya took her and never sendem back to husband. That kartiya bin huntem out that Tjangala, 'you can't work here — you got to get away. Don't want to see you round here. I can't give you this woman, I got to keep him'. And that man, they bin huntem out for good…That man, that Tjangala, bin come sneaking up, go inside boughshed. He gettem big mail bag, gettem rifle and bullets and puttem in mail bag…sneak up with rifle. He bin shootem now — that whiteman…He bin say, 'No one argue long me. If anyone argue, I shoot whole lot!' Angry for that woman, Napanangka. (Peter & Lofts 1997, p. 76)

In 2003 a senior desert man provided me with a similar version of the cause of the deaths of these two stockmen. While kartiyas had their views, Puntu held their own, very different memories of these same events.

As the police sought to pacify the northern areas, authors, such as Ernestine Hill, represented a new image of the recently 'domesticated' Aboriginal people. In 1930 she wrote of Kimberley 'blacks', who previously had been responsible for the deaths of half of the kartiyas 'in the very early days' but had now become 'genial' (Hill 1963, p. 89). However, there were exceptions. Despite her view that, 'the natives of Kimberley [were] merrier and more contented than in any other corner of the Continent', she commented that, 'the blacks are bad at Billiluna' (pp. 89, 336).

Pastoralists in the east Kimberley often worked on large properties, isolated from family and police for lengthy periods of time. They were aware that violence was being used against Aboriginal people, and many believed that the only way they could hold power and control, and protect their resources, was by the use of force. Matt Savage, a drover in the east Kimberley in the early part of the twentieth century, described his experience of coming to the Kimberley.

> When I first arrived in the North-West a white man was not expected to speak to a black at all, unless it was to tell him what to do. If you had a normal conversation with any one of them, the other fellows would say you were becoming too familiar and probably you would not last very long in your job. This did not apply so much to the black women who, after all, did have their place in the scheme of things. (Willey 1971, p. 52)

The 'scheme of things', as described in Ann McGrath's *Born in the Cattle*, included women's roles as sexual partners (1987). Most of the kartiyas involved in the colonisation of the east Kimberley were independent, itinerant and often single men (Clement 1988, p. 3). They treated Aboriginal men very differently from the women. It was important that a stockman developed a reputation for being 'hard on the blacks' as, according to Savage, 'the boys were little more than slaves' (Willey 1971, p. 52). If one ran away they had to be found and punished. If the appropriate person was not found another would suffice. 'A belt over the ear was usually enough to settle them down. I never found it necessary to shoot any of them, although others did' (p. 60).

It is in within this context of colonial expansion and contact violence that Catholic Pallottine missionaries arrived in Rockhole, south of Halls Creek, in 1934. They entered a world where Puntu remembered the violence that had been done to them, or to other Puntu, and where it continued to be enacted. Whether it was along the Canning Stock Route in the west, near Sturt Creek to the north, out in the east near the Granites or south around Lake Mackay, the Aboriginal people of each region held particular and strong memories of violence that had been done to them or their families. At the same time kartiyas were increasing in numbers and influence in the desert regions south of Halls Creek.

The intention to buy Rockhole Station arose from a particular interest by Bishop Raible in Aboriginal health, especially leprosy.[11] His intention was to set up a medical centre, a home for the old and infirm, and a school (Durack 1960, p. 99; Durack 1969, p. 243; Byrne 1989, p. 49). Without warning the Government of his intentions, Raible negotiated with Francis Castles to buy Rockhole Station, a sheep station close to Halls Creek, for 1400 pounds (Byrne 1989, p. 50; Nailon 2000, p. 112; Zucker 2005, p. 104). On 13 October 1934 Fr Francis Huegel, Br Henry Krallmann and Br Joseph Schuengel left Broome to take ownership of Rockhole Station (Schungel 1995).[12] Accompanying them were Aboriginal men from Beagle Bay, Paddy Meranjian, Willie, George Kelly and Phillip Cox (p. 1).[13]

In January 1935, at the request of the Western Australian Minister for Aborigines, Raible put his proposal in writing:

> …The Pious Society of Missions intends to establish a hospital
> for the treatment of Blacks and Half-castes at Rockhole Station
> in the vicinity of Halls Creek. This station is 22 miles west of
> Halls Creek…We are prepared to erect the necessary buildings
> in the near future, have the hospital staffed with trained nurses

of the Sisters of St John of God, and will be able to have our own doctor on the spot by the end of this year. (Raible 1935)

He then left for Germany to recruit staff. He returned with four Pallottine priests, two brothers and a husband and wife medical team, Hans and Ludwina Betz.

The Chief Protector replied to his letter:

> Since then [the January letter from the Bishop] the Royal Commissioner appointed to investigate aborigines [sic] matters has presented his report and consequent upon certain recommendations contained therein, which I might say coincide with the views of the Department, it has been decided to appoint a Departmental Medical Inspector of Aborigines to travel throughout the North. Such being the case, I am directed to inform you that while thanking you for the offer contained in your communication we shall be unable to take advantage of it. (Neville 1935b)

In the months while the Bishop had been away, the Moseley Royal Commissioner had recommended that a medical clinic be established at Moola Bulla Station and a medical inspector appointed for the north. Raible's proposal was therefore, in the official eyes of the Government, 'superfluous' (Neville 1935a). Not until 1 October 2006, more than seventy years later, was a doctor to live permanently in the Kutjungka region south of Halls Creek.

Greatly disappointed, and after persevering for a few more years, Raible sold Rockhole Station to Ernie Bridge in 1939 (Byrne 1989, p. 64). While the Bishop had been planning his new venture at Rockhole, the Pallottine linguist and anthropologist Fr Ernest Worms had been making yearly expeditions into the east and west Kimberley from 1933. In October 1938 and May 1939 Worms and Raible travelled south of Halls Creek into the more remote desert areas where they met desert people. The Bishop's intention became clear, as Fr Alphonse Bleischwitz later recounted:

> The attention of the Bishop had been drawn to the plight of the little known tribes south of Halls Creek — nomads wandering about over hundreds of Sand Ridges along the Canning's Stock Route and East of it in the Lake White Desert. So far nobody

had bothered about them — they were unknown in No Man's Land.[14] Billiluna was the last cattle station, 200 kms south of Halls Creek, but at that time it had never shown much progress. The bishop realised: here, at the edge of the desert, a new mission could be born. (Bleischwitz & Huegel 1995, p. 11)

Worms believed that assimilation was as inevitable for Aboriginal people as were the dangers of urban life and the benefits of Christianity. His conviction was that the best approach was for 'gradual assimilation in contrast to the more hurrying method suggested by certain governmental bodies' (Worms 1970, p. 378). He, as with other missionaries of that time, rarely distinguished between the values of Christianity and those of Western 'civilisation'. They saw themselves as different from station people whose interest in Aboriginal people was largely economical. Worms was clearly fascinated by particular aspects of the culture of Aboriginal people that did not clash with his own and the Catholic church's understanding of Christianity. Some have romanticised him and seen him as an exceptional visionary, such that 'he was accepted as a greater authority on the law than the leaders themselves' (Durack 1969, p. 286). To others, 'despite his unquestioned erudition, his commitment to the maintenance of Aboriginal culture [was] highly suspect' (Alroe 1981, p. 124). While Worms exhibited interest in the various expressions of Aboriginal culture, his attitudes and behaviour clearly supported the process of assimilation and the superiority of Christian beliefs over others. His views helped establish a rationale for later mission intrusion and intervention in Puntu cultural and social life.

Establishing a mission south of Halls Creek offered the Catholic church a rare opportunity to work with those who were perceived to be still strong in their culture but also able to receive the benefits of Christianity. Worms' advice, to be accepted by the Bishop, was to apply to the Western Australian Government for a lease of a million acres further into the desert and adjacent to the Canning Stock Route. In 1939 the search for an appropriate site began.

The three years after they departed Rockhole Station turned into a desert sojourn, 'like the wanderings of nomad shepherds'

(Durack 1960, p. 102). On 8 September 1939, Br Frank (Franz) Nissl, Paddy Meranjian, Bertha Paddy, Phillip Cox and Dick Smith left the station with a large herd of sheep, goats, horses, donkey and camels. The group travelled south-east, stopping briefly at Ruby Plains Station and four weeks later came to Billiluna Station. From there they moved further south-east, away from the Canning Stock Route, until they reached the end of the Billiluna station run. This was called Comet, the site of a broken-down windmill. They repaired the windmill and camped there for the next six weeks, waiting for Fr Alphonse and Br Stephen to join them from Rockhole with the truck. Finally, after looking for a better camping and shady place, they came to Tjaluwan, a large waterhole. Here they met a large group of about sixty Puntu, 'waiting for us as they heard of our coming'. It was Christmas.[15]

Due to a shortage of water the missionary band split up, one half staying at Comet and the other half at Tjaluwan. They continued to live in two groups for six months, but the summer rains did not arrive and once again they looked for a more suitable site. Tjumunturr, about 40 kilometres from Tjaluwan, was then found.[16] Here they found small waterholes with some good pasture for their sheep and goats. From this base the group searched further until they finally found a place where they believed they could establish a mission. Three years later, in 1942, they settled at old Balgo. They would remain there until moving to the present site of Wirrimanu in 1965.

The identity of the first group of desert people is not revealed. The Walmajarri recall that it was they who first met Bishop Raible. They have also maintained that old Balgo was on their land. Comet, Tjaluwan and Tjumunturr are close to the site of the present-day Malarn community and Walmajarri country. However, it is also possible that Kukatja and others were present at those early encounters.

Peile and Kingsley Palmer have suggested that the Walmajarri and Kukatja were traditionally close, shared land and inter-married (Peile n.d.; Palmer 1983, p. 519). Petri, quoting Worms, proposed that as some Walmajarri moved westwards from their country the Kukatja moved in from the south (Petri 1968, p. 65). The Walmajarri had been attracted to stations and settlements and some had moved north and west to Fitzroy Crossing (Kolig 1981, p. 18; Walmajarri Storytellers 2002, p. 3). Worms and Raible had made contact with the Kukatja in the two years prior to leaving Rockhole and it is possible that some Kukatja developed relationships with them. Horgan reported that in 1948 a large number of Kukatja walked into Balgo, followed later by Walmajarri (1976). Whatever the formation and reasons for those initial shifts and gatherings, the dominant group and language of Balgo Mission in a short period of time became Kukatja.

There is little evidence that people were systematically brought in or pressured by kartiyas to live at the mission.[17] The desert economic 'household' was usually quite small in number. Larger numbers of people would only have gathered for ceremonies and these would usually have lasted only for a week or two. At the mission people were living closer together, and for longer periods, than they had experienced previously. Ronald Berndt described the changing patterns of movement in those early days:

> The majority have remained for various reasons, not all associated with a reaction against the rigours of their home territories, because life was in some respects easier in the Desert than on the settlements. Many came only for short visits, but the usual tendency has been for such visits to grow shorter until they became virtually permanent residents. However, those who came in as adults do retain some ties with their own countries, or territories, and parties still set out occasionally for the bush, where they stay for varying periods. But except in a few isolated cases, they no longer envisage remaining there. (Berndt R 1972, p. 181)

Eubena Nampitjin, a prominent desert artist, came into old Balgo in 1955 and in later years supported the admission of young boys who had been living around the Canning Stock Route (Bleischwitz 1957; Crugnale 1995, p. 175; Warlayirti Artists 2001). Her story, and that of others, suggests that some desert peoples chose to come to the mission and to leave cattle stations such as Billiluna. They were also attracted by economic interest and a desire to sample new material goods. From that first gathering at Tjaluwan in 1939 Puntu were aware that they could get food at the mission. As they moved in and out of the region they also knew where they could locate many of their relatives and friends. People were also curious as to the benefits of this new desert company. However, such movements in and out of kartiya settlement were not new. By the 1940s Aboriginal people of the desert had been moving into and out of missions, towns and settlements for more than forty years (Berndt R 1972, p. 180; Kolig 1981, p. 21; Long 1989, p. 16). As with those who left the desert for Papunya and other communities in the Northern Territory, there were elements of timing, choice and pressure. It would seem that desert groups were spreading out 'fanlike' for some decades (Petri 1968, p. 168). However, it is also likely that activity around Woomera and Maralinga in the 1940s, and the setting up of the meteorological station at Giles in the 1950s, pressured the southern neighbours of the Kukatja who, in turn, pressured the Kukatja to move further north.

Desert people had not always confined themselves to specific and restricted geographical areas. Some groups were believed to be regularly mobile as they took advantage of vast areas and unpredictable desert rains. Some sites were believed to be 'jointly owned' and places where 'co-hunting' could occur. Anthropologists reported that in the 1930s and 1940s the Kukatja were moving north and occupying land of the Walmajarri who in turn were heading west (1968, p. 169). The Kukatja were also reported to be spreading into Warlpiri territory (Berndt R 1972, p. 181). Groups of desert people were moving away from some of the harshest desert areas well before the missionaries came to old Balgo in 1942 (Petri 1968, p. 168; Kolig 1981, p. 21).

In 1950, Alphonse Bleischwitz (Superintendent, 1939–57) wrote of the aims of the mission:

> The principal aim of the Mission, as of all religious missions to the primitive people, is to help these people become ideal Christians. The secondary, but important, aim is to endeavour to give them any positive good which our modern civilization is

able to give them, and they on their side are able to absorb to the
benefit of their general wellbeing…We hope in the near future
to have a school for the children, where they will be educated,
both in religious and secular matters. Further, we intend to
build dormitories for the girls and the boys. (Bleischwitz 1950,
p. 62)

Bleischwitz' emphasis on the priority of religious conversion
was not shared by all missionaries. Some argued for it and actively
promoted it. Fr Francis Huegel (1934–36, 1962–65) helped some
adults to be baptised but was criticised by Fr John McGuire (1958–
70) for his efforts. Fathers Joe Kearney (1950, 1955, 1957 and
1960) and Ray Hevern (1969–84) offered religious instruction
when people requested it. They put little pressure on adults to be
baptised. McGuire, who arrived at old Balgo in 1958, said he did
not baptise people, except at the moment of death: 'We feel a sense
of responsibility is the first thing, then a knowledge of hygiene and
the rudiments of education' (Harris 1965).

McGuire believed that Puntu needed to be first taught about
'civilisation' before they could accept Christianity (Finn 1963).
He instituted a style of administration that, like many missions of
the times, was strongly authoritarian.[18] For McGuire and Hevern,
running and maintaining the mission was their first priority.
However, children were treated quite differently from their parents.
They were removed from their families for the purposes of education
and the benefits of Christianity and Western 'civilisation'.

Not all dormitories in Aboriginal missions and settlements at
that time were the same. Some missions had chosen not to use them
and preferred to work through families, while others focused on the
girls, protecting them from 'from cradle marriages' and from getting
pregnant (Berndt C & R 1972, p. 113). At old Balgo,

children remained with their parents until they were five or six
years of age. When they began school — the first formal school
— they moved into dormitories and lived in the dormitories
right through their school age and afterwards until they married.
(Kearney 1974, p. 2)

The model of dormitories at old Balgo came from Beagle Bay, Balgo's 'parent' mission. It had provided Pallottine, and Aboriginal personnel, to Rockhole Station and later old Balgo. By 1951 there was a girls' dormitory, and a boys' dormitory by 1960.[19] Initially, neither was locked at night and there were no rigid restrictions between children and their families (Berndt R & C 1970, p. 66). However, this soon changed.

As in other missions, the missionaries found that children became unsettled if they returned to live in the camps or went hunting with their parents (Grayden 1957, p. 30). The missionaries deemed it necessary to increase the separation between children and parents. When Puntu first visited old Balgo they would occasionally leave and travel to other communities or they would go hunting. It was convenient to leave the children in the care of the mission. However, in time, especially in the move from old to new Balgo, the security around the dormitories became 'tightened' as the separation between children and families became reinforced. The Berndts described the change:

> In the late 1950's [Balgo] had no boys' dormitory, and the girls' dormitory was not rigidly policed but worked on an honour system: girls could come and go quite freely in the early evening, and on hot nights slept in the open beside the dormitories, looked after by the sisters in charge. Today [1972] both dormitories are operating, but only the boys are allowed to visit the Aboriginal camp; the girls meet their parents and other relatives in the central area in and around the church and the main institution buildings.[20] (Berndt C & R 1972, p. 134)

When the mission moved in 1965 the new site was carefully prepared. The various buildings were established in the shape of a large horseshoe: the church at the top, the convent and girls' dormitory on the east side, and male staff quarters and the boys' dormitory on the west. The playground and basketball courts lay between these two groups. What was significant about this site was the separation of the dormitories from where Puntu lived, in their 'camp', west of the boys' dormitory. Only on Christmas Day, and for part of that day, were the girls allowed to visit their families in the camp. A physical and social barrier between parents and children was maintained.

There is now a large number of Puntu in their forties and older who grew up in the Balgo dormitories. For more than twenty years young Puntu were separated from the holding and nurturing gifts of their parents and older relations. The dormitory system closed in April 1973, at least for the children whose families lived at Balgo.[21] For those children who came from neighbouring cattle stations, the dormitory system continued until the communities of Malarn and Kururrungku were established in 1979. When children began returning to live with their families in 1973, parents were now considered to be responsible for them, a responsibility which the mission had appropriated for more than twenty years.

Today, when Puntu look back on the dormitory experience they remember it as a 'hard' experience, especially in their separation from family. An interview about that time with a married man, now in his mid-fifties and with four adult children, went as follows:

> R: What do you think about that dormitory time when you look back?
> A: Mm…good training…not enough to go and visit my parents …it was a really hard life…
> R: It was a hard life?
> A: Really hard, a hard life.

Like many others of his generation, his views on the dormitory experience were mixed. He believed that he learned a lot during that time and there were 'good and strict laws'. He can speak English and has confidence to mix and work with kartiyas. While he has experienced many skills in order to understand and live in a kartiya world, he recognised that what he missed most was the company and support of his family. Now, as an older man who is looked on to lead and guide the community through difficult decisions and Law ceremonies, he has found such leadership and responsibility difficult to sustain.

The *Bringing Them Home* report paid relatively little attention to those who spent significant years of their lives in dormitories, removed from their families who were living in the same community as themselves (National Inquiry 1997). Despite the benefits Puntu perceive they received in those times, they have also described the dormitories as 'prison' times: 'they were a bit locked in, yeah, like they weren't really free'. They remember that if they tried to run away they would be caught and sent back. This separation of children from their parents and those of older generations threatened a severe wounding to the Puntu social body as it undermined the expression and reciprocity of kanyirninpa. Later, I will further explore this as intergenerational and intragenerational trauma of the 'separated' Puntu body.

However, dormitories did not simply separate children from their families. They could also be used as mechanisms for preventing young boys being taken into ceremonial Law. While this policy changed when Hevern came to new Balgo, McGuire believed that the 'old fellows take the boys away for horrible practices' (McGuire 1959). He not only spoke against the ceremonies for the young men, but also actively sought the elimination of their practice. He is remembered for undressing a young boy who was being prepared for his ceremonial initiation.[22] Another time, a young marlurlu (initiate), accompanied by a small group of men, walked from Billiluna to old Balgo. His task then, and as is still practised today, was to bring people from Balgo back to Billiluna for his final Law ceremony. After he arrived at Balgo the people performed the appropriate ceremonies, but when they tried to return with him:

> He (McGuire) try to stop that Law, culture, you know…he tried to stop all them people so they didn't…no one didn't, no one didn't follow me that time. I had to go back myself, and me and whatever family.

Now an old man, he remembered his father's shame when he returned to his community without his relatives:

> R: How did [your father] feel?
> A: Oh…that was really (he laughs)…they got upset, but they knew that Father was a little bit cheeky.[23]

Bishop Jobst noted in his memoirs that 'Fr McGuire used to send the young boys to Derby hospital for circumcision by the doctor. The elders did not object' (Jobst 2000, p. 29). Clearly, as a number of older Puntu have remembered, their families strongly disapproved. However, they had little voice, influence or power to object.[24]

What Jobst and McGuire perceived as a standard medical procedure was understood radically differently by Puntu whose society and identity depended on the ceremony of initiation for its social reproduction. It was, and continues to be, the means by which young males assume important religious knowledge that enables them to belong and participate in adult society. It is a ceremony, as Myers has described, that lies at the very centre of desert life:

> The production of the social person involves an elaboration of the ties of relatedness to others, the creation of a public self that takes priority over its private qualities, and the development of the ability to 'look after' others...in initiation, the strands of Pintupi social life are brought together at the fulcrum of the system: the construction of related individuals. (Myers 1986, p. 228)

During the time of Law the power and meaning of the tjukurrpa is transmitted, not just to the men, but to all of desert society. Puntu are empowered and renewed by this ceremony as it gathers and discloses the deeper meanings of ngurra (land) and tjukurrpa. The belief and conviction of some missionaries to do away with initiation practices was linked to their desire to do away with the associated 'promised' system, what Bleishwitz described as 'the custom of too early marriages' (Bleischwitz 1950, p. 62).

Apart from the attempted control over ceremonies and sexuality, missionaries also held power over access to regular food and water. I have mentioned how recorded stories of older women show that hunting for food was, with family and ceremonies, the most important and remembered priority of desert life. As Hamilton has noted, Aboriginal people moved towards kartiya society (in this context a mission) because it offered food. Their movement did not necessarily suggest they were interested in participating in the society that provided it (cited in Rowse 1998, p. 43). Some chose to move away. There are Walmajarri people who remember that they, and Wangkatjungka people, first met the missionaries but then moved further west when Kukatja people arrived.

It is not surprising — bearing in mind the occasional difficulty and frugality of desert life — that Puntu were attracted to a regular source of food and water. There was a ten-year drought (1957–1966) that affected Central Australia. The Walmajarri would later recall:

> For all its satisfactions, the hunting life was hard, sometimes precarious. The promise of reliable and plentiful supplies of food for little cost in energy was irresistible. (Walmajarri Storytellers 2002, p. 1)

The mission also provided a regular supply of sheep. Worms recorded that, by October 1959, 120 sheep at the mission had been speared (Worms 1970, p. 371). McGuire was publicly to comment, 'our biggest worry with the sheep is to prevent the blacks from killing them' (1959). In previous decades, when Puntu encountered kartiyas, and killed their cattle or sheep, they were often punished, sometimes arrested and even killed. Missionaries recorded that as early as 1939 at Tjaluwan, their first major meeting with Puntu, a sheep was found killed. The police were informed and three Puntu were arrested and taken back into Halls Creek (Byrne 1989, p. 76). McGuire complained to the Commissioner of Police about the killing of sheep, especially when those who had been arrested and served sentences for killing sheep returned and continued their practice (O'Brien 1959). He reported such behaviour to the Halls Creek police and men were arrested and jailed (Durack 1960, p. 116; Crugnale 1995, p. 63). This practice of arrest and imprisonment, and the use of police as a means of controlling and pacifying Puntu behaviour, I explore later in chapters 7 and 8.

Like the pastoralists, the missionaries found that the killing of their sheep (or cattle) seriously affronted their right to exercise control over land, food and water resources. Missionaries, like McGuire, believed that their authority was a right and not to be challenged. Tjaluwan established the precedent for an often-to-be-repeated confrontation where kartiyas found themselves frustrated by their inability to control Puntu behaviour.

The mission encouraged Puntu to settle and live a sedentary and new form of communal life. The policy of 'no work, no tucker' was introduced to avoid any accusation that the missionaries were fostering 'rice Christians'.[25] The missionaries saw themselves promoting one of the basic foundations of civilisation, the link between labour, wages and food (Gill 1967; Kearney 1974, p. 1). The Government also provided a financial subsidy for some who resided at the mission. These 'inmates', as the Government counted them, were either approved for 'education and care' — hence were young — or were in such a physical condition that they required medical attention. Hence, the subsidy encouraged the young to remain at the mission, while pressurising older men either to work for the mission to obtain or seek food in other ways.

Initially, Puntu were given rations one day a week.

> It would not be sufficient to last them for the whole week but only for a day or two. This was enough to keep them in contact with the mission. After a short time they would leave their children there because the children were a burden during their excursions in search of food. The children remaining at the mission would be fed, housed and clothed according to the meagre facilities available to the missionaries themselves...Any of the parents who wished to stay on the mission and work were allowed to remain and do so. They received all their food and clothing in exchange for the work they accomplished. (Kearney 1974, p. 2)

Myers and Folds have discussed this relationship between food and missionary activity in reference to the Pintupi (Myers 1986, p. 31; Folds 2001, p. 10). Myers' link between hierarchy and kanyirninpa suggested, according to Folds, that it was through rations that the missionaries achieved their power and authority. In *White Flour, White Power* Tim Rowse analysed the importance of food within the context of missionary activity (Rowse 1998, p. 80). He proposed that 'typically, missions and welfare officials rationed as an instrument of command — in order to stabilise and concentrate Aborigines for 'education' (1998, p. 44). Rowse has also referred to Myers to suggest that the link between kanyirninpa and hierarchy was present in some of the exchanges around food, distinct from reciprocity of trade as in the exchange that occurred involving women (1998, p. 44). The presence of kanyirninpa provided for Folds and Rowse the element of 'command' that stabilised mission life.

While there are clear links between kanyirninpa and hierarchy, such links were not uniformly established over all Puntu in Balgo Mission. Nor can it be said that by providing food for adults the missionaries were guaranteed authority over them. Certainly, a strong experience of relatedness was established and reinforced. However, rationing was used in a highly selective manner. The children, old people and mothers with young children were provided with daily rations. Men only received rations if the mission employed them. Initially, most of the men were not employed. They either had to obtain food from the women, hunt, find employment by the mission or seek work elsewhere. The provision of rations separated active men from their families as it also separated adults from their children. It concentrated the children for education while disenfranchising their parents. In this way, a form of kanyirninpa was applied to the children, to those who naturally sought the nurturance and protection of older people. It did not apply to the adults who were 'held' in very different ways. By feeding and holding the children the mission arrogated a new authority and relationship, especially as the children grew and matured.

Until Peile came to new Balgo in 1973, no missionary, after Worms, spoke any Kukatja or had studied anthropology. While wishing to be seen as different from the pastoralists in their treatment of Puntu, in some ways they were often quite similar. They sought to build economic bases amidst challenging and very difficult physical conditions. Like the pastoralists, most missionaries lived by the same principle once articulated by Tom Savage, 'We did not know what the Aborigines thought about it all. We would never have dreamed of asking them' (Willey 1971, p. 52).

What I have presented in this chapter is a particular picture that describes how contact between kartiya and Puntu was initiated and developed south of Halls Creek in the twentieth century. This relationship was often characterised by suspicion and fear as kartiyas entered the Kimberley in larger numbers to dominate the land and its resources. Balgo Mission arose within that context. While Puntu may have experienced a different relationship with the missionaries than with pastoralists, there were commonalities. Both largely denied the violence that had been, and in some cases continued to be, enacted on Aboriginal people and both saw their right to control the lives of Puntu. At old Balgo the Catholic church espoused its respect for the values of an ancient culture, but the missionaries moved firmly and clearly to change those values. The socialisation of the young into kartiya society was to be accomplished by their formal separation from their parents. Polygyny and promised marriages were to be replaced and people were to work if they were to receive rations and wages. These were the signs of a 'civilised' life. The change to a sedentary life separated Puntu from close and regular contact with their traditional lands, it reinforced the authority of the missionaries and it restricted Puntu social and ceremonial behaviour. It impacted severely on people's diet, and on their ability to hunt and gather, and it severely limited the ability of older men and women to provide and care for those they held.

While the mission may have seen itself as providing a 'less hurried' form of assimilation than the Government, the means and results were similar. The moral right of older Puntu to hold and look after younger generations was denied. The inter-connectedness between land, ceremony and holding was frustrated. The missionaries held great social, economic and religious power. They could make it difficult for Puntu to celebrate ceremonies, to visit relations and to have their young initiated. Missionaries had control over food and water, especially when the land around the mission became more difficult to hunt and was depleted. These interventions threatened the fabric of desert society as they attacked the foundations of identity and social reproduction. When children were returned to their families in 1973 parents were told to take responsibility for them. For twenty years they had been told that, not only would kartiyas take responsibility for their children, but also that Puntu were not capable of doing so.

As one who witnessed the change to the dormitory system in April 1973, I have been particularly able to watch those boys, then aged from 5 to 15, grow up into men in the following thirty-five years. Of that original group of forty-seven, ten have already died at an average age of 38 years. On one of my field trips in 2004, one of them was admitted to hospital after having a heart attack. He died a few months later.

The health of this man, and that of his fellow wati, cannot be easily separated from a history of growing up in the desert and the impact of various colonial and mission practices upon them and their families. One of the social practices that the mission heavily influenced was kanyirninpa. As kartiyas took responsibility for separating and growing up children, they prevented and wounded the ancient ways of social integration and reproduction. Older people were frustrated in their ability to grow up younger people and younger people suffered when older people could not hold them. The social and emotional health of Puntu society was radically affected. I now turn to examine this health in more detail.

3

Healers and Health

If I tell you somebody will sing you, you'd laugh at me, yangka?

What's this blackfella talking about? No one can sing people!

In bringing the previous chapter to a close, I related the story of a man in his early forties who suffered a heart attack. Shortly afterwards, he was taken, with some urgency, by the Royal Flying Doctor Service (RFDS) to Derby Hospital. A week later he returned to the region and I asked him how he was feeling. He replied,

> When I came back I found it hard to breathe. But yesterday the maparn took three dark red stones out of me [he points to his stomach] and now I feel much better. There is no pain now. They tell me I have to go back to Perth for a check-up. I am not going to have a heart operation, just a check-up.

In one short conversation this man summarised a number of competing interests in relation to his health. According to Western medical care he was seriously ill, but according to one of the local maparn (traditional doctors) he was recovering. Despite his own prognosis, a month later he was flown to Perth and underwent a heart operation. He died a few months later.

The Puntu of the Kutjungka region share a colonial and mission experience similar to that of many other Aboriginal people. They also share a similar range of biomedical health outcomes. These outcomes, and the broader discourses around Aboriginal health that encompass them, assume important meanings around the English word 'health'.[1] As suggested by the story just related, the Puntu of the Kutjungka region share understandings around 'health' that differ from those generally held by Western biomedical practitioners. Puntu attendance at community health clinics and their belief in particular health outcomes are seriously influenced by their own health beliefs, such as in the importance of maparn, the 'traditional doctor' or 'healer' (Peile 1997, p. 166).[2] As kanyirninpa is a deeply embedded value in desert life so also are concepts of what it means to be well, palya, and sick, nyurnu. To grow up in desert life is to grow up within a particular cultural context: being 'healthy' describes an embodied quality of living that includes the relationships a person shares with walytja (family), ngurra (land) and tjukurrpa (dreaming). To become a healthy adult male is to invite more than the expression of physical and bodily health.

In this chapter I will describe some of the main biomedical indicators of men's health in the region. Following that, I will give a description of maparn and their healing skills; how Puntu understand being well or healthy, palya, and how they understand being unwell or sick, nyurnu. This will, in turn, lead to a description of the health clinic and how the clinic engages the Puntu male body.

While there is a slowly growing body of knowledge about the current status of Aboriginal men's health, not much is known about the health of men in this particular region. Anthony Peile's work, *Body and Soul*, offers many valuable insights into Kukatja understandings around health, but little that specifically pertains to men (1997). Ernest Hunter's *Aboriginal Health and History* gathers valuable health data relevant to the Kimberley, particularly during those decades of great social change, the 1960s to 1980s, but the desert region merits only scant comment (Hunter 1993, p.187). In 1989 some of these desert men provided information for the Regional Report of Inquiry Into Underlying Issues in Western Australia (RCIADIC) (Dodson 1991, section 6:8). Within the past decade, and through some of the health data gathered by Mercy Community Health Service (MCHS), there is now some general mortality and morbidity data available for the region, encompassing the Halls Creek area.[3]

In mid-2002 some of the men in the region underwent Well Men's Checks.[4] Although limited in scope and representation, these checks confirmed the poor health of a number of men and indicated risks for further ill-health.[5] A high percentage of the men smoked tobacco (83 per cent) and drank alcohol (79 per cent); a smaller number smoked marijuana (*Cannabis sativa*) (29 per cent) and sniffed petrol (14 per cent), and were found positive for Sexually Transmitted Infections (21 per cent).[6] There was an almost equal group whose BMI (Body Mass Index) was underweight as opposed to overweight.[7] Nearly half of the group measured more than 6.6 for BSL (Blood Sugar Levels).[8]

If we accept the 2006 Census as a reasonable but limited indicator of the region's population, 719 people were living in the Kutjungka region: 460 in Wirrimanu, 144 in Kururrungku and 115 in Malarn (ABS, 2006). Of this group — which included kartiyas who were mainly staff — it would seem that there were about 632 Puntu in these communities. Of these were 317 were male: Wirrimanu, 209; Kururrungku, 58; and Malarn, 50. Approximately two-thirds of the men of the region live at Wirrimanu.

There are a number of statistical phenomena within this region that can be found in other Aboriginal communities across Australia. For example, in the Kutjungka region those under 15 years of age comprise nearly 40 per cent of the total population, but those older than 45 years constitute only around 14 per cent. The number of older people declines quite rapidly after the age of 44 (see Graph 1). The very high number of young people can also be found in other Indigenous communities. For example, in Canada 21 per cent of the population are under 15 years of age but this increases to 37 per cent for Indians, 38 per cent for Metis and 43 per cent for Inuit (Morrison & Wilson 1986, p. 612). As revealed in the second graph, not only is there a greater proportion of younger Indigenous people than non-Indigenous in Australia, but there is also a far smaller proportion of older people to help 'grow them up' (see Graph 2).

Of those young Puntu in the Kutjungka region who had been born between August 1977 and August 1986, and hence were between 15–24 years at the time of the 2001 Census, at least ten

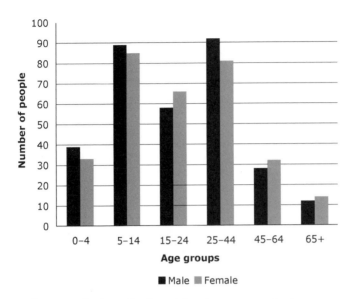

Graph 1. Distribution of male and female age groups in the Kutjungka region.

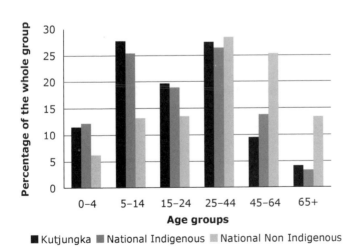

Graph 2. Comparison of Kutjungka region with Indigenous and non-Indigenous age groups within Australia.

had already died by August 2001. Three have died since the 2001 Census, two aged 16 and one aged 17.

Within the decade 1992–2001, nearly 25 per cent of all male deaths in the region were motor vehicle related. Some resulted from rollovers, others resulted when the vehicle broke down and those who were injured could not receive medical help for some hours. Similarly, alcohol has also contributed to the deaths of many men in this region, and has been a significant factor in many motor vehicle related deaths. Hunter identified the period of major social change in the Kimberley as,

> From the mid-1960s to the end of the 1970s. It was around the mid-point, in the early 1970s, that the restrictions on the sale of alcohol to Aborigines in the region were lifted. There was subsequently a sustained increase in the proportion of deaths from external causes — primarily accidents, motor vehicle accidents and interpersonal violence — consistent with the direct impact of alcohol on male behaviour. (Hunter 1993, p. 194)

This desert region has not been an exception. Some men have died as the result of an alcohol-induced illness, others as the result of alcohol-related violence; some have resulted from the desire to obtain alcohol at the Rabbit Flat roadhouse in the Northern Territory, 280 kilometres away from Wirrimanu.[9] Two men, who attempted to drive to Rabbit Flat in the summer of 1992, disappeared and have never been found; the following year, two young boys also died when a vehicle returning from Rabbit Flat broke down.[10] Three years later, another man died when his vehicle broke down between two communities. Within the past decade, more than half of all the deaths of young men under the age of 30, were influenced by alcohol. At least once a year, the region loses a young man through an accident or the result of violence; sometimes they are fathers with children. There are now a number of children and teenagers who have grown up without a father, some having been born after their father died.

The above statistics reveal a high-risk element involved in driving in remote areas, especially under the influence of, or motivation to obtain, alcohol. It also reveals the importance of mobility and alcohol for men, young men in particular. Roads are unsealed, vehicles are in constant need of repair and distances between the nearest communities vary from 50 to 120 kilometres.[11] Support services, such as emergency health care, are also seriously limited. There is evidence that in remote areas of this country young Aboriginal males (15–24 years) have a death rate twice that of Aboriginal youth in urban areas, with motor vehicle accidents being significant contributors to these death rates (Australian Institute of Health and Welfare 2000, p. 226).

In 2002 and 2003 there were the first cases of suicide in the region (and several attempted suicides), several charges of sexual assault (which resulted in imprisonment) and at least one incident of sexual abuse. These events all involved young men in the 15–24 year age group. While the incidence of suicide has, for more than a decade, occurred more dramatically in the West Kimberley, these three deaths of young men, two 16 years and one 17 years of age, suggest an emerging social and emotional health issue in this region (McCoy 2007b).

Puntu are aware that there are many sources and causes of physical pain and sickness, and that they have various means at their disposal to achieve personal healing and well-being. The following incident captures the complexity of sickness and healing possibilities that can interact in contemporary Puntu life:

> It was a Saturday morning when news had gone around the community that an older woman was dying. People came and filled the house where she lay, unconscious in her bed. Some cried as they watched and waited. Attending her were maparn, local church leaders and nurses. Each provided moments of care and attention, attempting to save her from death. The nurses maintained a drip, the church leaders prayed and anointed her with oil and the maparn worked to remove the sickness from her body.[12] After a long period of time the old lady suddenly stirred and a little later sat up in bed. She seemed oblivious to the large and concerned gathering around her and shortly spoke and asked for something to eat. The change in her physical state was remarkable. Later, the nurses said that she had recovered

from a diabetic coma but the church leaders and maparn also maintained that their interventions had made a significant difference to her recovery. Her family was happy and all those involved were pleased. She was alive and well, all due to the efforts of nurses, church leaders and maparn.[13]

There are three locations, or separate geographical spaces, where sickness and healing interact in the desert today. There is the clinic, often a small fibro-cement building, where a nurse, generally a female, is based. Her attention to sickness derives from a training in, and delivery of, a Western biomedical approach to illness and disease. There are local church leaders who provide, usually with prayer and holy oil, a Christian response to a person who is sick. They operate from the church or, if requested, visit those who are sick in the camp or in the clinic. There are also maparn in most of the communities. These are usually men, but can be women, who respond to people's sickness using a traditionalist model of diagnosis and healing. People usually seek their help in 'camp', where the maparn or the sick person live. Sometimes the maparn will visit the clinic, especially if a member of the family requests their presence. Today, most Puntu move quite deliberately in and out of these three geographical spaces. Sometimes, as in the story mentioned, all three groups will work closely together. As Janice Reid has summed up:

> People are pragmatic in their search for a cure of an illness: they will utilise whatever resources are accessible to them. It is not necessarily the case, though, that changes in practice reflect changes in belief. In Aboriginal communities, a coherent body of medical thought shapes the interpretations of misfortune among young and old. (Reid 1982, p. 196)

While Puntu attend the local health clinic or seek Christian healing, they also say that they visit the maparn first, especially if the pain originates within the body and they consider that their sickness may be serious. They admit that women can be maparn as well as men. As some would comment, 'there were women, some maparn, a long time ago'. Men believe that most of these women are no longer alive and their gifts and skills were not handed on (Tonkinson 1982, p. 231). They also believe that children can have maparn powers and cite the example of a young girl presently living in the one of the communities.

While both men and women have been maparn, such roles, as in other places, would appear historically to have belonged more to men (Elkin 1943, p. 123; Bell 1982, p. 220).[14] This does not discount the particular ways in which men and women provide and sustain healing, but in fact suggests an 'interdependence and complementarity' of healing roles (Bell 1982, p. 220). This would seem to apply in this region. Women appear to resort more to the use of bush medicines and provide healing as a group, maintaining their health through ceremonial women's business (Peile 1981, p. 29; 1997, p. 174). Tjarrtjurra describe these women and their healing powers (de Ishtar 2005, p. 3).

What has become clear is that maparn, especially men, continue to be active within this region and others (Cawte 1996; Ngankari 2001; Ngaanyatjarra et al. 2003). In 1960 Worms wrote, 'today he is mostly replaced by the white Flying Doctor' and in 1974 John Cawte noted, 'the end is in sight...and their total eclipse may take no more than thirty years' (Worms 1960; Cawte 1974, p. 27). Despite such observations, it is apparent that Puntu have maintained detailed, highly developed and intricate understandings of the causes of particular forms of illness and what can heal those illnesses. While these understandings are deeply embedded in strong cultural beliefs, this is not to say that they have not been influenced by contact with kartiyas and the provision of nurses and Western medical services (as also teachings and practices about Christianity) over more than fifty years. Puntu are conscious that they are living in a different world from their parents and grandparents. They are now exposed to relatively recent forms of sickness, and these have become important elements in their lives.

As a means of further understanding the work of maparn and the ways in which Puntu understand health and illness, I invited a number of maparn to paint something about their work. I suggested this for a number of reasons. Painting is now accepted as a medium of cultural expression within the region where paintings are done, not only for sale through Warlayirti Artists, the regional Art and

Cultural Centre, but also for outdoor walls or floors of buildings, for church ceremonies, as banners and as gifts for kartiyas. I wondered whether paintings might provide not only a helpful way of understanding people's health beliefs, but also enable those beliefs to be re-visited and discussed at further times. I avoided suggesting what they might paint, but requested they paint something about maparn 'business'. Some took up the offer and others didn't. Some appeared more comfortable with this medium of expression than others; some painted privately, others painted with the assistance of their wives.

The paintings express the distinctive personality of each maparn. They also revealed a close connection between healing powers and ngurra (land), the human hand as an instrument of healing, and a strong conviction that their 'ownership' of healing gifts were given to them to be used 'for others'. In the first painting (*Maparn* 1) Fabian Polly Tjampitjin, a young man in his late twenties, recounted the time when summer floods prevented maparn from two of the desert communities travelling to another community to heal someone who was sick. Their presence had been requested, as there was no maparn available in that community. While his own activity demonstrated that young maparn are continuing this tradition, it also revealed that there are sometimes no available maparn in particular communities. Some have died and some have given up their practice. This young man received the gift of maparn from his father's brother and he felt that people appreciated his gifts. However, for some maparn the decision to relinquish their healing work can arise from the pressure and beliefs of particular Christian churches.

Despite the combined efforts of maparn, clinics and church healers, men readily admit that they are not as healthy as their fathers and grandfathers. While conscious of the health messages round the dangers of smoking, drinking, 'getting the shakes', consuming too much sugar, tea and flour they also admit, 'we just can't stop; we like it too much'. Change to diet and lifestyle has left them without regular exercise and with added health risks and new diseases. However, they continue to maintain very particular and cultural understandings of health and illness.

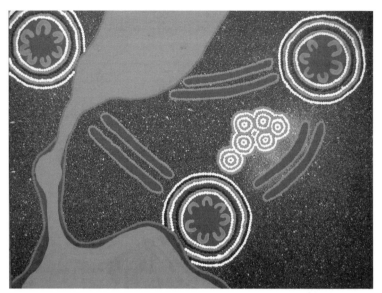

Maparn 1, Fabian Polly Tjampitjin

Not only is the term 'health' complex across cultures but it also suggests more than the absence of disease (Adelson 2000, p. 5). The most commonly used word that Puntu use today to describe 'health' is palya. Palya has been translated into English as, '1) good; correct; beautiful; 2) healthy' (Valiquette 1993, p. 185). It covers a range of possible meanings, depending on the context.[15]

When someone returns after spending time in hospital someone might ask them, 'palyan?', 'are you well?', and they will often reply, 'yuwayi, palyarna', 'yes, I am well'. The nurses or doctors may not consider the person to be 'healthy' — they may have an ongoing illness — but the person considers that they are palya. They are not currently experiencing pain, their body and inner spirit (kurrun) feel palya and they are home again with their family.[16]

'I'm glad to see you, palya, I'm happy to see you,' says one person to another they have not seen for a long time, 'I've been worrying about you.' Relatedness, especially with members of one's walytja, is important for the experience of health. Palya, as one man described it, summarises the whole of a person's life, the 'inside, outside, everywhere'. He stressed the word 'whole'. Palya can describe one's experience of bodily well-being. It can also describe one's spiritual well-being (the location and status of one's kurrun) and one's social well-being (one's connectedness with walytja). When a father described his feeling for his son, when he stopped petrol sniffing and came home, he used the phrase 'tjurni palya'. Inside (his stomach or tjurni) he felt good and happy. While palya can be located in the physical body, it describes the person who is in relationship: with others, land, cosmic and spiritual forces.

When a man described a men's gathering that would talk about issues that were relevant to the men he said, 'We'll be happy; our health will be happy.' Men's social relatedness, as I explore in the following chapter, is an important element of men's health, as are rituals such as those involving sorry business. A young man described how he would go to a sorry meeting feeling sad but walk away feeling 'happy'. The public gathering and social activity healed his feelings of sadness.

What is also common in the use of the word 'palya' is the person's belief that a physical, spiritual and social harmony has been established. In some cases it is highly personal and individual, in other cases it emphasises the balance of social and cosmological forces (Wiminydji & Peile 1978).[17] The person who returns from hospital, the young man who stops petrol sniffing, the men who gather together, and the ritual of a funeral can all be palya as they reveal the desire and effect of people to re-establish a balance and harmony between relationships. As Diane Bell described Kaititj women's understanding of health: 'health, happiness and harmony are intimately intertwined' (1982, p. 198).

Peile linked the word 'palya' with notions of the good and the beautiful and, quoting St Thomas Aquinas, suggested they described 'genuine aesthetic principles' (1997, p. 25).[18] His argument was that health consisted of the body being 'cold and dry' with a person's kurrun (spirit) lying in the area of one's stomach. Health, he proposed, did not describe harmony or balance between people (1997, p. 130). Later in this chapter I discuss his notions of 'cold and dry'; I suggest that such descriptions do not preclude an emphasis on the use of palya to describe health in terms of relationships. In fact, I suggest his use of 'cold and dry' can reinforce this argument. Like Peile, I have not heard people describe a sunset as palya (1997, p. 25). However, one Puntu related to me the following story:

> A car load of male Puntu was driving along a desert road and came across a group of kartiyas. This group had stopped their vehicle and were standing beside it, looking up at the sunset. Thinking that they were looking at some unusual heavenly phenomenon, the men asked them, 'What are you looking at?' 'What a beautiful sunset,' came the reply. The men got in their vehicle and kept going.

The men were amused and surprised that kartiyas would stop and admire something that, to them, was part of the regular experience of their desert life. It was not, as Peile has commented, that they were 'reserved in commenting on the beauty of something Europeans would speak about as beautiful', but there was no need for them to draw attention to something they considered normal. It is my understanding that the sunset would only have been singled out and described as palya if its relationship to Puntu had changed, causing it to be made better or improved. Peile described the Kukatja appreciation of the adolescent body as an example of palya. Perhaps, in this understanding, the adolescent body was palya because it was perceived to be in a process of development; it was in the process of becoming an adult body and, in this way, was both physically and socially beautiful. In my experience, the 'beautiful and the good' are not, for desert people, abstract concepts but linguistic metaphors used to describe the deeper harmony and interconnectedness that Puntu perceive exists in all desert life.

Palya suggests then an inclusive and relational understanding of health, a holistic notion that embraces not only the physical and the social, but also the spiritual and the cosmological. Maparn suggests the critical importance and inclusion of healers within that understanding.

Peile's notion of 'cold and dry' offered several important descriptors of the Kukatja body and its experience of health. The Kukatja word 'yalta' has been translated into English as, '1) cold; 2) healthy; 3) better; well' (Valiquette 1993, p. 354). The word 'lalka' (also larlka), as, '1) dry; 2) healthy' (Valiquette 1993, p. 66). And while yalta and lalka are not commonly used today to describe manifestations of wellness or illness, there seems little evidence that using the terms 'cold' and 'dry' necessarily excludes social and relationship aspects of health. As others have shown, Peile has been sometimes contradictory in his use of 'cold' and 'dry' (McGregor 1999, p. 225).[19] For example, when a child sniffs petrol their spirit becomes 'dry' and after drinking grog one feels 'cold' in the head (Peile 1997, p. 95). He has also described an experience of coldness that is associated with sorcery.[20] Neither of these examples would suggest an experience of health that might be considered palya.

Learning to cope with the extremes of heat and cold, as also of wet and dry seasons, has revealed that many Indigenous peoples experience health by monitoring their own bodies within the demands and extremes of physical conditions. The Cree, for example, define health in terms of their ability to stave off the cold (Adelson 2000, p. 87).[21] Hence, as Puntu say, if the body is exposed to excessive sun one can get sick; if one's body is too hot, one will move to shade, to avoid that heat. In a response to heat, the body seeks to be cool rather than cold. But if one's body is cold, one needs to find the warmth and experience of sweat to keep well, 'waru ngantjilpa palyarri', 'warming oneself at a fire will make one better'. It is my understanding that the desert physical body is ideally 'cool' rather than 'cold', as one of the signs of bodily health is the body's ability to be warm and to sweat. Hence, 'when they don't sweat... their body is out of, nganayi, control and when they sweat they know their body, ah it's sweating, I'm getting palya'. Peile also stated that the ability to sweat was a sign of health: 'I am strong [and healthy]. I go out in the sun with my bald head. Perspiration cools my bald head' (1997, p. 131). Hence, use of the words 'yalta' (cold) and 'lalka' (dry) to provide a detailed understanding of health can be problematic. However, they can provide valuable barometers and monitors of bodily health and sickness. They situate the physical body as preferably cool within an environment that is often hot, and preferably warm within an environment that can be cold. While it would seem to be restrictive and unnecessary to limit notions of well-being, health or palya to these two concepts, they can be valuable descriptors that sensitively locate the physical body within a social and ecological world.

There are different words in Kukatja that are used to describe sickness or illness, such as the word nyurnu. This has been translated into English as, '1) sick; 2) slightly sick' (Valiquette 1993, p. 173). Surprisingly, Peile does not refer to this word in his work. When someone asks another, 'nyurnun?', 'are you sick?', they would be wondering if that person felt sick or pain inside. There are also other words such as 'marnmarlarrinparna', 'I am feeling pain'. Or they might use the word 'mimi', '1) sick; 2) incapacitated by illness; 3) having a wound' (Valiquette 1993, p. 94). While Peile suggests that mimi can describe a range of experiences and being 'sick', this word would seem, at least in more recent times, to refer to those particular and exterior sores associated with sickness. Hence a sexually transmitted infection (STI) is referred to as mimi.

Sometimes Puntu also use the word 'ngawu', meaning, '1) bad; evil; 2) not functioning normally on account of sickness' (Valiquette 1993, p. 145), suggesting one is getting sick in a more serious and possibly life-threatening way. This form of sickness is generally caused by the sorcery of another that can be difficult to diagnose. Not surprisingly, ngawu can express both the form of illness but also the emotion associated with illness. A father, worried about his son sniffing petrol, might describe his feeling as 'tjurni ngawu', 'he is deeply worried inside' (his stomach). Similarly, if a young person feels cut off from family or friends he might say he feels ngawu, and this can lead him to extreme behaviour such as petrol sniffing, stealing and alcohol. These different words for sickness indicate that the emotions associated with sickness, like those around palya, reflect an important social and relationship dimension of illness.

There are many ways in which people can get sick. Some refer to relatively simple causes such as getting sick from eating food that was too ripe. The sun can make people hot and sick. In the second maparn painting (*Maparn* 2), a person has come to Joey

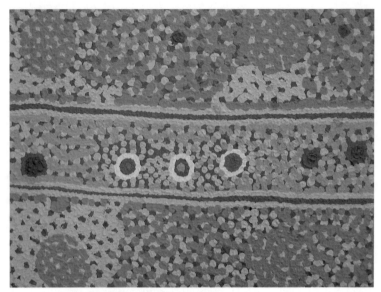

Maparn 2, Joey (Helicopter) Tjungurrayi

Tjungurrayi, also known as 'Helicopter', to be made well.[22] The three white circles are people: the person who is sick, the maparn and the person who has been made well. They sit between two lines or rows of tali (sandhills, the red horizontal lines). The green circles are the different communities of the region, and the country is full of bushtucker (yellow).

'Palyalarni,' the sick person asks the maparn, 'make me well', and the maparn cleans the inside of the person's body. In this case the person has a 'runny tummy' from eating too much bush food, such as kumpupatja or pura (bush tomato) or kantjilyi (bush raisins). The person has become well, palyarringu.

There are other forms of sickness. Headaches can come from 'cracks' in people's heads. The wind can make people sick: 'a stick can go through a person's body and make a hole and as the wind goes through the person they feel hot'. A person can have 'bad blood'. Their blood needs to be blocked from some internal bleeding. Or, it needs to be opened up from some blockage to the movement of blood. People can become sick from the actions of a murungkurr (tree spirit).[23] And wearing another person's clothes can make people sick (Peile 1997, p.134). This would seem to be an example of a more recent understanding of sickness which people have learned from contact with kartiyas.

A person can become sick if their spirit, their kurrun, shifts from its normal place. Instead of lying in the middle of the body, tjurni (the stomach), it could move elsewhere, such as to the back of the body or to the shoulder or feet. Or, if a person gets a fright, their kurrun could jump and then stay in the wrong place within the person's body. The maparn is able to put the kurrun back in its rightful place.

A further painting was done by a maparn in his forties, who grew up as a young man at new Balgo Mission and had then moved back to the Canning Stock Route with his family. He regularly returns to Wirrimanu. In this painting (*Maparn 3*) Flakie Stevens Tjampitjin has described a sick person, covered in murtu (red ochre) who has been brought by a family for him to cure. The people are surrounded by tali (sandhills) and also by many little maparn or healing powers.

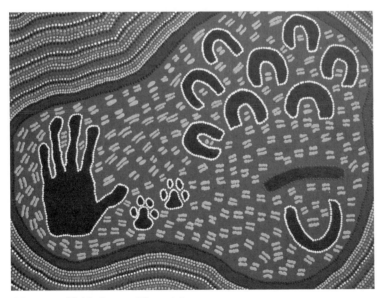

Maparn 3, Flakie Stevens Tjampitjin

His hand has touched the sick person and healed them. A kunyarr (dog) spirit accompanies him and helps him as he works.[24]

The most serious and dangerous forms of sickness for Puntu are those caused by sorcery. For example, there are 'lids', foreign and invisible objects that can fly up and enter into the human body. The derivation of the term 'lid' is unclear.[25] Some men believe that 'lids' are like lead or copper wire; they exhibit similar material properties to nails, copper and iron. Others suggest a 'lid' is more like a fingernail (milpiny), shell or pearl shell. Still others describe their qualities as like bullets. Lids are invisible to the average person. Only maparn have the powers to see them. They can move through the air and cause serious illness.[26] They can especially be dangerous at Law time.

Lids are not the only form of sorcery. Some people are believed to have the power to put sickness in another, as also the power to remove that sickness. Despite contact with kartiyas, and more recent forms of diseases, such as cancer, if people hear that someone is sick their first thought will be that someone has made that person sick. That people have the power to make others sick, not only leads to mistrust of others, especially strangers, it also can make people very frightened.

Maparn, especially the older and more experienced, are often sought for their healing powers. The final maparn painting (*Maparn 4*) was done by an older man, Bill Doonday Tjampitjin, who travelled the Northern Territory and Kimberley as a young stockman. He is now a respected and experienced maparn who has been asked by Puntu from the region to go to regional and interstate hospitals and heal family members when they have been seriously ill.

In this painting he has described a particular country where men can go to receive special maparn powers. The artist detailed the story of a man who once went there to get maparn powers, so that evil spirits would no longer frighten him. Not only is there a strong connection between ngurra and maparn, but also between the fear that some sicknesses generate, and the need for strong and available maparn to alleviate those fears.

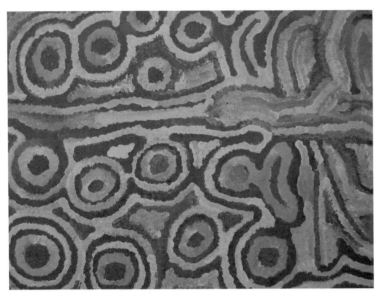

Maparn 4, Bill Doonday Tjampitjin

Most men, including maparn, say that 'new' diseases, including renal failure, diabetes, cancer or STIs, lie outside the powers of maparn. The difficulty Puntu have in dealing with these diseases is that they are perceived to be 'new'. 'The new diseases came out of nowhere,' said one man. They do not arise from an understanding of sickness that has guided Puntu in the past. Regarding cancer one maparn said, 'The maparn can feel them but will say, "You've got your own sickness, go and see a doctor."' Cancer does not belong to a memory of past illnesses but is associated with the colonial and mission experience. Recent changes to Puntu diet, lifestyle and health are also seen as interconnected. Kartiyas are therefore perceived not only as being instrumental in such changes, but also to have some power over these 'new' diseases. The rending of the Puntu social body, as described in the previous chapter, discloses an important link between the ongoing effects of colonisation, kartiya influence and power, and Puntu health. Disease, and the treatment of it, can be perceived to arise from the world that kartiyas control.

The one who is sick with cancer cannot easily ask a maparn the question, as they may have in the past, 'what wrong did I do to receive this?' or 'why are others trying to hurt me?'

Hence, the boundary that separates the work of maparn from that of the clinic and its concerns is not clearly identifiable. While one maparn said that his work is 'stronger' than that of a doctor because 'he can fix someone right away', another said that his job was to fix the person who could then get pain relief from the clinic. In this latter sense, the clinic is perceived to provide medicines in similar ways to bush medicines, but it also can be perceived to replace other methods of healing. Whereas in the past, people might have been smoked for a 'runny tummy' they might now go to the clinic for medicine. This is not to discount the use of some bush medicines. People continue to use pilytji or murtu (red ochre) on a person's body when they are sick. This 'ancestral blood' can, among other strengths, protect a person from a 'lid' that can't smell a person who is covered in pilytji.

One young man in his mid twenties told how he used maparn and also attended the clinic. He did not express concern or anxiety about having two very different explanations, or methods of healing, for his sickness. He allowed both to offer their own forms of treatment: 'one in the morning and one in the afternoon, like taking tablets'. He would go in the morning to the maparn and then in the afternoon to the clinic. He believed that both helped his condition but, he then added, 'I believe more in maparn'.

The provision of a clinic-based health care in the region can be traced back to the early days of old Balgo. At that time the Government permitted missions,

> the right of rural and pastoral pursuits on such reserves... provided the freedom of tribal life on outback reserves is not interfered with except in respect to medical considerations or other assistance as may be necessary in the preservation of tribal life. (Bray 1945, p. 13)

The Commissioner had noted that same year that leprosy 'was rising rapidly in [the] East Kimberley' (1945, p. 17) and the missionaries were well aware of their failure to establish a medical clinic at Rockhole some years previously. The first nurse, as also the first kartiya woman at old Balgo, was Allie Evans who worked from 1951–55 (Nailon 2000, p. 198; Zucker 2005). The Sisters of St John of God arrived in 1956. The Western Australian Health Department took responsibility for the delivery of health services from 1975–88, providing nurses at Wirrimanu, supported by Royal Flying Doctor visits. In 1989 the Western Australian state government put the service of primary health care in the region to public tender, and it was finally given to the Institute of Sisters of Mercy Australia (ISMA). The provider of the service was then referred to as the Mercy Community Health Service (MCHS). In 1990 this new service began with four resident nurses based at Wirrimanu, and four part-time Aboriginal Health Workers. Initially the sisters — not all were Sisters of Mercy — were based at Wirrimanu. They made regular trips to the other communities until 1996, when nurses began to live permanently in Kururrungku and Malarn. In 1994, MCHS initiated the formation of a locally based Puntu health organisation that led in January 1995 to the incorporation of Palyalatju Maparnpa Aboriginal Corporation Health Committee (PMACHC). The phrase 'Palyalatju Maparnpa' may have been translated as 'good health for all', but, as Fatima Lulu, the first health worker at Malarn wrote: 'The name we chose because it is important to us that the Aboriginal doctor is included by people first, after that then the Kartiya (western) doctor' (1999, p. 1).

In each of the communities there is now a health clinic. They usually include an open meeting area where people gather and where the nurse or health worker provides initial attention. There is also another room where people can be seen more privately. In the smaller clinics the files, notices and fax machine are in the front, open area of the clinic. The Wirrimanu clinic is much larger than those in Malarn and Kururrungku, and has extra rooms where nurses and health workers can attend the more seriously sick. This clinic is the second health clinic built in Wirrimanu since people moved there in 1965. In August 2001 it was announced that approval for a new clinic had been given (Mirli Mirli 2001). It was opened on 5 June 2004.

There is evidence that the present clinic system has marginalised the health needs of men, particularly due to the nature of the clinic's personnel, priorities and its geographical space. Historically, kartiya female nurses have staffed the clinic with the support of female health workers; there have been very few male nurses or health workers. As noted elsewhere, health clinics have become significant female domains where the majority of those who attend are mothers and grandmothers, often accompanied by babies and small children. Health concerns around infant sickness and mortality have clearly influenced this development. However, one consequence is that men's health has been compromised. In 1999 the MCHS concluded in its report, 'men's health issues are difficult to resource…due to the predominant female constitution of clinical workers in the health service' (O'Donnell 1999, p. 3).

The physical structure of a clinic can also create tensions across kinship and gender. Health clinics have been constructed with little sensitivity to Aboriginal values of space and kinship interactions (DodsonLane 2002, p. 15). Community clinics are generally small, enclosed buildings where patients and family are forced to sit close or facing one another. As the relationships that exist between men and women can extend from genial familiarity to strict respect (avoidance), men and women can equally experience discomfort and shame in these confined physical spaces. This can apply to men, especially when the person in charge is a woman and the majority of those attending are women.[27] 'What I mean,' said one man, 'like some men get shamed, see. They don't like going to sister.' Here, the 'shame' that is being described is more than embarrassment. The social and kinship dynamics that enable men and women to move and relate, within a wide range of personal interactions, are severely curtailed in the small physical space of a clinic. In 1999 a MCHS report noted, 'male attendance drops off sharply from age 10 upwards, throughout all male categories', and, 'adult males do not attend often, even when chronic disease has been diagnosed' (O'Donnell 1999, p. 3).

As discovered elsewhere, there is an important link between the status of Aboriginal men's health and the presence of Puntu male health workers, male health practitioners and the provision of clinics that are more culturally appropriate for men (Wakerman 1999; Menon et al. 2001; DodsonLane 2002; Brown 2004). The MCHS health report of 1999 stated the problem succinctly: 'the men's health programme is difficult to resource in the region when there is no male on the health service staff' (Mercy Community Health Service 1998–9, p. 15; 1999, p. 19). Four years previously, they had noted the value and importance of having at least one male on staff, an importance confirmed by research in the Northern Territory (O'Donnell & Lock 1995, p. 13; Menon et al. 2001, p. 7). As one man said, referring to his postponement in seeking medical treatment, 'I kept it as a secret for a long time, you know… [because]…there was no Aboriginal orderly'.

However these factors, in themselves, do not fully explain why, 'male attendance drops off sharply from age 10 upwards, throughout all age categories', and how it is that 'adult males do not attend often, even when chronic disease has been diagnosed' (O'Donnell 1999, p. 3). In order to understand the 'healthy' or 'sick' Puntu male body, it is also important to understand important elements in the social and contemporary construction of this male gendered 'body'. It was only after I witnessed the frustration and embarrassment of men as they entered the clinic, especially at those times of the year when men's Law ceremonies were being performed, that I began to wonder about that relationship between the 'outer' male physical body and the 'inner' and personal self.

The Kukatja word 'yarnangu' has been translated into English as, '1) body; 2) somebody; anybody; group of people' (Valiquette 1993, p. 358). Yarnangu can refer to both a 'physical body' and also a 'person', similar to the Pintupi yanangu (Keeffe 1992, p. 32). The link between the physical and the social body is particularly well expressed in Kukatja where a boy, who is being initiated, can be referred to as yarnangurriwa (literally, 'body/person-becoming'); he is becoming both an adult male body and an adult male person. As with other Aboriginal languages, Kukatja reflects not only a close linguistic relationship between the words used for 'man' and 'person', but also the close relationship of those words with ceremonial initiation (Evans & Wilkins 2001, p. 495). Hence, 'tjitjitjanu yarnangu punturringu', 'from being a child [his] body [person] became that of a man'. He was transformed, physically and socially, at initiation into becoming an adult male person.

The transformation of a boy into an adult person is accompanied by important cultural meanings that are intimately linked with his physical body (Willis 1997). His body, like the earth, sustains physical, social and religious meanings. These meanings are inscribed upon and within the physical body by the use of song, dance, ochre and painting as a man enters into the secret and sacred ceremonies associated with men's Law. His body is not just a vehicle of entry into men's 'business', a world that is carefully separated from that of women; his body becomes part of that secret and sacred men's business that belongs to all of desert life and its cosmic 'business'. Initiation transforms him, person and body, into an adult social body where new relationships are configured and developed.

When a wati (man) enters a health clinic he cannot separate his physical body from his relationship with the adult social body. His physical body, his membership of a male social body and his identity are intimately related, such that his 'inner' and the 'outer' bodies can be understood as 'pleated' together (Teather 1999, p. 9). His health, as Saltonstall describes the interplay between health, self, body and gender, 'need[s] to take account of the body as personal and socially situated in the construction of self (and other selves)' (Saltonstall 1993, p. 7). While his physical body is his vehicle of entry into the clinic's social space, it is not the only part of him that claims respect and attention. Sometimes this space evokes a dissonant response to his sick or injured body.

Elizabeth Teather introduced the idea of the pleat in her exploration of the geographies of 'life crises' or 'rites of passage' (1999, p. 1). In *Embodied Geographies: spaces, bodies and rites of passage* — where researchers discussed very different geographies such as 'schoolies week as a rite of passage', 'the transition into eldercare' and 'spaces and experiences of childbirth' — Teather sought to challenge that body of knowledge that neatly separated the human body into an 'inside' and the 'outside'. Her argument was more than a criticism of Cartesian dualism and the separation of mind and body. She sought new ways to describe the embodied self, the self and the body, the self and the world.

Teather turned to Elspeth Probyn, who had used Gilles Deleuze's description of 'the fold' or 'the pleat', to explore 'the doubledness of the body...constituted in the doubledness of body and self' (Probyn 1991, p. 119). This process of 'doubledness' was subject-ification, whereby the self was constructed within the world, and by the process of 'folding'. The 'outside' became enfolded within the 'inside' and the 'inside' within the 'outside'. Probyn approached the embodied self from a feminist perspective, wanting to include the body within a theoretical discourse, not simply as an objective entity separated from the self. She described Deleuze's idea of the pleat:

> this pleating ('la pliure') is thus the doubling up, the refolding, the bending-on-to-itself, of the line of the outside in order to constitute the inside/outside. While the outside and the inside are to an extent distinct, Deleuze's metaphors can be used as ways of figuring the intricacy of the one stitched into the other. (1991, p. 120)

Deleuze identified four different foldings within the work of Michel Foucault. Folding can be understood through the folding of material bodies, the folding between forces (power), the folding of knowledge (truth) and the folding of the outside (becoming) (Deleuze 1995, p. 104).[28] In the desert, the process of becoming an adult male ('yarnangurriwa', literally 'body-becoming'), suggests an embodied process where the adult male body ontologically changes in relation to social relationships and cosmic powers through an interaction with very specific social spaces. While acknowledging that all four foldings may apply to the desert adult male, here I wish to pay particular attention to the first folding, 'the material part of ourselves which is to be surrounded and enfolded' (Deleuze 1995, p. 104). This folding has been described as 'the body's material relationship with space: the ways in which bodies become embedded in the spaces around them and the ways in which spaces simultaneously become embedded in the body' (Malins et al. 2006, p. 511). It is within such a folding, or pleat, that the importance of an intertwining of the inner and outer desert male body can be better understood. At the time of male initiation, important meanings are enacted, inscribed and effected upon the male body. Simultaneously, these meanings fold back between the self and the desert social world. This is an example of what Deleuze described as, 'foldings that together make up an inside: they are not something other than the outside, but precisely the inside *of* the outside'(1995, p. 97).[29]

The pleat as metaphor, but also as an epistemological and ontological concept, offers a helpful insight into this desert male body that is neither an exteriority, separated from the activity of one's inner kurrun or larger cosmic forces, nor an interiority, disconnected from social and relational meanings. Dichotomies that can be imposed upon this desert body — separating the physical from the spiritual, the body from the cosmic, the person from the social — deny important relational aspects for desert people that are dynamic and essential for living well and palya. The pleat offers a way of understanding this process of subjectification, where an adult male wati lives within a dynamic of interior and exterior worlds, and with social and cosmic meanings that are inextricably linked with one another. It helps explain some of the meanings that men bring and embody as they enter the health clinic.

Hence, as I have explored through this chapter, living healthy or palya becomes the embodiment of harmony that exists between physical, social and spiritual realities. It can be further suggested that in living well and palya there is a folding, a subtle pleating of the inner and the outer person, the physical with the social, the kurrun with the cosmic world. The metaphor and concept of the pleat remove artificial and fixed boundaries between the desert self and others, between inner and outer realities and meanings. However, while the intimacy between the 'outside and the inside' is what a male wati embodies, this can become quite problematic for him as he enters the health clinic.

A kartiya nurse would likely say that she would treat a male Puntu patient as she would a kartiya. She would likely treat all footballers the same, for example. However this approach can marginalise, even trivialise, a Puntu and his health needs. The clinic will largely attempt to socialise him into its space using a biomedical approach to his human body. In this model his physical body can be treated separately from his kinship or social relationships. However, the male Puntu who presents himself in a clinic cannot separate his physical body from his adult and social identity. His gendered body expresses both his health and identity. Any man who has been through ceremonial Law will be very sensitive to the treatment he receives in a clinic, especially if the nurse is female. In some cases it will not affect his experience of treatment. However, if a nurse asks him personal questions in front of women, makes jokes about his health or body, shows little sensitivity about privacy, or loudly suggests he needs to be tested or treated for particular diseases, such as STIs, he may get very angry, shamed and upset.[30] At such times frustration is heard: 'Oh heh', asks one married man, 'don't we need a bloody thing, male nurse, eh?' The issue for the man is not that he won't be treated — although frustration can lead him to walk out of the clinic — but the cost and the risk of being treated. In the process of receiving treatment, other forms of care, important for his personal sense of well-being, can be ignored or trivialised. Not surprisingly, and to avoid these risks, men prefer to see male health workers, nurses or doctors. Young men, in particular, will seek the help of older men, as they learn to carefully negotiate their new adult status in a transformed physical and social body.

This is not to say that sensitivity or privacy is important only for men. Nor to say that women can't offer clinic care to men. Sometimes, especially in relation to pain relief, the clinic will be the first port of call. As one man said, 'Cold sick and headache they can go any sister'. A man might also negotiate his needs within the health clinic by asking another male to accompany him. He may do so for support and company, or he might be seeking assistance from the female health worker who has a more appropriate kinship relationship with his male companion. In these, and many other cases, treatment is achieved in an appropriate, nurturing and respectful way.

There will be times, though, when a man will seek clinic care from another man. He might postpone attending the clinic until he can see a male nurse or doctor at another time: 'If a man is ever sick with an STD he doesn't go to the [female] nurse, he feels shame and he will keep that sickness.' He might even travel to the nearest town and visit its hospital: 'I would go to Halls Creek,' said one man, 'they've got Puntu there'.

The need for a more appropriate and gendered approach to Aboriginal men's health has been strongly recommended in men's health gatherings, research and health policy within the Kutjungka region, the Kimberley and elsewhere (Guyula 1998; Wakerman et al. 1999; DodsonLane 2002; Lowe & Spry 2002; Wennitong 2002; Brown 2004; Working Party 2004). They have stressed that the health needs of men, their under-utilisation of clinic services and their experience of colonial history are all closely inter-connected.

Mark Wenitong, in *Indigenous Male Health*, has referred to the compromising of male role models due to fathers being either absent (in prison), or incapable (from alcohol). He has expressed concern for *'an increasing matriarchical family structure...that* may have damaging consequences for the identity development of young Aboriginal boys' (Wennitong 2002, p. 39).[31] Lowe and Spry, in *Living Male*, have commented that,

> many adult Aboriginal and Torres Strait Islander males have also experienced separation from their communities and families in early life: because of sickness, imprisonment or removal under government policies. As well as the suffering from such separations, these experiences have interrupted and impaired their cultural processes of growing up as Indigenous males: resulting, for many, in uncertainty and lack of confidence in their cultural roles of parenting; as fathers, grandfathers and uncles. (2002, p. 30)

Other Aboriginal men have emphasised the importance of older men taking up their responsibilities including those towards younger men (Adams, cited in Lowe and Spry 2002, p. 12). These reports, and associated research, indicate the various ways in which the health of the Aboriginal male body has suffered, and how there remain important historical, generational and gender issues to be addressed (Brown 2004; Working Party 2004).

Some health reports, however, demonstrate little understanding or appreciation of these gender issues in relation to health. For example, the 1999 Kimberley Regional Aboriginal Health Plan made no mention of the particular health needs of Aboriginal men or of women. The Plan noted that,

> people in communities outside the larger towns usually have no choice of doctor, or even a choice of the gender of the doctor they see (or any choice in the gender of the remote area nurse or Aboriginal health worker who may be the only resident staff member). (Atkinson et al. 1999, p. 68)

It offered nothing about the health implications of that lack of choice on either gender. The National Indigenous Australians' Sexual Health Strategy (1996–97 to 1998–99) confirmed,

> an urgent need for an increase in the number of Indigenous health workers, especially men given the under-representation of men, and because of the gender specific nature of men's and women's business. (ANCARD 1997, p. 92)

However, it did not explore the 'gender specific nature of men's and women's business' nor possible reasons for 'the under-representation of men'. This lack of attention to gender ignores the particular impact of history on Aboriginal women and men, and the specific ways in which male and female bodies have become wounded and sick.

My intention in this chapter has been to explore the cultural and gender factors that affect Puntu health. Being palya in desert society invites physical and social well-being as a person faces the presence of cosmic forces that can cause serious sickness, even death. Maparn provide an important healing service as they assist fellow Puntu to move from experiences of being nyurnu or ngawu to that of being palya. The health clinic, on the other hand, offers a very different geographical and healing space that has, over the years, developed into a particularly female domain. While the clinic offers tangible health benefits, it also presents particular obstacles to the adult male body (yarnangu) when social and ceremonial meanings have been inscribed upon and within it. In the following chapter I will look at the social construction of the Puntu male body in relation to the practice of kanyirninpa, where new holding relationships develop as boys become men. These relationships bear important consequences for male sociality, men's praxis and their health.

4

The Male Praxis of Kanyirninpa

You need your fathers, especially if you are a man.

The current and critical status of Puntu health is not the result simply of history, remoteness, a change of diet, or an increase in smoking or alcohol consumption. While these and other factors are relevant, there have been a number of external forces that have severely impacted on the way in which the Puntu male body is individually and socially constructed. The pleating that exists between the physical and social male body, yarnangu, expresses a palya or health experience for men that is essentially relational. Health expresses a wellness that is both individual and social. The experience of kanyirninpa critically affects the embodiment of palya, as it influences the ability of men to experience and participate in the meanings and social regeneration of their desert society. To hold and grow up those younger than themselves, men need to have experienced the holding power of older men. The expression and experience of holding and being held by other men, is a critical ingredient of men's physical, emotional, social and spiritual health.

While clearly 'a feminised praxis', kanyirninpa is also a masculine praxis. Women and men both express physical care as 'a demonstration of relatedness' (Finlayson 1989, p. 96). Unfortunately, it has been noted, 'the specific role of fathers in child rearing is very poorly documented'.[1] Women play an important part in the holding and 'growing up' of the young, a process that they and many grandmothers continue today. However, at ceremonial Law, and beyond that time, a particular aspect of male kanyirninpa is identified. Men take, and are expected to take, their part in holding and 'growing up' young men. Any emphasis on 'growing up' young people that focuses only on the part of women limits the experience of kanyirninpa within contemporary desert culture. It can also exclude men from their significant holding opportunities and responsibilities.

For young desert men a critical moment comes in their lives when they move away from being held by their mothers and, to a lesser extent, from their fathers, into becoming adult males. From that moment they experience being held by men in a totally new way. Myers argued that as the older men led the ceremonies and transmitted important ritual knowledge, they powerfully reminded the young men that authority, nurturance and the tjukurrpa (dreaming) were all intimately related (Myers 1986, p. 220). The power of kanyirninpa for desert society was disclosed and reinforced at this time. Those who claimed authority needed to show they offered 'security, protection and nourishment' (1986, p. 212). At that moment, when boys ritually died and later rose as men, desert society was renewed. The cycle of social meanings around walytja (family), ngurra (land) and tjukurrpa (dreaming) was reinforced and deepened see Kanyirninpa model, p. 21). These Law ceremonies depended on the activity of both male and female Puntu and, without their activity and participation, society could not initiate the young into the meanings and mysteries of their adult lives. McGuire's and others' attempts to prevent, or restrict, ceremonial Law acted directly at the heart of desert, not just male, identity.

While I have attended a number of Law ceremonies, I do not intend to disclose any of their details. There are important restrictions placed on those who move within the Law not to divulge their secret or sacred elements. I have witnessed a number of times when men have expressed great concern that kartiyas and wati (initiated men) have revealed secret knowledge. Once, when ceremonies were being conducted in a nearby desert community, the local kartiya storekeeper photographed people as they entered the area near the store, a break from their ceremonial activities at the nearby men's Law ground. Some of the older wati approached me, the only kartiya who was in the Law at that time, to stop him. Although men and women were moving in a public space, they were doing so within the context of ceremonies that were still occurring. To the storekeeper, who believed he had the permission of the local chairperson to take photos, people were moving within a public, and therefore non-secret, space. Some of the senior men saw it quite differently. There was clearly a separation between the activities in the Law camp, and those that happened around the community store, but there was also a continuity. The appropriation of Puntu Law by a kartiya and his camera was held with great suspicion and some anger.

I need to add that I do not intend to compare the Law ceremonies of today with those of the recent past, as some anthropologists have done (Berndt, R 1972, p. 199; Kolig 1981, p. 122; Myers 1981). Nor do I intend to describe the process of how young women become adult, as it would be quite inappropriate for me to do so. However, one important distinction can be made between the social processes whereby young men and women become adult. I mentioned in the previous chapter how linguists have demonstrated an important etymological link in Kukatja, as in other Aboriginal languages, between the words for man, body and person. Evans and Wilkins have pointed out that the link, and the shift, between the words for 'man' and 'person' are driven in the desert by the cultural significance of initiation (Evans & Wilkins 2001, p. 495).[2] When a young man enters the ceremony of initiation he can be described as yarnangurriwa; he is in the process of becoming both an adult body and person. Puntu have said to me that yarnangurriwa can apply to both men and women. However, it applies particularly to young men through the inter-connection of the physical and the social in the ceremonies of initiation. Young women become adult women, but the process of their physical and social transformation does not occur in the same public and formally celebrated way as it does for men (Berndt, R & C 1985, p. 180). This is not to deny the process and significance of young women becoming adult, but to note that male initiation continues to remain a key public ritual that involves all adult Puntu. It also remains the only secret and sacred ceremony that is performed by Puntu on a regular basis, and that excludes (largely) the presence and influence of kartiyas. I also want to emphasise that today the process of ceremonial initiation continues to exert an important influence over the lives of both old and young desert men, as it does also upon all who live in Puntu society.

Anthropologists, such as Ronald Berndt, Robert Tonkinson, MJ Meggitt and Fred Myers, have described extensively the ceremonies of initiation for young men of the Western Desert (Tonkinson 1978, p. 67; Berndt, R & C 1985, p. 166; Meggitt 1986, p. 281; Myers 1986, p. 228). They have outlined the process whereby young boys were introduced to the sacred and cosmic world of the tjukurrpa, to finally re-emerge with a new status (Berndt, R 1974, p. 4). Myers portrayed these ceremonies as 'the premier cultural event', linking the construction of the social person to that of kanyirninpa:

> The production of the social person involves an elaboration of the ties of relatedness to others, the creation of a public self that takes priority over its private qualities, and the development of the ability to 'look after' others. (Myers 1986, p. 228)

Here, Myers is reinforcing a key aspect of kanyirninpa that lies within the process of yarnangurriwa. The process of a boy (marnti) becoming an adult (wati) reinforces relatedness with walytja and learning how to hold others. Clearly, Law stresses the importance of relatedness, the high priority of cultural awareness and knowledge, and living in multiple and dynamic relationships. In the Law, older men bring all men together. Some may have recently disagreed, argued or even physically fought with other men who attend. These, and other differences, are put aside for the duration of the Law.

The young men who share their first ceremonies of initiation are called yalpurru.[3] They share for life a close and personal bond and are encouraged to hunt and socialise together. They should never fight but look after one another. There are also other relationships that arise as a result of these ceremonies. Tjamparti and pilali refer to those who perform the ceremony and their immediate relations.[4] Not only do those who are initiated enter into new and important kinship obligations, but their families do as well. These relationships can be put under pressure when men move in different social domains and have other forms of social relatedness. Later, I explore how men negotiate these relationships in contemporary settings such as playing football.

Even in the 1970s Myers indicated that change was occurring in the life of the Pintupi. He provided an example of kanyirninpa where a man became a 'real father' to a young man, held to account after a fatal car accident (Myers 1986, p. 212). The young man, his wife's son by a previous marriage, feared that he might be killed in payback for two who had died. The older man stood up for this young man and accepted responsibility for his 'son'. In return the younger man deferred to the older man who was now 'looking after' him. This was a revealing example, not simply because it exposed the continuing importance of kanyirninpa for Pintupi young men, but also because of its context within a changing social world. As Hunter later pointed out in relation to the Kimberley, it was from the early 1970s that motor vehicle accidents led to a dramatic increase of deaths of men aged between 15 and 30 years of age (Hunter 1993, p. 82).[5] However, even before the 1970s the context in which older men held younger men had changed. This has not denied men's desire for kanyirninpa but it has revealed the serious difficulties some men have experienced in obtaining or sustaining it.

In his painting about 'men's health' (p. 100), Jimmy Tchooga Tjapangarti, an older man, chose to paint himself with his sons, and the other young men he has 'grown up', sitting around a fire. This man has four sons, has looked after some of the sons of his deceased brother and has also 'grown up' other young boys. As he described his story it is clear that a hierarchy exists with him as the 'father' (the largest 'U') at the top of the painting. At the bottom of the painting he has drawn symbols representing men's Law. It is not necessary to describe these in detail but to stress the connection he made between himself, his sons and the Law. As he said, 'I taught them really…they took my footstep and everything'.

Men's Health 1, Jimmy Tchooga Tjapangarti

He described his relationship with his sons with much pride and how he 'put' his older sons into the Law. He believed he continued to hold them even though some of them were married.[6] 'Why they stick together? Because they want to get experience from me, go through the Law and get more experience from me.' The painting revealed the reciprocal nature of kanyirninpa and its close relationship with walytja: as the father continued to take responsibility for his sons, especially by teaching them and introducing them to men's Law, they in turn sat with him and supported him. They submitted to his values and authority; they acknowledged that through him the ancestral tjukurrpa was transmitted to them. He was proud that his sons had listened to him and kept out of trouble. And he was confident that, in his case, this next generation would pass on the Law: 'You know, when old people pass away these can take over'. Desert culture would continue through his sons taking on and living the Law.

Here, an older man, father and grandfather, demonstrated the relationship that existed between himself, his sons, the other young men he has 'grown up' and men's Law. The painting also reflected something about his walytja. While there was no mention of his wife, and her significant role in care and nurturance over the years, he recognised that his family was particularly close and strong. They had taken in, and looked after, children from other 'families', and not only from his deceased brother's family. None of them had been to prison or sniffed petrol. They were strong in following ceremonial Law. Not only had the sons gained confidence, knowledge and strength from their father, but the older ones were now competent and proud in what they knew and what they could do when in the Law. However, not all young men have experienced the same holding security and care that this man and his wife have been able to provide.

As a marnti a young boy grows up under the primary care of his mother. When men's Law ceremonies are about to begin, there is a formal and public occasion when everyone in the community will gather. At those times a marnti will sit with his mother, other women and children. There is, however, one occasion during men's Law ceremonies when he will be permitted to move with the women to the edge of the men's Law ground. This occurs prior to the final ceremony, after the tjamparti have been selected and introduced to the gathering of all Puntu. The whole assembly of men and women walk to the men's Law ground. There the women dance for the boys to be initiated. After this, the marnti run in line through the gathering of assembled wati to be thrown by them into the air, a moment of joy and laughter that contrasts the seriousness of the occasion. This leads to the women and boys being chased back to their camp and then the final Law ceremony, with only wati present, begins. Until that time, when he is taken for his own ceremony of initiation, this is the closest that a marnti can ever approach the men's Law ground. That moment, when boys run through the gathering of men and are thrown by them into the air, is repeated at every men's Law ceremony. It reminds the marnti that, within the seriousness of men's Law, there is also present a quality and company that he can enjoy and anticipate receiving.

As boys reach about 11 or 12 years of age they become aware they are approaching the age for Law. They can be heard asking questions that reveal their growing interest. In return, the wati sometimes tease, but reveal nothing of detail, and conversations begin among members of the boy's family. The father and mother will talk with key men and women in their family and gradually a decision will be made. As any Law ceremony involves the Puntu of other communities — sometimes inviting them to come in return for previous ceremonies they sponsored — negotiations will occur with the senior men and women of those other communities.

Once the initial ceremonies of the Law are completed, young men are expected to move away from their mothers and younger siblings and move more in the company of men. His mother might say to his older brother, 'nyuntulu kanyila ngampurrmarra', 'you hold him and look after him'. Until this time he will have experienced being held by his mother and father, or by other older relations who have looked after him and grown him up. Now is the time for the older men to take hold of him. They are not to literally hold him, as he was held as a child, but they are to exercise a similar relationship of care, protection and responsibility for him. It is up to them to help grow him up.

The young man might move from living with his parents to living with his uncle or with other single men. He will look to his older brothers, and those men who are a little older than him, to teach and show him how to act like a man. From attending further Law ceremonies to coping with alcohol, from relating with women to playing football, a young man will seek the company, advice and support of older men. He will be advised as to appropriate conduct during ceremonies, and how to express new relationships that arise from those ceremonies. Men will advise him how to drink and deal with hangovers, how to relate with women and get married. In essence, they will teach him how to move around and act as a wati, as an initiated man. These are important years for a young man. His gendered and adult role in Puntu society is constructed and strengthened with the help of older and other men.

When a young man first 'enters the Law', he experiences being held in an analogous way to when he was held as a child. This experience is based on the authority of older men, their power and intimate knowledge of the Law. It is an authority that teaches, nurtures and protects those who are young, as the Law is not only a place of great cosmic power but also one of danger. One of the roles of older men is to watch over the younger men to ensure they do not do — or become exposed to — anything that could lead them to getting injured or sick. Hence, when men are travelling for ceremonies, or if a small group of men have gone with a marlurlu (initiate) to bring others to Law, men want older men to accompany them. They acknowledge the protection such company provides.

After his time of seclusion in the bush, following his initiation in the Law, the young man will return with his yalpurru and other men to his walytja and community. It is often late in the day, a week or two after his initiation. There is an open space between the men's Law camp and the community houses. It is a public ceremony, which kartiyas will often be invited to attend. He walks with his fellow yalpurru, hidden behind a large blanket or sheet, carried by other young men. His panytji (brother-in-law) comes forward and kneels on hands and knees, offering his back for the young man to sit on. The young man comes out from behind the covering and sits, facing away from his mother and the other women, who come forward to cry over him one last time. His first action, when he comes out of the Law is to sit on the back of an older male relative, facing away from his mother and female relatives — a strongly symbolic gesture. He is no longer a boy dependent on his mother. Now, older men will hold and carry him. That radical separation between son and mother, which began when he was first taken from her presence into the Law, is reinforced once again.

In his radical transformation into becoming an adult male, a young man now belongs in the world and company of men. In this world and company he is held by older men in ways that promise further holding when the ceremonies are completed.[7]

The sensitivity, energy and intimacy that men share with one another (the journey for Law and the ceremonies are linked in one extended ceremonial space) provide a significant male sociality. This sociality and space, separated very clearly and strongly from the presence and scrutiny of women, who have their own rituals, is also very clearly separated from kartiyas. This ceremonial time provides one of the clearest examples of Puntu agency, belief and commitment. It also reveals the importance of Puntu male sociality and company.

One time, as the men settled into their swags, on a journey to another community for Law, a young man announced, 'I didn't come here to sleep, I came here to tell stories.' Men will often sit around talking long into the night on such journeys. The company and context provides its own particular nurturance for relaxation, conversation and enjoyment. On the journey and as the ceremonies are being performed, it has become clear to me, sometimes the only kartiya present, that this is a time like no other for Puntu men. Not only are the older men in control, the younger men active and energetic, but there is also an experience of male company and unity that is only partially glimpsed outside Law times, on occasions such as sorry business or football. Apart from the sacred and secret nature of the Law, it seems that 'going to Law' does more for men than simply preparing them to participate in ceremony, or to provide a break from the daily stresses of family and community living. At these times, I have both witnessed and experienced an important quality of men's behaviour with one another. Men are relaxed, open with each other, talkative and keen to share stories. There is humour and occasional teasing. Differences are put aside. There is no violence, acrimony or overt jealousy. Under the umbrella of very serious and sometimes physically demanding cultural 'business', men enjoy an energy and relationship with one another that I have rarely experienced or witnessed elsewhere. Here, they share food and water, cigarettes, mattresses and blankets. A physical, religious and social environment provides them with enjoyment, trust, learning and affection. The Law provides a powerful and intimate homosocial experience.

Clearly, men enjoy their own company, separate from women and away from kartiyas. Beyond those times of ceremonial Law, men's gatherings are believed to be a proven method to discuss and resolve problems, for the young to sit and learn from the older men, and for the young to be constrained from doing simply what they like. Ceremonies provide those special moments when men 'all join in together' but, because they are so few, it also invites them to explore gatherings outside that of ceremony time. I discuss this further in the following chapters.

This spatial separation of men from women allows both men and women to perform their own gendered ceremonies, but it also allows for ritual moments when men and women gather together (Berndt, C & R 1983, p. 68). This gendered separation, and the intimacy of the male experience, indicates the continuing importance and value of male geographical space where place and meaning are linked. Here, older and younger men come united for ceremonial purposes within a place (which can vary but is usually based on a ceremonial men's Law ground in each community) over which they have power and control. If kartiyas are present, they are small in numbers and they come under the jurisdiction of the older men. Activity within this defined place connects the men with cosmic meanings that link the generations of men, past and present. Men recognise that these social situations are existentially very different from the meetings and encounters they have outside Law. They also recognise the difficulty of connecting or linking the meaning of such moments with the social and daily activities of contemporary life. In the following exchange an older man reflected on the problems of Law business competing with other and more recent demands on Puntu:

> A: See we got this new thing, eh? Computer stuff now. I don't
> know. I like to see them working together. Like we have those
> certain times, you know, when we start working together like

March to September. And then that time comes, September comes around, we can go back to our ways, you know.

R: Law time?

A: Law time, business, Aboriginal way. They can sort of learn in that period of time, you know?

R: March to September and September to March being Law time, culture time?

A: Yuwayi, March to September, and from September to February, in that time we can do Law business and we can be happy, you know. If they know where they come from, where they were, where they stand and everything, we'll be happy.

What this older man wanted was more time for men's Law. He recognised that the conversations often held around 'Law' space expressed two very contrasting views by Puntu and kartiya. Kartiya attitudes towards men's ceremonies over the decades have shifted between the extremes of outside interference and total indifference.[8] In more recent years, kartiyas have often distanced themselves from these ceremonies by describing them as 'Aboriginal business' and encouraging their celebration during the summer season when kartiyas usually take their annual holidays. The discussions and comments that kartiyas made, often benevolent in intent, revealed at times an irritation that much of the Law lies outside their understanding and control. This irritation was particularly noticed when the performance of ceremony constrained the movement of people around the community and their availability for tasks in the community office and other places. Staff also showed exasperation when they were informed that certain roads were 'closed', due to the movement of Puntu and other Aboriginal groups for Law.

Kartiyas can also make it difficult for Puntu to celebrate Law ceremonies. Pressure can be applied by kartiya staff on those who have jobs in the community not to travel for Law or be absent from their work. Payment of wages through the Community Development Employment Programme (CDEP) can be withheld if people attend ceremonies out of 'formal' holiday time. Stores can refuse to open at those times that fit in with the ceremonial timetable and a large influx of visitors. Garages can make it difficult to repair vehicles or provide fuel to assist visitors returning to their communities. And while they do not attend the ceremonies, and often have little knowledge about what occurs, kartiya staff can apply pressure for ceremonies to be postponed or completed by a certain time. In the summer of 2003 the older men postponed one Law ceremony so that the young man involved could attend kartiya 'law'. The young man was bailed to appear at court at a later time, and the Law ceremony was then conducted to fit in with the demands of his bail.

Kartiyas, especially those who hold positions of power in communities, share little — if any — understanding with the older men about the timing, costs or implementation of ceremonies. Kartiyas who live inside (and outside) the communities can influence the planning and execution of ceremonies. Older Puntu, men and women, have been marginalised over many decades and their authority to determine and define ceremonial space has been severely restricted and compromised.

In addition, some young and married men are not attending Law ceremonies as they did in the past. There is less compulsion or pressure from older men, and there are more alternatives, such as people taking summer trips and holidays to other communities. Ceremonies are also physically challenging to perform in midsummer, when the temperatures rise into the forties and airconditioners are available in an increasing number of homes. Some men are showing signs, even at a young age, of increasing obesity and the desire for less physical activity. In recent times, some men have become concerned about health risks for themselves and their sons at ceremony time. However, at such times, and despite pressure to minimise ceremonial Law, Puntu persevere with the performance of regular and annual ceremonies.

Moreover, some Christian churches have opposed the conducting of ceremonies. As one mother described it:

> A: I think it's all the other churches finding it hard, see, but Catholic do really, you know, how Catholic they like culture and church too, you know, but same with other church they don't like culture.

R: Making it hard for some people?

A: Yeah, like for some, like people like us.

R: Mm. So working it out is not easy?

A: Not easy, like pastor...like pastor and priests, you know, it's a bit hard pastor say another thing, priests say another thing but...

R: So what do the people say?

A: People do say, 'oh, we can't do culture' but some say, 'oh, because Ngarpu (God) gave us culture too', 'Jesus gave us culture'...

R: That makes it hard, doesn't it?

A: It's hard, true.

The preparation, gathering and journey that men and women make for ceremonial business can be demanding and difficult. Men's Law is generally performed at the hottest times of the year. It can also be very wet, and hence also the most difficult time for road transport. But it is achieved, often on a number of occasions, each summer. In addition, family members have to buy gifts for the ceremonies, supplies have to be procured and vehicles have to be obtained for journeys that can be hundreds of kilometres long. A convoy of vehicles (if the people are moving to another community for Law) needs to move as one 'body'. Not only does it need to arrive at that other community within a designated time (especially if other groups are travelling to that community) but, if there is a marlurlu, his must travel last in the convoy. If a vehicle breaks down the whole convoy must wait until all can move together. Coordination, planning and timing are critically important as ceremonies also need to be performed by the wati prior to entering the community they are visiting.

What traditionally helped incorporate young initiated men into adulthood, namely being inducted into further religious knowledge and getting married, has changed significantly in recent decades. Young men in their twenties remember the months of seclusion they endured after they were initiated in their teenage years. Even within the past decade these times of seclusion have been greatly reduced. It is now rare for men to spend more than two weeks in isolation after their first ceremonial experience. Men offer two reasons for this: there are fewer older men capable and willing to lead such seclusion time, and young men are generally less interested in experiencing the challenges that such seclusion, particularly during the hot summer months, promises.

Both young and older men have also expressed concern that the knowledge of the Law is not being handed on to younger men. As older men pass away, especially those who were born or grew up in the desert, they take much knowledge of the Law with them. They also take a confidence about land and ceremony that their sons, many of whom spent time in the dormitories, do not have. As one older man reflected:

> Nowdays the old people pass away and take stories with them
> and teach their sons a little bit. Sometimes they die and take
> their Law. And we're worrying about that.

Further reflections on growing up as a young man were offered by Brendan Ross Tjangala, who offered this painting (*Men's Health*, 2; p. 110) when he was 21.[9] In it he provided three different stories (panels) that he called his 'book' and 'story'. In the first panel (left) he described when he was getting into trouble, around 15 years of age. He was part of a teenage world where there was petrol sniffing, alcohol, girls and marijuana. One young man accompanied him as he got into trouble but then turned back. Another turned around and went with him. From this behaviour he ended up in prison.

This story represents what is common for many young men of his generation. After entering ceremonial Law he re-entered the kartiya world of 'adolescence'.[10] He spent ten or more years as a single man, not quite a 'man' in kartiya society and not fully a 'man' in Puntu society. He faced many risks to his health: car accidents, petrol sniffing, alcohol and imprisonment.

In the earlier painting, where Jimmy Tchooga described holding his sons and those he grew up, he exemplified that relationship between holding and relatedness. In this second painting, the emphasis is more on the relationship between holding and autonomy. Kanyirninpa values autonomy, but it also constrains it.

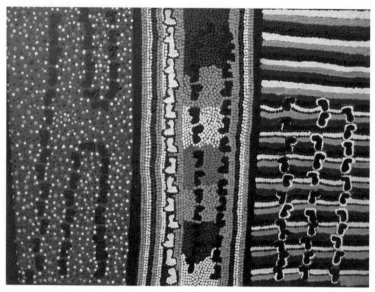

Men's Health 2, Brendan Ross Tjangala

It is not uncommon to hear a young man say, 'I'm a man and I've got nobody, I could do what I want' (Brady 1992, p. 75; Martin 1993, p. 12). Or parents and members of a family might hear, 'you not my boss anymore, you can't tell me what to do'. As adults hear these and similar statements they recognise that the young man is claiming what he has a right to claim, his autonomy. For, having been through the ceremony of initiation, they respect that he now has the adult right and independence of a wati. His mother, and other women, are particularly sensitive not to infringe upon his new autonomy. But they can also hear such statements as cries for help. They hear his loud and outspoken cries inviting someone to hold him, and for older men to take a stronger role in his life. In these cases it is not so much the fear of 'surrender' to the demands of adult responsibility and kartiya society they hear, but the felt absence of an appropriate and nurturing male company. The strident and loud claims for personal autonomy result from an absence of male holding.

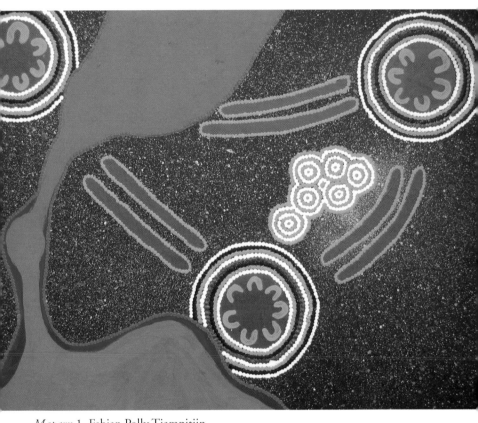

Maparn 1, Fabian Polly Tjampitjin

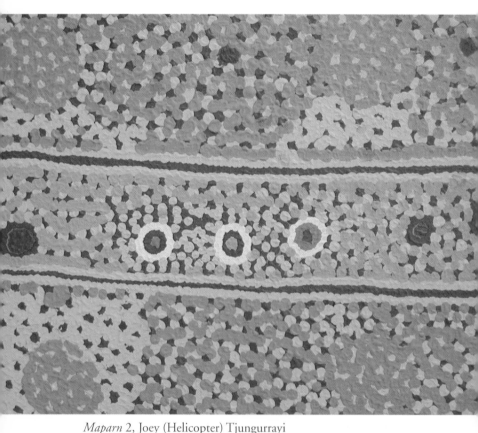

Maparn 2, Joey (Helicopter) Tjungurrayi

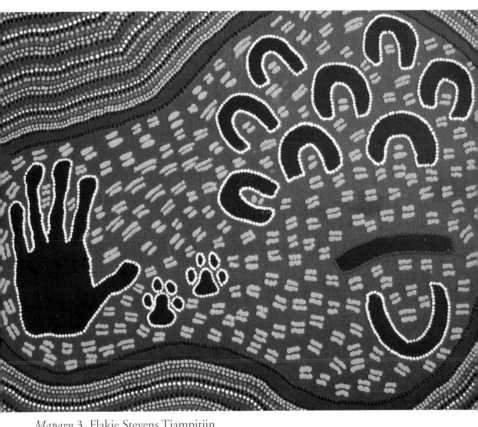

Maparn 3, Flakie Stevens Tjampitjin

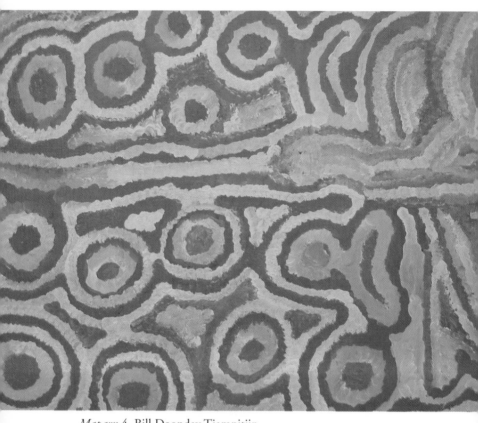

Maparn 4, Bill Doonday Tjampitjin

Men's Health 1, Jimmy Tchooga Tjapangarti

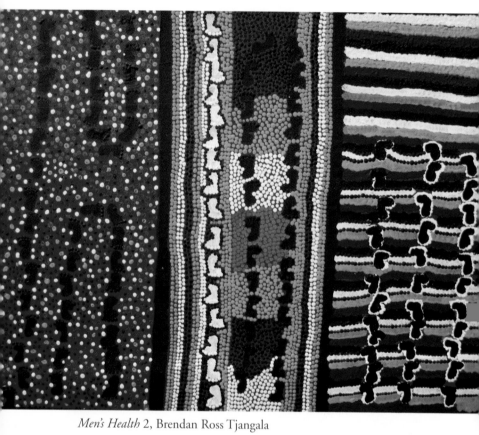

Men's Health 2, Brendan Ross Tjangala

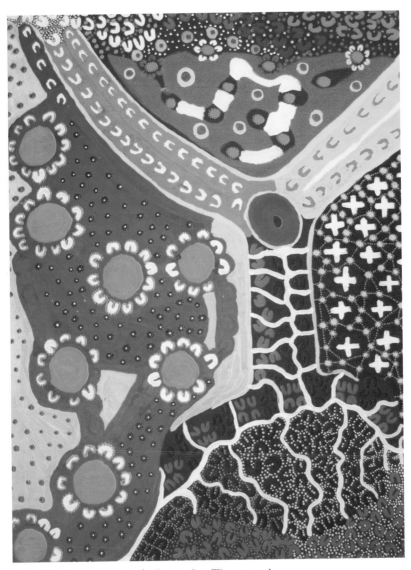

Men's Health 3, *Cross Roads*, George Lee Tjungurrayi,
Harold Gill Tjapangarti, Trevor Mudji Tjampitjin and
Ricky Woggagia Tjapaltjarri

Petrol Sniffing, four young men

Some researchers have interpreted these and similar statements as attempts to delay 'the inevitable embrace of mainstream life' (Brady 1992, p. 96). The message that most young Puntu men communicate to me is that they look forward to their moment of initiation, but with mixed feelings of anticipation and anxiety. They anticipate the time when they can join the ranks of other men with the privileges and male company it affords. At the same time, they are anxious about the journey they must take to get there. This 'ticket', as one young man described it, provides the only means of entry by which a desert 'boy' can enter the world of being a 'man'. Becoming a man opens up many new and exciting personal possibilities for him, in relation to self-esteem and stature, as well as adult male company. Without it he remains a marnti. If he does not go through men's Law all men will know and it is likely he will be teased. When desert men visit Halls Creek they can be quick to point out that they themselves are 'wati' while some of the men who live in the town are simply 'marnti'. In their home communities, men are well aware of who has been through the Law and who has not, who are 'real' men and who are not. In recent years, wati have put pressure on men who have come into the region and married to go through their Law: 'They're married to our people, you know, our families; they should be part of us.' Some, kartiyas and Aboriginal men from other areas, have done so and some have refused.

In the second panel (middle) of Brendan Ross' painting he has described a time when he was drunk. It was a time when he began to listen to and follow older men. There was a kartiya and an older Puntu friend who told him 'to stop doing silly things'. He listened to them and, as the painting shows, he turned around from what he was doing, a reference to his criminal behaviour and subsequent time in jail.

It is not uncommon for desert men to spend some time in jail. On most occasions, when a man is charged, alcohol is also involved. This young man moved, as do many young men, away from petrol sniffing to taking up alcohol and a different lifestyle around it. He began to travel around with older men, spent time in town drinking, and took the risk of being arrested and spending time in jail.

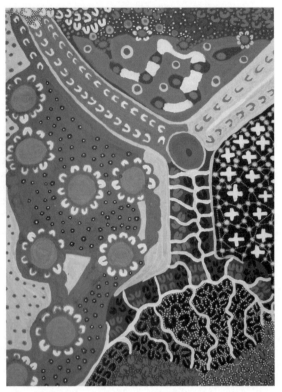

Men's Health 3, George Lee Tjungurrayi, Harold Gill
Tjapangarti, Trevor Mudji Tjampitjin and
Ricky Woggagia Tjapaltjarri

This period of a young man's life, where he and other young men
are 'at risk', is described in another painting done by a group of
young men when they were in their early twenties.

These young men called the painting *Cross Roads*, which they
completed after a weekend camping trip with other young men and
some male staff to talk about living at Wirrimanu. They described
the painting:

> Some of the young men and women find themselves at the
> cross roads of their lives too early, and without help they make
> decisions that cause serious problems within their families and
> the community…For the young men: drinking alcohol, sniffing

petrol, breaking into places, arguing with parents and also leaving school at age 13 or 14…For the young women: drinking alcohol, sniffing petrol, leaving school, not listening to parents.

The painting showed the two major roads that young desert people could take in life. One road (left) is where they tried different things like sniffing, drinking and marijuana. As the footsteps show they could come in and out on that road as they experimented with drugs and other things. The other road (right) was the road they could choose as they got older. It could prove safe and healthy or not. As they approached the crossroads (blue circle with red centre) they passed their community, and other Aboriginal communities, on the left side. On the right was the cemetery, a salutary reminder that many have died. At the very top are those who were adults: they included men who have been through the Law. Some had settled down and some had not. Some were still 'running wild'.

The painting revealed the particularly vulnerable and risky period of life for young Puntu. Not only do they face the dangers of drugs such as petrol, marijuana and alcohol but, in their own words, they 'find themselves at the cross roads of their lives too early', having to make decisions about drugs 'without help'. Their families can be 'broken' and they can experience great tensions with their parents. There is no one older available to help them find a better road. The promise of becoming adult, a wati, is experienced within the context of living as an adolescent. Young men feel particularly vulnerable when risk behaviour takes them outside the protective company of older men.

In the second panel of his painting Brendan Ross described the help and advice he received from two older men. One of those was a slightly older friend; the other was myself.

I was surprised when I heard him say that the kartiya (the white footprints) in the painting referred to me. I was not aware that anything I had said or done had made the difference his painting suggested. He reminded me that I once accompanied him back from Broome prison. He was being released around the same time I happened to be in town.[11] The older men in prison were concerned that he might get stuck in Broome, as he needed to wait a day until the bus departed for Halls Creek. They even suggested he ask if he could stay the extra day in prison to avoid the problems he would meet when he was released.[12] I offered to arrange transport so that he could come home directly with me. I picked him up from the prison, found a place for him to stay, and provided meals and transport that enabled the two of us to get back to the desert. That occasion meant far more to him than I had imagined. In the desert kinship system I am his older brother, and for that brief period of time I acted as one. It came at a time in his life when he was looking for such company and support.

In the third panel of his painting (right) he described himself walking with his wife and young baby. He saw that his life had now significantly turned around. Compared with his life before, he now saw that he had a 'future'.

In this panel he has described an ancient ideal: he has a wife and child, the beginnings of a family. This is his future: the three sets of footprints. In his painting Jimmy Tchooga saw his 'future' in the lives of his sons. They had taken up what he had taught them and they had continued in the Law. Brendan Ross saw his future in being married and having children. In both cases their hope for the future sustained them, but it also provided them with a sense of responsibility to hold and look after their families. In both cases stress was placed on the importance of male company and relationship. For the older male, it was expressed in hierarchy with the young men of his walytja gathered around him; for the younger male, it was expressed in the influence his peers had on him and that of older men to help him at an important turning point in his life. These two men are more than thirty years apart in age. They have experienced life very differently and yet they both share something in common. At the heart of growing up as an adult male lies the importance of the relationship that men receive from other men, and which they, in turn, pass on to the next generation of men. The experience of being held offers men the capacity to hold and grow up others.

As indicated in *Cross Roads*, in contemporary desert society holding and 'growing up' young people can be a difficult and frustrating experience for both young people and their parents. If young people do not receive the food or care they want, they can get very upset. When young people revert to behaviour their parents do not approve, parents can despair. The young can threaten to hurt themselves or even commit suicide. In one case a family offered a young man a car if he would stop sniffing and drinking. In other cases parents have threatened to leave their children to the consequences of their behaviour. Like a final act of desperation they threaten to cut off a younger person. Such a threat reinforces the importance of holding, as it gives notice of the final and ultimate sanction, the removal of personal attention and care. Unfortunately, it can also reinforce in some young people the feeling that they are alone, that no one cares for them.

Many of the men in this region, between the ages of 30 and 60, spent some of their lives in the mission dormitory, physically and socially isolated from their families for long periods of time. Today, most men do not live on, or regularly travel, their traditional lands. Stores now provide meat which men once hunted; Centrelink, together with CDEP, shape and re-arrange economic relationships within families; church personnel, community advisors, television, teachers, stockmen and police continue to provide different, sometimes conflicting, models and experiences of kartiya behaviour and masculinity. It is within this social and historical context that Puntu masculinity has been constructed and continues to change. Some of the young men in the region have lost their fathers through accidents and premature deaths. Fathers have moved away, married again or have gone drinking in town. There are young men who were only babies or very young when their father died or when they were given to someone else to grow up.

A young man in his twenties, married with a child, looks at some of these young men and comments, 'all those young boys grew up themselves...they grow up lost. Well they think they're lost well they're going to do something bad'. The absence of kanyirninpa affects the personal and the social. The one who feels 'lost' is unable to live within the demands of relatedness and the limitations of autonomy. A young man in his early thirties also uses the same word 'lost' in describing the lack of personal boundaries that result from an absence of not being held:

R: And what happens when no one is holding you?
A: You feel lost.
R: You feel lost and what happens, what do you do when you're a young man?
A: You just break loose.
R: Break loose?
A: Yeah, go anywhere.
R: Why do you do that?
A: I don't know…because you haven't got someone who can, you know…you need someone to teach you the right way.

There are also serious consequences that carry into the following generation. The older cousin of one young man, who had recently married and had a child, expressed her concern about him, and others like him: 'sometimes we have young fathers who's never been held onto by an older person'. She is worried that, because he did not experience being held by his father when he was growing up, he doesn't know how to 'grow up' his first child:

A: He's looking for his father to hold onto him.
R: Because he can't grow up his child by himself, and his wife?
A: Mm, cause he doesn't know how to…pass it on.
R: That responsibility?
A: Mm, being responsible for his daughter, for his little family, cause ever since he's been a kid his father wasn't really holding onto him.

In this case the young man returns to stay with his father, sometimes with his child, but sometimes by himself. He does not have the confidence to 'step out' from his own family, hold his child and look after her.

There are serious consequences if a person did not experience being held as a child or young person. It can lead to extreme forms of autonomy, as it can also lead to extreme feelings of loneliness and isolation. The voice that cries, 'I can do what I want', can be interpreted by adults as the voice of a lonely person who calls to be held. One man, now in his early thirties and father of four young children, describes what it would be like for him to feel the absence of holding:

A: If I had nobody holding me…I would just…
R: What would you do?
A: Do anything…what young boys doing now…
R: You mean you'd do whatever you wanted to do?
A: Yeah.
R: You'd go off and you wouldn't care for yourself or you wouldn't care for other people?
A: Care for myself…wouldn't care for myself…wouldn't care.

Holding provides an early, unconditional state of being cared for. It invites a reciprocal relationship. While its absence does not preclude the possibility of a young person discovering a balance between personal autonomy and family relatedness, it makes that discovery more difficult. Holding reinforces the importance of both, and the delicate tension that exists between them. If a young man has not experienced the foundations of holding before his initiation, he enters that rite of passage even more vulnerable to what might be offered at that time.

Van Gennep described three stages of a rite of passage: separation, transition and incorporation (Gennep 1977, p. 21). When anthropologists have described in great detail the initiation rites of desert men, they have generally given more emphasis to the first two stages, separation and transition. They have focused less on the third and final stage, incorporation. It is this often less formal but equally important, threshold by which kanyirninpa incorporates young men into the social well-being of contemporary desert life. The presence and continuity of ceremonies of the Law, however difficult they are to maintain and sustain, do not provide an automatic guarantee that young men will make that final incorporation. As I have already indicated, there are a number of signs that show some young men are struggling to become adult. There are also signs that some are quite resilient and creative and will seek the experience of being held by older and other men in new situations.

In 2002 the ABC filmed a documentary about policemen living in the Kimberley region of Western Australia. It was called *Kimberley Cops*. One of the weekly episodes told the story of a 12-year-old Aboriginal youth who came to ask the local police sergeant, based at Halls Creek, if he could live with him. This young man was being 'grown up' by his grandmother, even though both of his parents were still alive. As a young boy he did not think anyone cared for him. He did not have his own bed, would often go hungry and was regularly left to fend for himself.[13]

As the story was recounted:

> [Neil] was surprised when a teenage boy asked if he could sleep at [his] house so [he] could wake him up in time to get to school. I said, 'No, no way in the world! I can't have a kid come and stay in my house.' And he assured me it would be all right with his grandmother, who was looking after him. So we went around and saw his grandmother and she said, 'Yeah, that's fine', and he sort of went from staying one night here and there to staying five nights a week. [At my] house one day...[he] told me we needed to have a chat. He and his gran wanted to know, 'if I'd bring him up the rest of the way'. (Roy 2001)

Sgt Neil Gordon is not only a policeman, he is also a kartiya and single. He does not have any children and his family live in Perth, some thousands of kilometres away. In 2003, that young Aboriginal man continued to be 'grown up' by Gordon. Four years after coming to him, still a teenager but now older and more independent, he continued to be grown up under the care and support of this older, kartiya man. He would introduce Neil as, 'Neil, he looks after me'. In recent times four other Aboriginal youths, 13 years of age, have come and asked Neil whether they can stay. Three of those four have no living fathers.

If young men, especially around the early teenage years, do not find older Aboriginal men to help grow them up it is not surprising that some might look to kartiya men to hold them. As they seek to become adult, they will pursue the experience of holding that only older men can provide. I have already mentioned a time, some years ago, when a mother in a Northern Territory community asked me if I could take her son and look after him for a while. In the next chapter I will describe the time when some young men stayed with me when they were trying to stop petrol sniffing. In those other times when I 'looked after' young men — taking them hunting, speaking up for them in court or coaching them football — I always received support from their families. No one ever asked if they could stay or live with me, as they did with Neil Gordon, nor did I ever seriously consider it a possibility. But, now, as I watch young men associate with older kartiya and Puntu men, I am less surprised that they seek their company.

In this chapter I have focused on kanyirninpa as it applies to men and how a specific male praxis is initiated when a marnti becomes a wati. Not all young men experience the full potential of this praxis, yet its possibilities remain to influence, moderate and change male behaviour. As a boy grows into adulthood his desire for further autonomy continues to be countered by his desires for relationship in walytja. Older men help to provide this balance, where their authority nurtures as it directs, and encourages as it teaches. In this regard, the company of other men assumes a priority, as does also the capacity of older men to influence those who are younger. Unlike kartiya young men who stay longer at school, have access to books, libraries, tertiary education and computers, these men rely more on one another for information, counsel, example and correction. One man explained quite graphically how another man had shown him what a woman was like. He had grown up in the boys' dormitory where, he said, 'I didn't know what woman was like, whether they were boys or girls.' Men learn from their older brothers and their 'mates'. Despite those forces that continue to compromise and undermine the capacity of older men to hold younger men, there are signs that young men continue to seek, sometimes creatively and sometimes with great risk, that experience of being held by older men.

For some young men too, petrol sniffing provides a context for experimenting with drugs, peer relationships and alternative forms of social behaviour. It can also disclose a need within them for older male company. For those who are older, the game of football provides a 'space' where they can enjoy each other's company. And prison has become a common experience for many Aboriginal men, particularly in Western Australia. Despite the restrictions it places on a person's freedom, it also can be seen as an option with some attractive possibilities.

The 'journey of personal discovery' for young men covers much more than petrol sniffing, football and prison. For most, the rite and process of initiation into Law continues to represent the most significant pathway into the possibilities and potentialities for becoming adult men. Despite the many difficulties in maintaining these ceremonies — the growing lack of older men with knowledge, pressure to restrict their occurrence by some kartiyas and Christian groups, and even the attitudes of some Puntu themselves — these ceremonies continue. At the heart of their celebration is the Puntu experience and knowledge that their participation and involvement contributes to the continuation of their society in the generations that follow.

For men, the changes that occur through Law to their physical yarnangu also represent significant changes to their social yarnangu. These changes cannot be effected without men gathering together under the watchful care of older men. This particular form of male sociality reinforces the significance and possibilities of further male company: men travelling together, older men guiding and watching over younger men, men learning, engaging and competing in the company of other men. This gathering and sharing reveal a deeper energy and power that lies within the relationships that unite the physical, social and spiritual. When men experience those moments they enact meanings that derive from an ancestral past, and with those men who have been handed these ancient traditions. In such sociality they experience confidence, strength and dignity — individual and communal — that enables them to face the future with greater confidence, but also with a positive belief that they can hold and grow up those younger than themselves. This is an embodied and deeply healthy experience for all.

In the following chapters I examine these three different social constructions of Puntu activity in relation to petrol sniffing, Australian Rules football and prison. I will explore the experience of holding and how it continues to influence young men's behaviour within these contexts. Each of these social activities discloses elements of kanyirninpa that reinforces values for men's health in today's world. They also reveal particular risks within the male praxis that continues to seek the values embedded within kanyirninpa.

5
Petrol Sniffing: More than a risk

All this mob who are on petrol...they're missing
something in their lives.

In the following three chapters I intend to explore the relationship between kanyirninpa and three activities that significantly affect the health of the men of this region: petrol sniffing, Australian Rules football and prison. Petrol sniffing exerts its greatest influence on young men (and women) in their early teenage years; football attracts an older group of men; and prison, or juvenile detention, can involve both younger and older men.

The social theories that have been proposed to explain Aboriginal involvement around petrol sniffing have generally followed two paths. There has been an emphasis on the effects of colonial history and the consequences for people in physical dislocation from traditional lands and resulting cultural disruption. This history, including missionary activity, the dormitory system and the imposing of kartiya authority, has deeply affected the ongoing ability of Aboriginal society to reconstruct itself. The key ingredients of this history have become, in effect, powerful social and health determinants that have led to the prevalence of behaviours such as petrol sniffing. This theory concludes that sniffing is a symptom and result of the breakdown of traditional family structures (Langton 1990; d'Abbs & MacLean 2000).

Another emphasis has focused on the ways in which individuals and groups of Aboriginal people have sought their own initiative, their agency, in the face of colonial experience. Sometimes this has been described as actions of autonomy where people have sought to exercise control over their lives. Sometimes this has been described as resistance, where people actively resist the ongoing pressures and domination of colonialism and post-colonialism. In this explanation people demonstrate resilience, conviction and creativity in ways they variously oppose, resist and seek to maintain those values that are of most importance to them (Folds 1987; Brady 1991a & 1992).

The approach of this chapter, while not negating the value of these ways of understanding petrol sniffing, examines this phenomenon within the changing transformation of social relationships in Aboriginal society. Holding offers a window to this change.

The particular reasons why Aboriginal young people sniff petrol are many and varied and they have been extensively documented (Nurcombe 1974; Morice et al. 1981; Folds 1987; Brady 1992; Biven 1999; ; Mosey 1999–2000; d'Abbs & MacLean 2000). The health dangers of petrol sniffing have also been well established (Brady & Morice 1982; Maruff et al. 1998; d'Abbs & MacLean 2000; Cairney et al. 2002). In 1992 a survey of 837 Aboriginal communities reported petrol sniffing in 6.7 per cent of communities and, 'of the 35 documented deaths from petrol sniffing between 1980 and 1988, all but one involved young men and 20 involved 12–19 year olds' (Boss et al. 1995). In the Anangu Pitjantjatjara lands it has been estimated that thirty petrol sniffers (all male) have died between 1983 and 1995; twenty-five of that group were 24 years or younger (Roper & Shaw 1996).

Within the desert regions of Australia there have been a number of initiatives to combat sniffing (d'Abbs & Maclean 2000; Senate 2006). Of greatest significance, in terms of cultural affinities and kinship connections to the Puntu of the Kutjungka region, has been the program run at Yuendumu in the Northern Territory. Here, sniffers have been taken from the community to Mt Theo, a small, isolated community some two hours away. In 1994 this program, which also worked on improving the social environment of young people when they returned from Mt Theo, reduced the numbers of sniffers at Yuendumu from seventy to zero over a nine-year period (Stojanovski 1999; Preuss & Brown 2006).

The three activities of male praxis that I am about to explore need to be understood in the context of previous chapters: the meaning of kanyirninpa as a social praxis, the desert experience of history, contemporary expressions of men's health, and male praxis that arises out of male ceremony and sociality. They also need to be understood in reference to the differences that exist within families and communities. Not all young people sniff petrol, play football or go to prison; and in a particular family some of the young men may sniff and some may not. Within the cultural and geographical boundaries of shared history, men demonstrate variability but also individuality. At the same time the patterns of male behaviour around petrol, football and prison demonstrate a deeper paradox within their lives. As men continue to seek a more healthy adult life, often within the context of male holding experiences, they also enter areas of life where their physical and social emotional well-being are placed at risk. One young man was well aware of this paradox.

> R: In what other ways do young men especially feel good about themselves?
> A: Other ways, young men? Yeah, but it would seem unhealthy to other people.
> R: Go on…
> A: Going into town, having a few drinks.
> R: Feel good about themselves doing that?
> A: Talking with mates, especially if they go with mates.

My own interest in petrol sniffing began in the 1990s when I was based at Wirrimanu. When sniffing occurred many of the kartiya staff became highly anxious. They had heard stories about petrol sniffing from other places: the possible violence of sniffers, the brain damage they were experiencing and the serious risks involved when encountering them. While one could spend many days without coming into contact with sniffers, there were the regular signs of their activity: cut garden hoses, makeshift smelling containers and the pervasive smell of petrol. When sniffers attracted other young people to their company, children were noted to be absent from school, and occasionally there were signs of property damage.

Because they usually sniffed after dark, and mostly out of sight, it was relatively easy to ignore the sniffers. However, when they moved to sniff late at night near staff accommodation, their noise and behaviour caused kartiyas to express their frustrations. When it then became evident that the council, police and wardens would not do anything about it, a group of Wirrimanu church leaders took some initiative. In 1999, they called two community meetings of parents and young people. It was these initiatives that led MCHS to invite Anne Mosey, a community researcher, into the region to investigate and advise (Mosey 1999–2000). In February 2000, a magistrate's court was held at Wirrimanu and some of those who appeared were petrol sniffers, charged with offences related to their sniffing. They were all placed on probation and sent home on condition they gave up sniffing. Later that same day, police found some of them sniffing in one of the petrol sniffer's homes, against the specific agreements of their release. The police publicly criticised the parents and took their young son into custody.

That evening a group of church leaders met and decided to act. They gathered some of the main sniffers, expressed concern about their sniffing and asked if any of them wanted to give it up. When the group said they did, the adults prayed over them. They then looked at me. Where could these young men now go? I offered to look after them for a few nights, as a bridge between sniffing and returning home.

For the next three nights four young men, aged between 13 and 18, stayed at my house. They were fed, had showers and slept at night in front of the television. During the day two went off to school and two to the adult education centre. They would come back at night for a meal, television and rest and after a few days eventually returned to their homes. The sniffing temporarily stopped, causing one of the senior women of the community to comment: 'I see the problem now. Our young people need to be cared for, not hit…they need to have a place where they can go to, be fed, share stories and watch TV. They need a good home.' For those few days she saw that I cared for and looked after these young men in ways that mirrored the praxis of kanyirninpa. And for those few days they were happy to stay together and not sniff. It disclosed the potential of holding to draw young people away from petrol sniffing.

In this Kutjungka desert region people remember that petrol sniffing has been part of their memory and experience, with episodes of high and low, regular and intermittent participation, for more than forty years. Some of Anne Mosey's interviews about petrol sniffing were published in *Petrol Sniffing and Other Solvents* (Biven 1999). In addition, and in order to gain a wider perspective of the experiences of sniffers, during my 2001–04 research I interviewed (as a group) a number of the young men who were still sniffing. I also invited them to take photos, using disposable cameras but did not suggest what sort of photos they might take. In this way I hoped to gain a more accurate understanding of petrol sniffers, their interests and perspectives.

I accept that there is an important distinction between 'intermittent' and 'chronic sniffers'. Some young people sniff, on and off, over short or longer periods of time while others, usually older, are regular and continuous users. In this region sniffers have generally been, to quote the descriptions of sniffers elsewhere, 'intermittent', 'recreational' and 'experimental' users (Morice et al. 1981, p. 39; Mosey 1999–2000, p. 13; d'Abbs & MacLean 2000, p. 7). The experience of sniffing has regularly drawn young boys, and in more recent years young girls, into its ambit for different lengths of time but not into their late twenties or early thirties.[1]

Mosey quoted Mark Moora who said he learned to sniff from his uncle around the time of old Balgo in the years 1942–65 (1999–2000, p. 12). Whether he learned at the old mission or elsewhere is not clear. In the course of my collection of field data in 2001–04, I interviewed Fr Ray Hevern (Superintendent 1969–84) who remembered young kids in the boys' dormitory having cans of petrol under their beds in 1969. Peile referred to 'isolated occurrences of petrol sniffing among some young men', probably around the 1970s. He used sniffing as an example of a sick or 'dry' body: 'A child sniffs petrol. As a result of sniffing petrol, the spirit inside [the body] it becomes dry' (Peile 1997, p. 96).[2]

In early 1997, a large group of young people were sniffing petrol around the old girls' dormitory at Wirrimanu. Since then groups have sniffed intermittently in the community (Mosey 1999–2000, p. 13). In February that year, also at Wirrimanu, a young girl of 14 years died as the result of an assault. Petrol sniffing was identified as one of the key factors in her death. In the very serious payback that followed, older members of their families publicly punished all petrol sniffers. No one was exempt and the punishments were severe. The next day the alleged offender was apprehended, and he received payback by all the family of the deceased, including ritual spearing. He was then taken in police custody to hospital, later charged and served time in prison. The death had a severe and long-term impact on the young girl's family and, while it firmly placed in people's minds the realisation that petrol sniffing could lead to death, it did not put an end to sniffing.

In recent years, a young man has ended up in hospital after receiving burns to his leg when sniffing; another young man has been hospitalised with pneumonia. There have been other injuries. The fire that burned down the Wirrimanu community storage area was blamed on petrol sniffers, as was that which caused the destruction of a Wirrimanu community vehicle (1999–2000, p. 13). There have been a number of occasions when sniffers have been assaulted and when they have caused damage to vehicles and property (1999–2000, p. 13). No one has died as the direct result of petrol sniffing although the three young men who committed suicide in 2002–03 had been, at one time, petrol sniffers. After the suicide of one of them in 2002 sniffing stopped for a few months. However, it recommenced in 2003 and continued into 2004.

There are dangers in oversimplifying the general causes of petrol sniffing and their manifestations within particular communities (Brady 1991a, p. 29). For example, in this particular region, petrol sniffing has been generally restricted to only one of the four communities, Wirrimanu. This community is the largest of the four regional communities, has the largest kartiya administration and it has been in existence longer than the others.[3] When I looked carefully at the group of young men presently aged 15–24 and living in the region, I found that around half had been or still were petrol sniffing. This latter group of more than fifty was almost entirely associated with Wirrimanu.[4] If young people from the other Kutjungka communities have wished to sniff petrol they have usually come to Wirrimanu and joined the sniffers there. It is likely that Wirrimanu, compared with the other three communities, offered a tradition of this activity, a larger geographical and social space in which it could occur, and an existing group of sniffers that one could easily join.

Petrol is the most easily available drug for young people in the desert and offers certain pleasures. Whereas in the cities young people might have access to chrome-based spray paints, glue, marijuana or heroin, here young people have relatively easy access to petrol. While it has become a drug of choice for some, such a choice has been influenced by its increasing availability in community vehicles since the late 1970s. Young people could access these petrol-driven vehicles but they could not use them to acquire alternative drugs, such as alcohol, which required the ability and financial means to travel (Brady 1991b, p. 21).

The research that I conducted in the region in 2001–04 indicated that petrol sniffing has arisen out of three interrelated contexts. There is a history of lived experience that has encouraged younger people to follow the sniffing behaviour of older generations. There has been a lack of parental care in some families that has caused some young people to seek support in the company of peer groups. And there has been the opportunity provided in petrol sniffing for young people to choose a 'passage' in life to assist them move between childhood and young adulthood.

Older brothers and relations can have a significant influence on the behaviour of young people and petrol sniffing appears to be no exception (Brady 1991c, p. 2000; Biven 1999, Appendix C, p. 71). A young man of 19 years described how he learned to sniff and then showed others: 'Someone learned me…and I've learned [names] because I'm the oldest'.[5] This young man is the eldest child in his family. His father lives elsewhere and he is not close to his stepfather. He only had one uncle in his mother's family, who died when he was very young. He has not found it an easy process growing up, has experimented with drugs, had a baby with a woman who does not want to live with him at Wirrimanu, and he has even attempted suicide. As he talked about his deceased uncle, and his experiences of growing up, it was evident that he looked to older men for company. At the time I interviewed him he was no longer petrol sniffing. He saw it as his role to help younger men, only a few years younger than himself, to stop sniffing.

In the context of male kanyirninpa, Puntu believe that one of the roles of older brothers and relations is to teach and guide those who are younger. Hence, it is not surprising if young men follow the example of older brothers. Milton James has argued that one reason why young people sniff petrol is that someone 'gave them the idea' (James 2004). Here, I am suggesting that there can be a strong influence by older brothers or relations on younger ones to sniff. In some families there is no history of petrol sniffing. In others, petrol sniffing behaviour has developed as young men have followed the examples of older sniffers: 'I followed one big man', remembered an old man who described how he first learned to sniff when he was ten: 'he was the leader, he was older than us' (Biven 1999, Appendix C, p. 74). As some of the older men threaten, hit and encourage younger men to leave petrol sniffing, their own history of being sniffers can, paradoxically, motivate younger men to take it up and try it. These older men are living examples that not only can a young man begin sniffing and then leave it, but that the effects of petrol are neither dangerous nor fatal. Referring to the effects of petrol on sniffers in the past, one man, now in his late forties, is alleged to have said to Anne Mosey, 'it didn't hurt them...we're okay'. Obviously, it is difficult for him to tell his youngest son to stop sniffing when he doesn't appear to have suffered seriously from his own experience of it.

The absence of older brothers or relations within the petrol experience can also work to motivate a person against petrol sniffing. One man compared his experience of sniffing, 'I didn't really have anyone to look at' with his experience of drinking alcohol, 'I've got family members who drink'. Both could make him physically sick, but with alcohol he had older relations around him who would take care of him when he was drunk and vulnerable. He, like the rest of his peers, was influenced to move from sniffing petrol to drinking alcohol because of the company, and the support, it promised. If he had remained sniffing, as some have done in other regions, he would likely have become more socially isolated and possibly more physically ill (Chivell 2002, p. 1).

Puntu, men and women, share a number of common perceptions and judgments about the causes of petrol sniffing. They believe that sniffing results when parents are absent or not seeming to care for their children: 'all this mob who are on petrol...like their parents away...they're missing something in their lives'. Or, they might suggest, sniffing results from, and in reaction to, parents' drinking. The sniffer is believed to be upset and angry at those who are drinking and reasons: 'you won't stop, well I won't stop too'. The walytja (family) dynamic that Puntu believe is operating would seem to arise from their understanding of kanyirninpa and its associated responsibilities that began at birth. If kanyirninpa does not continue to be provided, as would appear to be the case for some young people, petrol sniffing is perceived to be a result but also a response to that lack of holding. Whether stress is placed on the parents or the sniffer, the poles of tension that lie at the heart of kanyirininpa can be identified. The care that is owed by older people is contrasted against the loneliness and isolation of the individual sniffer. The authority and responsibility to care by those who are older is contrasted against the autonomy and irresponsibility of those who are younger. Sometimes, members of the community will blame the family, and sometimes they will blame the sniffer, but usually both are ultimately represented within the context of a sniffer whom, they believe, is 'looking for family to support him'.

I have previously discussed the critical importance of older men, including fathers, in the social and developmental life of young men. Some research has indicated that the absence or death of fathers is one factor in petrol sniffing (Nurcombe 1974, p. 68; Morice et al. 1981, p. 8).[6] This is not an easy factor to identify as the majority of young men presently aged 15–24 have absent or deceased fathers. Some fathers died when these young men were very young, others as they were growing up. There is also a variation in the way fathers have become 'absent'. Some have remarried and have moved to live elsewhere, while others have spent large amounts of time drinking in town. There are also some whose sons have been brought up by other family relations. Clearly, there are various ways in which the relationship between sons and fathers has been experienced, severed or re-configured. Of the more than fifty 15–24 year old young men presently living at Wirrimanu (of whom about 70 per cent have sniffed at one time), approximately 30 per cent have deceased fathers.[7] What currently distinguishes those who have been petrol sniffers, from those who have not, is that 40 per cent of those who have sniffed have 'absent' fathers. This figure drops to around 20 per cent for those who have not sniffed.[8]

Apart from talking with those who had sniffed in the past I also spoke with some who were still sniffing. Over the years I had managed to obtain trust with some of these young men, such that they did not run away when they saw me approaching, as they often did when kartiyas came near. A group of them were happy to arrange a time to sit and talk about their petrol experience. They decided a time and place and I offered to provide them with breakfast (it was mid-morning). Some were happy to take photos using digital cameras, on the understanding they would get a copy of the photos they took.[9] There were five that eventually met, an average age of around 15 years. They had all been taken through the first stage of Law and were friendly and outspoken in the interview. They were aware of the dangers of sniffing, referring to more than one other sniffer who 'got no brain'. They could see that what was happening to other sniffers could also happen to themselves and affect their health.

The conversation turned to their fathers. One had a deceased father and three were experiencing problems with their fathers at that time. The father of one sniffer had left the community: 'he's got a new girl'; the father of another one often went away which, they said, caused his son to sniff. I asked the group about the third one (A, B, C and E are speaking about D):

A: Sometime he sniff.
B: Sometime.
A: When his father go to Halls Creek, you know.
R: He sniffs then?
A: Yeah.
R: But when your father here do you sniff?
A: Nup.
R: But he was yesterday, this morning?
C: He went halfway.
A: Because father going to town today.
D: Halfway...
E: When he go to Halls Creek [name of father]...when he drink grog and he'll go for sniffing.
R: He leaves him here, you mean?
E: Yeah, when he leaves him here.
R: Why do you think that?
E: He get sulky.

There were other occasions where both adults and petrol sniffers identified a connection between sniffing behaviour and absent or deceased fathers. One of the sniffers in the group just mentioned admitted that he sniffed when his father went away, but would stop sniffing when his grandmother told him to. The other sniffers confirmed this. He went on to say that he would take it up again, 'sometime when they're away'. Here, he is referring to the absence of his father (and stepmother), as his father separated from his mother and re-married. His older cousin, who lives in another community, later informed me that she believed it was the absence of his father that prompted him to sniff. His grandmother looked after him but it was the care and attention of his father that the young man sought. At that particular time she made reference to another young man who had 'been drinking since his father died'. Clearly, this young woman believed that the relationship between a young man and his father was so important that it could cause great harm to young men when such a relationship was severed.[10]

I once asked about a sniffer who had left one of the other Kutjungka communities to join the sniffers at Wirrimanu. His father was dead and his mother had 'grown him up'.

R: When he was sniffing who was looking after him?

A: Nobody.

R: Nobody was looking after him?

A: He's only got his mum and sister and a brother who's not old enough to hold onto him; he's only got two uncles who's alcoholics.

In these cases, where a father has died, it can be difficult for young men to find older men who can provide the male company they need. This can prove even more difficult for those whose fathers are kartiyas (and hence have no extended Puntu relations on their father's side) or where their father or mother's family live a long way away.[11] The father of one young man, now in his twenties, died in a motor vehicle accident when his son was only 3 years old. As a teenager this young man was a petrol sniffer, spent time in juvenile detention and later some time in prison. As he grew older he found significant support from his uncles and his other 'fathers' (his father's brothers), who lived in the Northern Territory. Despite this support, he continued to feel the loss of not having his own father as he grew up. He would say, with much feeling, 'you need your fathers, especially if you are a man'.

Sniffers are 'hurting inside' said one father, whose own children have sniffed petrol. 'They're missing something in their lives'. They are not perceived to be responsible for the loss they have suffered. While it would seem that his comments suggest some criticism of his own holding abilities, he does not suggest this possibility. His sister, also married with children, some of whom have sniffed, made a similar comment. She believed that young people were sniffing, getting into trouble and mixing with the wrong group because no one was holding them (Senior 2003, p. 201).

On two separate and unrelated occasions women described the lives of two young brothers whose mother had died, when they were quite young (their father had died previously). That they are not, nor have been petrol sniffers, was explained as a consequence of extended family members taking care of them when they were orphaned. Their lives were contrasted against those young people who do have family and parents to care for them, but are absent and do not provide that regular, essential kanyirninpa relationship. To these women, both mothers and living in different communities, it was the offer of a new holding experience that made the significant difference to the lives of these young men and kept them away from petrol.

As I've previously stated, family members have explored different methods to prevent sniffing. Physical violence has been tried. One young man described how he gave a 'big hiding' to a young relation that caused him to stop sniffing. Others have described how they prayed, 'promised a car', reasoned and encouraged. Petrol sniffing can cause much anxiety to the parents and family of those who sniff. One father described his feeling as 'tjurni ngawu' ('sick in his stomach'). He felt sick when he saw his son sniffing. These various attempts to constrain sniffing contrast the apathy that kartiyas perceive Puntu families have towards their children who are sniffing (Mosey 1999–2000, p. 22). As Brady has explained, the range of freedoms that a young desert person experiences is much greater than those tolerated by kartiya families (Brady 1992, p. 73). These freedoms increase when a young man enters the Law. The phrase, 'I'm the boss now, it's my body', indicates both a claim and right to personal autonomy (1992, p. 75). Family members find it difficult to constrain another's right to their autonomy, even when they risk hurting themselves. The Mt Theo petrol project explored different ways to 'convince' sniffers to leave Yuendumu using the support of police, families and elders. In 1998 Comgas (Community Gasoline, also known as Avgas or Aviation Gasoline) was introduced into some communities as an alternative to petrol.[12] In April 2004 it replaced unleaded petrol in Wirrimanu.

The efforts to try to overcome sniffing can prove daunting. Parents, who wish to exercise a holding relationship with their children, can feel particularly frustrated and inadequate in their inability to help those who come under their care, and who continue to sniff. One wife described her husband's reaction: 'I give up', he said, 'let them die' (Biven 1999, Appendix C, p. 72). In many ways the withdrawal of care or concern, as noted before, is a threat of the ultimate sanction. A mother described the despair of the father of a petrol sniffer: 'Oh, no good, now just leave it', he said, 'for petrol sniffers, nothing we can do.' In his case this appeared to be true. His son, nearly 20, had sniffed on and off for a number of years. Only when he was in prison could his parents safely assume he did not sniff.

In some cases sniffers express strong feelings of anger and hurt. Puntu can interpret such behaviour as responding in obvious and logical ways to a particular type of care that has been deprived them. Parents who are seen to have deserted their holding responsibilities will be strongly criticised and the 'sulky' behaviour of young sniffers will be interpreted as a logical reaction to the felt lack of an appropriately deserved holding relationship. In this context sniffing is interpreted as 'reasonable' behaviour. But it is also dangerous. And herein lies the contradiction that is sometimes found in the differing behaviour and attitudes by Puntu towards petrol sniffing. While many adults and parents criticise and act against sniffing behaviour, it is not always or consistently condemned. What Brady describes as 'a high level of tolerance, and a lack of decisive intervention, on the part of adults' arises from more than 'non-authoritarian socialisation practices and a belief that petrol sniffers are unamenable to rational instruction' (Brady 1991c, p. 199). Some adults perceive a logical, protest element in sniffers that is both understandable and tolerable, especially if the person is a young adult who is entitled to respect and autonomy.

One 15-year-old teenager, whose father had died some four years previously, became a very active sniffer while also involved in considerable criminal behaviour. His life revolved around that of sniffing, breaking and entering, and causing damage to places, such as the school. His mother and stepfather tried to reason with him but for months there appeared to be no solution. After several months of sniffing, according to his stepfather, 'from here, sniffing and everything...someone just picked him up and all of a sudden he bin go to school'. In a dramatic reversal of direction this young man's life suddenly 'picked up'. He returned to school and took up playing Aussie Rules. While his stepfather had been talking with him and encouraging him to play football, what occurred was still quite unexpected. When he appeared in court, twelve months after the offences he committed, the magistrate was surprised by the change in his behaviour after such a short period of time. He, like a number of other young men in the desert, have been known suddenly to leave their use of petrol and move on without it. Their entry into a peer-focused use of petrol, their intense activity around it, and then their sudden exit from it, suggests that petrol sniffing, in this desert context, exhibits for some young people the characteristics of a 'rite of passage'.

In suggesting that petrol sniffing may be understood in this way, I am using the word 'passage' to describe what has been called a 'journey of personal discovery' (Teather 1999, p. 1). And, like other 'journeys of personal discovery', it demonstrates those three key elements described by van Gennep: separation, transition and incorporation (van Gennep 1977, p. 77). I am not, however, comparing it with the more formal and established rite of male initiation, but as an example of a contemporary form of personal transition (Brady 1992, p. 95; Teather 1999, p. 20).[13]

When one man described his earlier petrol sniffing experiences he said, 'when we used to do it there was only men...we was our own little gang'. As he implied, the pattern of sniffing has changed, even within the last decade. Now, young men and women sniff, and often together. The desire to sniff within a peer group continues to remain strong. Moreover, the priority of emphasis upon family relationships shifts as sniffers focus more strongly on their own group and allegiance to that group. Turner has described this first phase of separation as a range of symbolic activity that signified that a person was now different within the social structure (Turner 1969, p. 94). In this case, petrol sniffers are clearly separated by being identified with behaviour that is morally judged and socially marginalised.

Even within their own community sniffers are often ostracised by many. When I asked one man who used to sniff about this, the conversation went thus:

R: Why [are] young fellas into petrol?
A: Mm...being accepted...petrol want to be in a gang mainly, cause the other gang don't want them, the drinking gang or the good boys' club.

R: The good boys and the bad boys?
A: Yeah.

While most of those who become sniffers usually leave petrol to take up alcohol (some do both, but they are rare) they can, as sniffers, be ridiculed, shamed and physically threatened by 'the drinking gang'.[14] Those who sniff petrol can be depicted as 'bad boys' and those who drink alcohol as 'good boys'.[15] The behaviour of these 'good boys', who sometimes go 'looking for all the sniffers' (to attack them), acts to further confirm the sniffers in their behaviour. The moral distinction between 'good drunkards' and 'bad sniffers' reinforces the separation of sniffers from those who do not sniff, and also from their families. It is a separation that can cause family members to feel powerless, shamed and alienated within their community and in the company of kartiyas (Mosey 1999–2000, p. 22).

Petrol sniffing can also be understood as possessing a transitional or liminal dimension. The spatial and social distinctions that are usually observed between genders in the communities are not strictly observed when there is sniffing. Sniffers, especially in more recent years, have crossed those clear and public gender boundaries, and such behaviour is usually done at night in ways that accentuate their marginal role within the community.[16] As they move around after dark, sometimes stealing petrol or breaking into vehicles or houses, the sniffing lifestyle contrasts and opposes the work, activities and priorities that characterise desert and community daily life.

Folds describes such activity as 'resistance', especially in relation to the school. He argues that sniffing is an expression of rebellion, a protest against powerlessness (Folds 1987, p. 56). While sniffers clearly engage in behaviour that is sometimes angry, violent and destructive — even among themselves — it is not surprising that the school they went to bears the brunt of their attention. In this region most, if not all, sniffers attended school prior to sniffing. It is a relatively safe and secure place to gather at night, a place the young are familiar with. At the same time their sniffing at the school provides a powerful message. It signals to those children who are still at school an invitation to sniff. It signals to the school, probably the most significant institution that puts pressure on sniffers to leave petrol, their desire for its attention. It also signals a protest against the school, its kartiya authority and any hold it may claim over them. That they return to it, often at night, confirms conflicting elements of their attachment to it and their desire to be separated from it. The school represents their desire for transition from something familiar into something new.

When young people begin sniffing different forms of social and geographical separation occur. This does not mean that such separation remains always fixed or static, as some family members can make great efforts to break that separation and put an end to sniffing. However, sniffing behaviour threatens walytja and community harmony and the enduring quality of desert values. Through the expressions of individual autonomy, sniffing symbolises great power by its ability to question the possibilities and effectiveness of kanyirninpa.

In the summer of 2002 a group of visiting Law men, with a marlurlu (initiate), were coming for ceremony into Wirrimanu. The community gathered, late in the day, watching for the signs of their approach and mindful that all needed to be seated and gathered when the group arrived. When some remembered that there were petrol sniffers in the community, who could walk across the paths of the Law group, many people went anxiously searching for them to urge them to join the assembled group. They wanted to avoid any conflict, punishment or sickness that might be caused if the proper protocols for Law were not followed.[17] In some ways the families sought to protect the sniffers. More importantly, they were protecting themselves. The sniffers, to use Mary Douglas' description, were 'matter out of place', not the sniffing (Douglas 1966, p. 35). Their sniffing placed them in a liminal state that was extremely dangerous. If they, even inadvertently, crossed the paths of those engaged in the Law, their families as well as themselves could suffer. At this time the sniffers were seen for the danger they represented, a far greater danger than the effects of the actual petrol sniffing itself.

Not surprisingly, sniffers become physically thin. Sniffing and hunger have long been closely associated, sometimes interpreted as cause and effect. One argument has been that food causes feelings of nausea when people are sniffing (Folds 1987, p. 62). Another interpretation is that sniffing dulls hunger pains or causes hunger to be forgotten (Morice et al. 1981, p. 23; d'Abbs & MacLean 2000, p. 11). Sniffing has also been proposed as a way by which sniffers achieve power over their bodies (Brady 1991a, p. 30). One young sniffer commented that sniffers 'don't need feed'. He was suggesting that sniffing reduced the desire for food. He was also saying that he had experienced being hungry before taking up petrol sniffing and this helped him cope with being hungry. Hence, I think it can be argued that 'thinness' results partly from this suppression of hunger. But, it also would seem to be a consequence of sniffers living and moving outside those regular, daily times when stores are open, and food and money are being transacted among walytja. As sniffers separate themselves — or find themselves separated — from the usual geographical spaces where food can be obtained, they confirm their liminal space. Their thin bodies symbolise their marginalised place.

There are occasional fights between sniffers and sexual activity that avoids the scrutiny of older family members or the police. Sniffers can spend the day sleeping, away from the attention, teasing or criticism of others. As they describe their various experiences the most dramatic are those of sensory stimulation, often encouraged in the presence of music. The hallucinations, visual and aural, may cause them to be frightened, but their pleasure attracts further sniffing (d'Abbs & MacLean 2000, p. 12). The group of sniffers explained:

> A: We sniff and sometime we listen [to] tape and we have a good time.
> R: You have a good time?
> A: Yeah…
> R: What's having a good time?
> A: Because we see lots of funny things, you know, they look funny.

R: You see funny thing when you [are] sniffing?

A: Power, powers, sometime you look nothing, like snake, you know.

R: You see a snake?

A: Yeah, it make you cry.

R: In your mind?

A: Yeah, in your mind, but it make you spin around.

While a frightening experience of sniffing can cause some to put petrol aside, it also offers an exciting, unpredictable and individual experience. Although sniffing has a strong group and 'gang' dimension, for many it also offers something very immediate, sensory and personal.

> I started feeling good, happy and laughing. I saw nice bright colours, things appearing on the ground, patterns, I seen the moon and stuff coming down from the moon. I hear things, music, soft music. (Biven 1999, Appendix C, p. 68)

The liminality of the petrol experience is also expressed in those cases where very young sniffing males are no longer 'boys' (in the kartiya meaning of attending school), nor are they 'men' (within kartiya and Puntu social meanings). Most male petrol sniffers have begun sniffing at the end of their primary school years, before they have entered the Law. Some of the adults at Wirrimanu have suggested that the young men have taken up sniffing to draw attention from the older men, in order to be put in the Law. This may be difficult to establish, but what is evident is that sniffing offers young boys a particular geographical and social space between the end of primary school years and their entry into men's Law. The young men know that eventually they will be taken into the Law. For some, desiring to join the company of older men, petrol sniffing provides a means by which they can obtain their attention. It is likely that some of these older men might believe that these young men will cease sniffing if they are initiated, and given the opportunity to become adult men.

However, it has become apparent that petrol sniffing does not necessarily cease when young men have been initiated, despite the strong injunctions at Law that they leave such behaviour behind.

When these young males are sniffing, often at night, disassociated from regular community activities and wearing darkly coloured clothing, they live in what Turner described as a 'betwixt and between' state. Sniffing allows them to live for a period of time between being a 'boy' and being a 'man', between being a 'marnti' and a 'wati' (Turner 1969, p. 95).

The third stage of this rite of passage, incorporation, can vary in its timing and method. Some young men sniff only once, some sniff for a limited period of time, and others continue to sniff on and off for some years. This suggests that young desert men make the transition from petrol quite differently. Presently, there are no long-term and chronic sniffers in this region, as there are in some other Aboriginal communities.[18] In these cases, it would seem, re-integration into an adult male and social world has been postponed. However, as in the example of the 15-year-old petrol sniffer previously mentioned, incorporation into a social and masculine yarnangu (body) can happen quite suddenly and surprisingly. At such times the invitation that holding offers young men, as a significant means of incorporation, can be noted.

Those who have experimented with the use of petrol describe very different experiences that led them to stop. One suffered frightening hallucinations when he saw himself dying as the result of sniffing. He only sniffed 'one time'. Another did not like the headache it provided and sniffed only once. Generally, giving the sniffer a 'belting' is not considered by those who have sniffed, or their family members, as helpful in causing that person to stop.

There are occasions when a sniffer simply decides that he has had enough. One young man, now around 21 years old, lost his father about three years ago. His younger brother is still sniffing. Here, he describes what prompted him to finish with petrol.

> R: What made you stop petrol sniffing?
> A: Oh, age.
> R: Age, what do you mean?
> A: Go big. Changed my life.
> R: Did somebody make you stop or you stopped yourself?
> A: I just stopped myself.
> R: What happened to you?

A: I stopped myself.
R: Anything happen, any reason?
A: Thinking about my life.
R: Thinking about what?
A: Own body.
R: Your own body?
A: Mm, and damage to my brain.

That moment, when a person made the decision to leave sniffing petrol, was sometimes triggered by the advice of an older person. Men have mentioned prison warders, and older male friends, who have helped them at that time. Change in behaviour has also been effected when men have become aware of the damage and pain petrol has caused their own bodies, but also to the Puntu social body. The following comments were made by a young man who described the time when he decided to give up petrol.

R: What is the worse thing that happened to you?
A: Worse thing?
R: That made you feel really ngawu.
A: Petrol.
R: Petrol?
A: Petrol killing me.
R: You could feel it killing you?
A: Some friend of mine…some people dying from petrol.

Early in 2002 a group of young sniffers were invited to leave Wirrimanu and live at Yaka Yaka, some 120 kilometres south. They knew there would be no petrol in that community, but were happy to live under the care and attention of a slightly older Puntu, who himself had been a petrol sniffer, and a kartiya who worked in the community office. They exchanged a petrol world for a new and very different social experience. They later recounted and painted their story: *Petrol Sniffing* (p. 142).

The painting describes two worlds and two very different experiences. The petrol world (upper left) represents a group of young people stealing petrol from a motor car, sniffing as they listen to music, a boy and girl going off together and a pair of sniffers fighting. They exchange this night-time world for a day-time one. In this latter world (lower right) they are taking rubbish to the

Petrol Sniffing, four young men

tip and spending time out bush, camping and hunting. Where, as petrol sniffers, they had experienced little social contact with others in their community, here at Yaka Yaka they became involved in the day-time life of that community. They worked around the community, camped out and went hunting. They were well fed, relaxing at night with a video and sharing of stories. They were happy in this time, learning new things such as how to play golf, which they played on the community oval before sunset. They felt supported and cared for by the community and in return believed the work they did helped the community. A number of older men supported them and looked after them. One of the sniffers later commented how he felt 'free', another that he felt 'trusted'. They agreed that they had 'fun' and learned new things.

While there are a number of reasons why the group did not remain at Yaka Yaka beyond those few months, their incorporation into a life away from petrol reflected a number of similar occasions when young men have stopped petrol-sniffing behaviour. When Brady pointed out that 'people abandon a dysfunctional drug use only when it begins to interfere with too many valued aspects of their lives,' she showed that marriage could attract young men away from sniffing, just as having a child could attract young women (Brady 1992, p. 193). While it is not unusual for young men temporarily to put aside petrol sniffing for football carnivals, funerals or law ceremonies time there is evidence that deeper, 'valued aspects of their lives', can influence them to put aside petrol sniffing entirely. For some this can be found in the supporting company that male kanyirninpa provides.

Within this desert region there is evidence that it is not the promise or possibilities of kanyirninpa that attracts young men to petrol sniffing. On the contrary, it would seem that they suspend the holding experiences they have previously experienced for an alternative peer experience. Their use of petrol is, as Mosey has described it, 'opportunistic, rather than chronic' (Mosey 1999–2000, p. 13). Here, petrol sniffing often occurs at an age when young boys are beginning to become aware of an imminent and significant shift into the adult male (Puntu) world and adolescent male (kartiya) world. Sniffing provides young people with a bridge from the world of childhood into impending and demanding Puntu and kartiya worlds. In these worlds, adolescence can be perceived as exciting but also frightening.[19] Sniffing offers young people geographical and social space; it provides 'breathing space' where, in a risky and dangerous context, new forms of social companionship, sensory experience and autonomy can be explored and realised.

Some young men do not seek or need the rite of passage that petrol offers. Older men and others in their families assist their passage into adulthood, without a need for the 'space' that petrol sniffing provides. Some sniff for only a short period of time and are only superficially touched by the experience. However, there are others who find it difficult to abandon sniffing and make the transition into adult life. As Brady has commented, 'if there are no valued aspects to life, then there is simply no compulsion to abstain' (Brady 1992, p. 193). Kanyirninpa, however, can provide those valued aspects. In the following chapter, I will examine how some young men experience the value of holding within the sphere of Australian Rules football.

6
Football: More than a game

R: *Football's good?*

A: *Yeah.*

R: *In what way?*

A: *Like joining in together now. Back then they
had corroborees.*

Australian Rules football has been popular among the men of these
desert communities for more than twenty years. It provides an
energetic social and geographical space for exercise, discussion and
male group activity. It is not surprising to see large groups of men
travelling to football carnivals during the winter months, or even
playing games before sunset in the heat of summer.

In this chapter I will explore how this particular expression of
'football' is an example of contemporary kanyirninpa, where young
men seek the company of older ones. As men attend ceremonial
Law during the hot summer months, the dry, warm winter season
provides a new and significant extension of 'men's business'. In a
number of ways football offers young men the continuity of being
held by older men that began and was promised in Law. The game
also offers a range of body and social skills, many of which desert
men have practised and enjoyed with other men for thousands of
years. It enables them to engage and compete with kartiya men.
As a valuable context for exercise and recreation, football can
also place important values of desert society under tension. The

construction of its competitive style can also put desert relatedness and responsibilities under stress, with repercussions for men, their families and communities.

My own introduction into desert football occurred when one of the local coaches invited me to help out at football training (there are two football teams at Wirrimanu and there is one team in each of the other communities). While I had been involved in Australian Rules football for a number of years before coming to the desert, it was only after some time of living in the community that this invitation was offered. Football training was not a regular event, but generally only happened when men were preparing for a sporting carnival to be held in the immediate future. At those times it would not be unusual at Wirrimanu to have two teams training on the red, dusty community oval during the late afternoon. The number of assembled young men was often more than forty, which would cause kartiya staff to wonder where such a large number came from. A relatively smaller number would generally have been visible around the office, store and adult education centre during the day.

It was not the desire for training that drew the men. Their evident and focused energy was prompted by the knowledge that a sporting carnival was approaching. If the games were to be played elsewhere this would entail travelling, sometimes several hundred kilometres, for a long weekend of sport. Vehicles might leave on a Thursday and return — assuming they did not break down and detour home via the pub at Halls Creek (in Western Australia) or the alcohol takeaway at Rabbit Flat (in the Northern Territory) — sometime during the following week. If the carnival was held at home, other teams would arrive and games would begin on a Friday afternoon, with the final game usually on a Sunday evening or Monday morning. Sometimes the games, to the frustration of community staff and schools' administrations, could extend even longer. Football could assume large slices of time in a young man's life during the dry weather months of the year.

There are a number of qualities that distinguish desert football from that played in most urban centres. All the ovals in the Kutjungka region are dirt — each community has one oval — and men often play in bare feet and sometimes in socks, shoes or football boots. Despite their toughened feet men can suffer quite deep cuts playing in bare feet on these ovals. Tackling hard or throwing someone onto the ground is avoided unless the game is taken more seriously, such as in 'finals' matches. Games are usually two 'quarters' in duration and are umpired by two men who move casually behind the play. Players often pair up with friends. Such pairing can reflect strong and enduring expressions in desert culture of the use of the dual number (Willis 1997, p. 82).[1] Kukatja, unlike English, uses particular expressions when describing persons in groups of two.[2] Friends, men and women, can sometimes be seen walking together in pairs (marlpa). Young men often match up at football where the desire for competition does not bear much relation to the oppositional aspects often found in the Australian Rules games played elsewhere. Games are also less structured. While men play according to set positions they show less interest in formal tactics or game plans. Training is to help men develop some fitness for the games that lie ahead, to prepare and get organised, not to devise new ways of playing or strategising against the opposition.

Spectators will arrive, even at training, and there can be good humour and banter among the players themselves, and also between players and spectators, on such occasions. I remember one particular training night. The sun was setting and a large group of men was sitting on the oval, discussing the trip that lay ahead. One of the senior players said to me, 'talk to us'. He was not asking that I talk about anything particular, just that I talk and extend that time at the end of training. The relaxation of the group was evident and palpable. Training was over and the men were happy to sit, relax and be together. While they would eventually get up and walk home to find a meal — note the gender separation and expectations around sport and meals — they wanted to linger a while longer. Sometimes in Law, and sometimes on camping or hunting trips, this spirit of a settled, attentive and relaxed group of men is evident.

Young men have been known to put aside petrol, girlfriends, families and work commitments if a truck offers them a ride to a football competition. The possibility of travelling together with other men, even for those too young to play, proves a strong incentive for old and young. At such times a particular aspect of holding can be noticed. Older men, coaches and mentors, make the important preparations. It is their responsibility to negotiate with other communities and try to obtain football jumpers and equipment, not that of the individual players. The older men accompany, guide and watch over those who are younger.

I asked an older man, a father of four sons who play football, whether he saw himself as holding the younger men when he went off with them as their manager or coach. 'Bloody hell, yes,' he replied, 'I am responsible to bring them back.' He then went on to describe the similarities between these situations and Law, when he and older men accompany younger ones. He was clear: older men accompany young men to look after them, advise and keep them out of trouble. They will tell them about the communities they are entering and how to conduct themselves when they are there. When he takes these men he is seen as holding them. Families will perceive him as being responsible for them, and for bringing them safely back home. If something tragic happens or someone gets seriously hurt he will be blamed.

Gatherings for football, like those at ceremonial time, can involve large groups of men preparing and then travelling long distances to other communities. Both football and the Law are highly valued expressions of male sociality. As in the quote at the beginning of this chapter one desert man, now a coach, likened football to the social corroborees of the past, where men gathered for social and recreational pleasure. He knew that making comparisons with the Law was both dangerous and problematic. As a young man in his late twenties, his authority to coach football meant very little in times of ceremonial authority or influence. Yet he also acknowledged that these times of male gathering were important for his 'mates' and other young men.

When describing football men use many similar phrases. They talk about the importance of 'joining in together', 'coming together', 'getting together'. A father, whose son has been playing football with the men for a few years, first learned to play when he attended boarding school in Broome in the early 1970s. It was his generation that brought back knowledge of the game to the desert. We were talking together about men's health.

R: And do you see times when the young men are happy?
A: The only time I see it when they play together.
R: Playing sport?
A: Yep.
R: That's the only time you see them happy together?
A: When they are together.

He was not suggesting that health for men was simply about men gathering or being together; he was suggesting that when men gathered important social and kinship connections were made. The young experienced being cared for and nurtured, problems could be aired and discussed, and young men's problems or activities (such as petrol sniffing, stealing or alcohol) could be addressed.

A: To come together and talk…talk about other issues and mixing and sharing… If we come together and talk a lot about the problems or things like that, we'll be happy. Our health will be happy. We know that everyone is happy…It used to happen long time when we had the old people going, the old men to one side, the old ladies to another side and we had the young people, like my group, we used to go…you [would] listen to what they're thinking.

The influx of vehicles into these desert communities in the late 1970s provided people with new and independent means of travel. And football provided a context and an additional reason to travel. Football carnivals served to reinforce relationships between families that until then only occasionally saw one another at funeral or other ceremony times. As noted in another state: 'You only meet your mob at football carnivals and funerals' (de Largy Healy 2001, p. 13). Football allowed social networks to be maintained and be developed. For young men, 'football means that you get to meet some people and make new friends'.

On one of my visits to the Kutjungka region during the month of August, I accompanied a group of men to Yuendumu for their annual sporting carnival. With us was a young man, around 16 years of age. This was the first time he had visited Yuendumu and had the opportunity to meet members of his extended walytja (family). Part of his excitement, apart from playing football, was to get to know his family and to experience being cared for and fed by them. Football carnivals offer many opportunities to renew contact, share stories and extend one's family network. It is also a valuable time for young men and women to meet. For young men there are also the opportunities to compete, to show off skills and win a trophy.

Sporting carnivals also provide opportunities for important cultural values to be expressed and publicly maintained. In recent years I have witnessed how families have used these public gatherings to pay respect to those who have recently died and, in some ways, extend the ritual of sorry business. If the deceased was a footballer, for example, the playing area needed to be 'opened up' before competition could begin.[3] This could be achieved by a group of women moving in single file around the oval, crying and sweeping the ground with leafy branches. Women, sometimes accompanied by men, often perform this ritual after one has died, removing signs of where the deceased has been and walked. On other occasions, games of football have only begun after players and supporters had formed parallel lines at the centre of the oval. As the line of people from one team passed in front of the other, people were able to express their respect for the deceased by shaking the hands of those on the opposite side.

Some years ago, during a football carnival at Wirrimanu, play stopped late in the afternoon and everyone gathered at the oval. The men sat in front and the women to the side and rear. A number of families were concerned about a young man who was clearly very sick. An older man had been accused of performing sorcery. He was brought forward, made his protestations and then began to work as a maparn on the sick young man. The football carnival provided the opportunity for many to gather. It also provided a public geographical space where a serious accusation of sorcery could be addressed. That games ceased for that afternoon was never questioned. The gathering confirmed the place of the young man in the concern of family and friends. It confirmed the integrity of the older man, and it strengthened the network and priority of relationships within the sphere of football.

In recent years there appears to have been a shift by Aboriginal people in the Kimberley away from attending rodeos to football. This shift in interest and attendance may have been influenced by the fact that football has now come under greater Aboriginal control than have rodeos. But there is further evidence, around very disparate parts of Australia, that Aboriginal gatherings around sport, particularly football, enable significant cultural values to be shared and promoted. I will mention three very different sporting associations: the Garbutt Magpies Sporting Association in Townsville (Queensland), the Rumbalara Football Netball Club in Shepparton (Victoria) and the Clontarf Football Academy in Perth (Western Australia). In these examples, as in many others, football can be seen to celebrate and promote important meanings for many Aboriginal men, their families and communities.[4]

The Garbutt Magpies Sporting Association was formed in 1955.[5] Like the Rumbalara Football Club it has also existed under various names but was re-admitted into the Townsville League in 1978.[6] The Rumbalara Football Netball Club was established in 1972 and accepted into the Goulburn Valley Football League in 1997 (Department of Rural Health 2001, p. 16). Like the Garbutt Magpies Sporting Association it has also encouraged non-Aboriginal members and players but within a cultural framework that stressed Aboriginal leadership and values that promoted kinship, communal celebration and well-being (2001, p. 18). Both Clubs have experienced being suspended from competition and both have made efforts to resurrect themselves. They have drawn strong family and community support when they play and in the various other activities they have promoted. The Clontarf Football Academy in Perth in 1999 began offering young Aboriginal men the opportunity to play football as they attended Clontarf Aboriginal College. This initiative resulted in significant increases in male students at the College where playing football enabled education, health and employment possibilities to be explored.[7]

These three examples — Garbutt Magpies, Rumbalara Football Netball and Clontarf Football Academy — each from a very different part of Australia, reflect important Aboriginal initiatives around sport, and in this case Australian Rules football. The desire of Aboriginal men to play football is matched by families and others wanting to be involved. But these initiatives have not come easily.

The context in which Aboriginal people have been involved in sport within Australia has its own particular history of discrimination and racism. Some Aboriginal sporting clubs have worked to exist within larger sporting and kartiya-controlled organisations; some have succeeded, some have failed and some have been banned.[8] While the number of Indigenous players within the Australian Football League (AFL) has increased significantly over recent years, the rhetoric and descriptions of such players have not developed to the same degree.[9] The media often represents players as 'mercurial', 'bearers of silky skills' and 'enigmatic'. The Krakouer brothers were once described as 'magical and mesmerising', 'possessing telepathic qualities', 'always knowing where the other was as if by some sixth sense' (Harris, 1989). There has been a consistent labelling and stereotyping of Indigenous footballers and their abilities without much serious reflection (Hallinan 1999, p. 4). Only a few commentators, such as Martin Flanagan, have tried to explain Aboriginal football as an expression of different cultural notions of time, space and place (Flanagan 1988, p. 115).

Racism in Australian Rules became publicly exposed in 1993 when Nicky Winmar, an Aboriginal player, lifted his jumper and pointed to his skin when facing abusive Collingwood supporters. In 1995 another Aboriginal player, Michael Long, accused Damien Monkhurst of racial abuse. The representations and experiences which Aboriginal players suffered were not unlike, in many ways, those earlier experiences of Aboriginal people in the Kimberley of the 1930s: people were either romanticised or they were treated as inferior. They were exoticised as beyond comprehension or relegated as being below understanding. While recent events within the AFL have demonstrated the willingness of the sport to embrace Aboriginal players, these events have arisen from a relatively recent experience of racist attitudes and behaviour in all sports affecting Aboriginal people (Tatz 1987, 1995; Godwell, 2000; Tatz & Tatz 2000).

Clontarf Aboriginal College in Perth has demonstrated an important link between young Aboriginal men and their experience of football. While only functioning for a few years it has shown an ability to attract but also hold young men. It has drawn young men back into formal education and also offered them the possibility of developing skills for long-term employment. It has seen itself as 'using football as a vehicle, to improve the education, discipline, life skills and self esteem of young Aboriginal men and so equip them to participate more meaningfully in society' (Clontarf Football Academy 2002). In some ways Clontarf's success is not surprising. The young men are at a time in their lives when they are seeking to move, with the help of other men, into adulthood. While they demonstrate other interests, such as socialising with young women, it is evident that playing football provides their primary focus and source of energy. Older men, kartiya and Aboriginal, provide a context that can be compared with those found in desert holding relationships. In both places young men are cared for, taught and looked after by older men within clearly defined gendered and social spaces. A particular form of male sociality is offered that provides deeper meanings and explanations for the specific energies of young men at this time. In Clontarf, in the desert and other places, football provides an essential ingredient, motivation and context for the construction of particular forms of Aboriginal masculinity.

While much that is said here could possibly be applied to other forms of male sporting activity, there is evidence that Australian Rules football distinctively engages Aboriginal men. As a game it is significantly different from soccer and the two rugby codes that are played in Australia. It provides a sport that is played in a relatively wide, open space. It allows a large number of players, more than in other football games, to move ahead of the ball as it is being passed and it offers various ways in which the ball can be carried, passed to others or kicked. The rules allow a wider range of foot and hand skills than soccer, and with less of the direct and physical confrontation than is found in the two rugbies.[10] These would appear to be significant factors in its appeal within many Aboriginal communities.

Despite Geoffrey Blainey's comment that 'it is unlikely that this Aboriginal game influenced Australian football' (Blainey 1990, p. 96), there is some evidence the game of Australian Rules had Aboriginal origins.[11] A game called Marn Grook was played at Cummeragunja Mission in the late 1800s (Potter n.d. p. 12),[12] (Cummeragunja was first established in 1881 on land on the New South Wales side of the Murray River.) The game that was played there was similar to one played by Aboriginal men in western Victoria in 1881:

> One of the favourite games is football, in which fifty, or as many as one hundred players engage at a time. The ball is about the size of an orange, and is made of opossum-skin, with the fur side outwards. It is filled with pounded charcoal, which gives solidity without much increase of weight, and is tied hard round and round with kangaroo sinews.
>
> The players are divided into two sides and ranged in opposing lines, which are always of a different 'class' — white cockatoo against black cockatoo, quail against snake, &c. Each side endeavours to keep possession of the ball, which is tossed a short distance by hand, and then kicked in any direction. The side which kicks it oftenest and furthest gains the game. The person who sends it highest is considered the best player, and has the honour of burying it in the ground till required next day. (Dawson 1981, p. 85)

Some important similarities can be drawn between the game observed by Dawson some 120 years ago and that played in the Western Desert today. Both are games where competition, skill and enjoyment are considered important. Both may be claimed as 'men's business', which is not the same as Law or ceremonial business. Football is not a secret or sacred event, nor have Aboriginal men ever claimed it to be one. Those who play football with distinction cannot claim authority or status beyond the sports arena.

As Dawson noted in 1881:

The sport is concluded with a shout of applause, and the best player is complimented on his skill. This game, which is somewhat similar to the white man's game of football, is very rough; but as the players are barefooted and naked, they do not hurt each other so much as the white people do; nor is the fact of an aborigine being a good football player considered to entitle him to assist in making laws for the tribe to which he belongs. (1981, p. 85)[13]

Despite Australian Rules being sometimes described as an 'inclusive' game for men and women, it remains in the desert solely within the male domain. This would also appear to be true of the game played in 1881:

Games are held usually held after the great meetings and korroboraes [sic]. Wrestling is a favourite game, but is never practised in anger. Women and children are not allowed to be present. (1981, p. 84)

Today, within the desert, women are not involved in the planning or execution of the game but they are significant spectators. Women appear to enjoy the spectacle and the company of other women and walytja that accompanies sporting carnivals. Men also feel better about their performance when women are watching. As with ceremonial Law, the separation of gendered groups is important. In both ritual activities men could not perform their role, or celebrate their place without the support and affirmation of women.

The skills that are needed within the football arena are very similar to those that men have developed and learned over many years as they hunted in the desert.[14] Hunting requires many finely honed, separate and practised skills. It requires the concentration, coordination and focus of many senses. The body needs balance as physical movement combines strength with speed, timing with coordination. Men had to learn how to move quickly, patiently and silently through the bush, sometimes pursuing low-lying and low-flying objects of prey. Sometimes the men hunted in groups where non-verbal communication occurred through the use of hand and facial signs and gestures. Hunting concentrated body skills where the hunted was observed, tracked, chased and caught by men who had learned to move together. The male body moved in harmony with other male bodies forming a concentration of energy and purpose.

In 1935, HH Finlayson, from the South Australian Museum, described the final stages of a hunt by a group of desert men. While his depiction of 'the other' borders on the exuberant and exotic — he is aware that he is describing something very foreign to his own experience — it recognised the skills of hunting, the intensity of commitment and the emotions associated with capturing a prize. He described the scene where a fire had been lit to drive out the prey and the men had then moved in:

> The three men, muscled like greyhounds, are breathing short and quick; they swing their weight from foot to foot, twirling their throwing-sticks in their palms, and as they scan the advancing flames their great eyes glow and sparkle as the climax of the day draws near. It is their sport, their spectacle, and their meat-getting, all in one; and in it they taste a simple intensity of joy which is beyond the range of our feeling. (Finlayson 1955, p. 57)

What Finlayson portrayed as sport, spectacle and 'meat-getting', Marcel Mauss described as a 'technique of the body' (Mauss 1979, p, 106). Hunting is more than a precise physical or biological skill. It combines social, mental and physical techniques nurtured within ancient and intimate connections to the land and often in relationship with other men.

> His skill as a hunter is largely based on his powers of observation. These again depend on his ability to receive and to retain, very swiftly, visual impressions of extraordinary minuteness of detail. (Finlayson 1955, p. 57)

Hunting remains an activity that confirms male identity, male company and male nurturance. Men did not hunt simply for themselves. They also hunted to display their skills and demonstrate their responsibilities to provide and care for others.

When the hunting 'technique' is applied to sport, such as football, its use can be varied and creative. Approaching a kipara (bush turkey), facing a tjarrampari (perenty goanna) or chasing a muntuny (black headed python) also require hunting skills, albeit of a different nature. They involve different body techniques involving the coordination of eyes, hands and feet. Men do not describe themselves as 'hunters' on the football field, but they bring with them another context of learned body techniques in relation to the land, to that which is hunted and in relation to other male hunters. The activity, energy and agency that men bring to football suggest a strong embodied connection between men and a history of shared values and enjoyment. At the heart of this valued experience is the ability of men to move physically and skilfully across the land with close attentiveness and with a heightened sensitivity to fellow male company.

Winning a football trophy and the hunted 'meat-getting' also bear similarities. As a man brings home the success of his hunting to share among walytja, so the hard-earned trophy from a football tournament is similarly treated. I have often found it instructive to watch how a trophy can be given away to a relative, left on display in the community store or simply left lying around the community. Winning a trophy is important but Puntu do not collect trophies. There seems little interest in having trophy cabinets or collections. The game holds 'goals' far more important than can be represented in a physical object. One time I asked a senior footballer, one of the most talented players in the region, about the game. He took pride in his football, bought the right boots, played in different competitions and won awards.

R: Is the winning important?
A: Not really.
R: Not really, what's really important?
A: Having a game, I suppose.
R: Having a game with your mates?
A: Probably. Having a game with your mates or just getting out there, trying to be the best, I don't know, something like that.

He is not suggesting that he doesn't like to win. Nor will he avoid the celebrations if his team wins. But it is within a larger male space that he experiences a positive sense of himself and his skills. The game provides him with the opportunity to extend and test himself as part of that male group.

In this region young men pay careful attention to the Australian Rules played in other places. They watch the games on television, read the newspaper articles and note the personalities, behaviours and idiosyncrasies of different players. The clubs they support, and the players they emulate, resonate in their conversations and dress. However, they are not simply assimilated into all aspects of the game. They do not repeat all they see and hear. They negotiate important cultural values within this sporting arena.

This negotiation can be most clearly seen in those particular relationships — beyond the usual ones of desert kinship — where great respect needs to be shown to another, such as one's yalpurru or tjamparti. These relationships arise within men's Law. The first relationship, yalpurru, invites close and enduring friendships as it refers to those who were initiated together. Yalpurru should never fight or hurt one another. The second relationship, tjamparti, requires great respect (demonstrated by formal avoidance) as it refers to those who performed one's initiation. I wondered how men negotiated such relationships when they played on opposite and competing teams:

> R: What about if your yalpurru on the other side? Do they worry about that?
>
> A: No, that's a part they hate, you know (laughs). Well, I mean, footy is footy, and the name of the game from white people. It doesn't matter yalpurru you can bump him anywhere, that's the name of the game.
>
> R: And what about your tjamparti on the other side?
>
> A: Tjamparti, you can do it again.
>
> R: You can do it again?
>
> A: That's the name of the game.
>
> R: But do you feel that that's good?
>
> A: Bit, a bit, you know, after game: 'Oh, I've been feel, bump my tjamparti and my yalpurru.'
>
> R: You don't like that?
>
> A: After the game (laughs).
>
> R: You feel bad after the game?
>
> A: Yuwayi, feel bad.

R: And you say something to him, or wiya?

A: Yeah, say if you tjamparti on the other hand, tell the other fellas, 'say sorry to tjamparti for me', you know.

R: Tell the tjamparti you're sorry.

A: Yeah.

R: So that's the hard one, that working out between kartiya style and cultural style?

A: Yuwayi.

When men adopt the kartiya expectations of a game, where they can — and are expected to — tackle one another with great vigour, they also need to deal with Puntu expectations. Games are played in the public arena and hence one's behaviour is manifest for all to see. In particular, tackling another player can be problematic where games are played on rough, dirt ovals. It does not take much force for a tackle or a bump to be interpreted as personal and excessive. This can lead to strong words. Sometimes there are fights, sometimes games stop. Playing football creates new forms of tension between men when they are playing against those to whom they are obliged to show respect. A man should never fight or hurt his yalpurru and should show great respect to his tjamparti by avoiding personal contact with him.

Obviously such demands cannot be easily exercised on a playing field. Such observances can be especially difficult for players when teams are trying to win games: supporters call out, emotions rise, forceful physical contact is made and players get angry. Men handle these tensions in different ways and some men feel these tensions more keenly than others. A number of men have said to me 'football is football', 'there is no family inside', 'no pilali is in the field'. They have carefully demarcated football imperatives from their cultural obligations. They leave their cultural obligations at the boundary to the oval. 'This is a kartiya game', they say, where new rules require new forms of behaviour. However, at the same time they can also be heard to say, 'one is not supposed to hurt family'. Clearly, there is tension and men are aware of it. While it would seem that men can safely move from one arena of values to another, such accommodation is not always easy or seamless.

That men do negotiate these tensions, largely successfully, can be seen in the way they play. Most kartiyas who watch Puntu play football rarely notice that kinship relationships affect the way men play football. Much less do they notice those other relationships that have originated in Law, that continue to operate strongly off the football field, and which determine male behaviour. Men have learned in football to put pressure on an opposition player, while avoiding an encounter that becomes too personal or confronting. Men have also learned to refine their skills to avoid being tackled. That men do negotiate these tensions reflects the obvious enjoyment that they experience in such gatherings, despite the serious risks they encounter in transgressing important relational boundaries.

Football, as in the cases of petrol sniffing and prison, provides its own elements of paradox in relation to health. While it is celebrated for its provision of male company, its exercise and the enjoyment if offers both men and women, it can also be viewed with concern. Women have articulated some of the dangers they perceive while men, also aware of these dangers, are less likely to name or discuss them publicly. As desert society works carefully to avoid public acrimony and violence, one danger in football is that it can cause tension within walytja and among extended family members.

Many of the people, for example, who now live at Malarn grew up at old or new Balgo. Not only do they have walytja living at Wirrimanu but they visit, maintain regular contact and exchange goods with their family relations. Football competitions, often based around the formation of community teams and the prize of a final trophy (or cash prize), can set community teams or members of those teams against others. If any tension arises from such a competition it can flow over to family members in both communities. One of the women who live at Malarn, who has strong family connections with Wirrimanu, expressed her concern:

> A: Like, you know, it's just a game but people get enemy with each other.
> R: They can get serious?
> A: Serious.
> R: So that's not…?

A: In that football they get out of control.

R: They can get out of control?

A: They get enemy towards each other because of trophy and money, you know, which that football is like just destroying, you know, friend and family.

R: There's a bad side to it?

A: Bad thing, yeah.

R: But sometimes when I see them going off together?

A: Happy, you know.

R: Happy when they're together?

A: When they're happy together and playing together.

Football brings great pleasure to families when they see their male relations together, exhibiting their skills and enjoying a game. But there had been occasions, as this woman remembered, when football led to arguments on and off the football field. When men argued, fought or hurt one another — and brought their families into the arguments — she believed that football ceased to be a healthy activity. Her anxiety was that football brought men together with the advantages of male company and recreation, but it could also create divisions between the people of the different communities of the region. It could be both healthy and unhealthy for Puntu at the same time.

Her younger male cousin, who plays football, referred to the tensions that he sometimes experienced between the men of these same two communities. Arguments from the football field could be carried over into Halls Creek when men went there to drink. He would find himself caught between his relations in one community and the men from the other community where he lived. Football, women and beer, he suggested with some seriousness, did not mix well. He then made an important comparison between playing football and the experience of men's Law. In both cases men could get angry, but the difference was that in Law the old men possessed the authority that kept anger and violence in check. Kanyirninpa kept men together but when it came under pressure, as in the case of football and alcohol, the authority that older men provided in the Law was absent.

In this context, the experience of the Clontarf Football Academy is worth comment. The young men who went there have been described as 'naturally aggressive or angry young people', comprising a wide variety of Aboriginal male youth from different parts of Western Australia. However, in the three years of Clontarf playing football, regularly presenting a number of teams for competition, there had only been one fight during a game. In 200 games of football only one player had been sent off the field. These young men are, on average, slightly younger than desert footballers, varying in age from 14 to 18 and coming from different communities. They also play a lot of football, some of it under great pressure to win. However, it is evident that the way in which these young men approach football constrains their frustrations and anger and the possibility of on-field violence. This does not suggest these young men don't tackle hard or take their game seriously. In fact, they have a reputation for the opposite. But it does indicate that an authority has developed around football at Clontarf that limits the possibilities of male aggressive and violent behaviour.

It could be argued that one of the foundations of Clontarf's culture, and its success, is that those who coach and mentor these young men hold them, and with their ability to hold comes their authority. These young men choose to be at the College and they accept the values that the teachers and coaches set before them. They also accept the restraints that are placed on their behaviour. In some very particular ways this holding is analogous to that experienced at Law. The young desert man just mentioned described the authority of the old men at Law as one that constrained men's anger and the possibility of violence: 'in Law time they listen to the old people'. It is this quality of listening and respecting that lies within kanyirninpa. When old men watch over and hold younger men in the Law they provide a context where young men exercise restraint. Their behaviour expresses individuality and skill but also an awareness and respect for others.

In a similar way, the autonomy of the young men at Clontarf is restrained. The authority of the older men encourages behaviour where young men can exhibit skill, individuality and competitiveness, but within a sociality, respect and enjoyment that relatedness provides. When young men do not come under authority, and restraint on their behaviour is lessened, the possibilities of violence can increase. Hence, in the desert, when playing football, and without the presence of an appropriate guidance and authority, men might play a more 'kartiya' style of game that places higher value on opposition and confrontation. A similar antinomy to that described earlier about alcohol will be revealed: sociality and restraint will conflict with the pressure to compete and win — especially if there is a financial trophy or other award. However, like drinking, men may choose the risks associated with playing because of the benefits they perceive being offered.

There is more to the game of football than the exercise and control of male behaviour, however.[15] When Gerard Neesham began coaching Aboriginal students at Clontarf,

> he recognised that during the football sessions the collective energies of the group were much more focused and positive than during other times during the day. (Clontarf 2002b, p. 2)

The collective experience, outdoors and with other men, promoted 'more focused and positive' behaviour. When desert men move to play a game, they exhibit a number of the same qualities that they do when they are about to go hunting with other men: the thrill of expectation, focused anticipation, the enjoyment of supporting company. When Desmond Morris suggested that 'many of our primeval, tribal hunting patterns are still with us, lightly disguised', he was interpreting contemporary examples of collecting, gambling and travelling as well as all forms of games and sports (Morris 1994, p. 65). Football provides a contemporary space in which some Aboriginal men maintain and develop ancient hunting techniques. These experiences provide a source of energy for men as they result in personal and group satisfaction. However, as also with some kartiya men, excessive attention on football can become distracting to the point of being obsessive.

Playing football can lead men away from their responsibilities to others. The prevalence in the desert of football carnivals and games, once the wet season is over, encourages men to travel. This can cause young men to absent themselves regularly from their family and communities. Football has been known to draw men away from family, work and other responsibilities for days, even weeks, at a time.[16] In addition, family members have wanted to travel with them and watch them play. This has impacted on the work that needed to be done in the community, as well as regular attendance of children at the school. One of the region's school principals remembers when a compromise was finally reached:

> What used to happen was the young men would go off on Wednesday afternoon or Thursday for football carnivals and the women and kids would follow on the Friday, after school finished. So, there was that change in the community where they knew it was important for the kids to be at school and very few kids went. Sometimes, some of the senior boys would go because they want to get on the truck and head off too, but there was a change in community attitudes as well.

This compromise, while it kept the younger children at school for longer, did not resolve the consequence of men being absent for lengthy periods of time. The wives of the players recognised the value for their men in playing football, but they also saw it created other problems:

> R: What do women think about men playing football?
> A: I don't think it's really good but they enjoy it (laughs).
> R: You don't think it's really good?
> A: Well two ways I always think, you know. It's kind of inter-fering with our culture and then but it's good for them but now we're living in two…I don't know, we're trying to fit into two worlds (laughs) a kartiya world and an Aboriginal world.
> R: And not easy?
> A: And not easy, yeah.
> R: But the men like football?

A: The men like football, but sometimes we're losing our culture because of football, too. 'Cause they always going away and not working and like, it's football, football all the time.

R: What is it that football is giving them?

A: Joy, happiness to be with men, you know (laughs).

R: To be together with men?

A: To be together, yeah…and in another community, you know, a big gathering time for the weekend and everyone catching up with families and friends.

R: Meeting other people is good?

A: Meeting other people.

R: Being with other men, you think, is really important?

A: Being with other men but I still think football is important too because men are together.

The difficulty for this young woman lies not within the game itself, but in its power to draw men away from other valued activities. She once commented that hunting was important for men because it enabled men to spend time together in the bush, even though community stores had interfered with the ability of men to hunt and bring home food for their families. This, she believed, impacted on their self-esteem. Here, an articulate and active young mother expressed her concern for a particular male praxis. She recognised that men needed the company of other men but they were also needed in their communities if their families were to cope with the challenge of living in Puntu and kartiya worlds. In one example, restraint — in the form of older men expressing their authority — proved the answer. Again, the school principal remembered:

> At one stage they were always take off here, there and everywhere for football carnivals. And everybody would go. And I remember the stage when the old men told the young fellas, and that was enough, they couldn't keep going to football, and things quietened down.

Without the expressed authority of the older men these young men would have continued, possibly indefinitely, to travel and play. Without the restraints of older men some young men cannot easily constrain their own behaviour. They will seek the benefits which male company provides but not within their own families and communities. While this points to the value and importance of football for men it also, as the wife of the footballer explained, can provide serious dangers with the neglect of other cultural values and relationships.

Football is clearly a highly valued social activity for many desert men.[17] It is a healthy experience where male sociality is strengthened, exercise experienced and which all Puntu enjoy as they engage with close and extended members of their walytja. The defined geographical and social space of football reinforces for younger men some of the values that they experience in Law. Men enjoy the company of other men, are tested for their courage and skill, and their behaviour is supported and encouraged by the authority of older men. Football enables men to grow in self-esteem and confidence as they play with other men, a spectacle inviting the interest and support of women. At the same time football can undermine some of the relationships that Puntu hold as important. Where violence occurs or where men are absent from their families for lengthy periods of time, such behaviour, a consequence of unrestrained autonomy, can lead to unhealthy consequences for both men and women. Such male praxis creates tension with others, a serious risk to important relationships and avoids those areas where male presence and responsibility are needed.

Football incorporates young desert men into a male world beyond the arena of the Law and, at the same time, into a kartiya football and wider male world. For men to play football and respect both Puntu and kartiya values requires much skill. The provision of holding provides a context where such skill can be entertained and protected. Men can bring their own 'learned body techniques' to the game. They can also seriously shape and influence the way in which kartiyas play football. However, without the company, nurturance and authority of older men and the values they express through kanyirninpa, football activity will risk the paradox of expressing both healthy and unhealthy outcomes for young men.

7

Prison: More than a holiday

*I think some Aboriginal people like going
to prison.*

Spending time in prison has been a common experience for many
men of the Kutjungka region. There are few older men who have
not spent some time in prison or in the police lock-ups of Halls
Creek or other Kimberley towns. A very small number, relative
to the total of those who have been imprisoned, have experienced
long prison sentences. These longer sentences have usually been for
serious assaults, rape or manslaughter. Most sentences, however,
have been of short duration and are alcohol related. At any one
time there might be more than twenty men from the Kutjungka
region in a Western Australian prison; there may also be male
juveniles in one of the Perth detention centres.[1] During the time
of this research desert men in detention were usually held in either
Broome or Roebourne regional prisons. Broome prison (minimum
security) is preferred as it is closer to the desert communities and
enables greater possibilities for family contact. Some women from
this region have also spent some time in prison but they constitute
a very small number.[2]

In this chapter I want to examine men's experience of prison in
the context of the male praxis around kanyirninpa. The history of
Puntu and their involvement in the criminal justice system reflects
similar patterns and experiences to that of other Aboriginal men.
Puntu are also faced with few choices when arrest, court and prison

occur. Despite this, desert men are able to use the prison system to some advantage through the values and meaning that kanyirninpa offers. However, as with petrol sniffing and football, the paradox of healthy and unhealthy outcomes is also disclosed.

Over more than thirty-five years living and working with Aboriginal and Torres Strait Islander peoples I have visited men, women and juveniles in detention in Melbourne, Townsville, Darwin, Wyndham, Broome, Roebourne and Perth. As a researcher for the Royal Commission into Aboriginal Deaths in Custody I was given the opportunity to visit Broome and Roebourne prisons (Dodson 1991). During the 1990s the prison authorities in Broome gave me permission, whenever I was visiting, to move around the prison and talk with prisoners in their cells or wherever they wanted to talk. In July 2002 I attempted to obtain permission through the Western Australian Ministry of Justice to interview desert men in prison as part of this research, but the protocols they had established took several months for final approval. Hence, the information provided for this chapter arose principally from interviews conducted with men in the desert. Some women also provided comments upon the prison experience of their husbands and male relations.

Clearly, there are serious issues around the high rates of detention of Aboriginal people within Western Australia. The over-representation ratio of Aboriginal people in Western Australian prisons was 21.7 in 1993, more than for any other prison jurisdiction in Australia (Cunneen & McDonald 1997, p. 30).[3] The proportion of Aboriginal prisoners in Western Australian prisons has doubled within a generation (Chappell & Wilson 2000, p. 208). Western Australia also provides the highest over-representation of Aboriginal juveniles aged from 10–17 years in Juvenile Corrective Institutions, an over-representation ratio of 65 (Cahill & Marshall 2002, p. 20). Such a large over-representation has resulted from a reduction in the number of kartiyas in juvenile detention where 'the high ratio results from a decrease in the rate (and number) of non-Aboriginal people in juvenile detention, rather than an increase in the rate (and number) of Aboriginal people being detained' (2002, p. 20). Not surprisingly, Cunneen and McDonald have commented: 'Western Australia is notorious, nationally and internationally, for its disturbingly high level of involvement of juveniles (especially Aboriginal juveniles) in the criminal justice system' (1997, p. 172).

Desert men have not been exempt from the experience of prison nor the social, historical and political influences that have led to imprisonment becoming a 'normative' experience for so many Aboriginal men in Australia, and within Western Australia in particular. In the decade 1990–2000 the level of Aboriginal imprisonment within the total prisoner population of Australia rose from 14 per cent in 1990 to almost 19 per cent in 2000 (Cunneen 2001, p. 56). Carach et al. have noted that 95 per cent of Aboriginal people who are imprisoned are male (1999, p. 4). In the Kimberley 90 per cent of those who pass through the prison system are Aboriginal (Colmar Brunton 2002, p. 1). The enforcement of particular laws, the attitudes and behaviour of police, the availability of legal advice, decisions by the judiciary and the offering of alternatives to imprisonment have all been part of an historical, social and political system of law enforcement that has impacted severely on the imprisonment of Puntu since colonisation (Beresford & Omaji, 1996). These issues were fully and carefully examined in the Royal Commission into Aboriginal Deaths in Custody (Johnston, 1991). The *Regional Report of Inquiry into Underlying Issues in Western Australia* examined a wide range of social, political and historical factors that have influenced the arrest and incarceration of Aboriginal men in Western Australia (Dodson 1991; Langton 1991). In the following chapter I want to return to some of these issues around the over-representation of Aboriginal men in prison, as an example of intergenerational trauma upon the Puntu social body.

Meanwhile, it is important to note that Western Australia has a distinctive and long history of Aboriginal imprisonment. Mark Finnane has observed:

> Western Australia stands apart from the other colonies in that large numbers of Aborigines were imprisoned during the course of expansion into the north. So great were the numbers

of Aborigines imprisoned that one might argue that the latter
pattern of large-scale Aboriginal incarceration in that state was
conditioned by this not so distant historical experience. As
early as 1840, Western Australia established the country's only
prison specifically for Aborigines, at Rottnest Island. But by the
1890s the colony had a number of other institutions that were
primarily 'Aboriginal' prisons. (Finnane 1997, p. 35)

I have already mentioned how, in that first encounter at Tjaluwan
between missionaries and Puntu in 1939, missionaries called the
police in response to the killing of some of their sheep (Byrne 1989,
p. 76). Three men were arrested and taken into custody. Since that
time the powers that police have exercised over Puntu, together
with the experiences they have remembered, have resulted in Puntu
holding ambivalent attitudes towards the police. While police can be
called for assistance and help, they are also remembered as the ones
who regularly removed men from their families and communities
for imprisonment. Those who were arrested during the first decades
of the mission were taken away in chains. The Kukatja word for
policeman is 'wayirnuwatji', 'the one with the chain' (Valiqette 1993,
p. 336). The Berndts commented on police practice where 'several
Balgo natives are said to be taken to Hall's [sic] Creek in chains late
in 1959' (Berndt, R & C 1960, p. 10). They noted that 'witnesses'
were treated by the police in a similar way. It was around this time
that police were also undertaking 'leper patrols' where suspected
Aboriginal lepers were taken to the leprosarium in handcuffs and
chains (Rees, C & L 1953, p. 110).

At Balgo Mission the missionaries would request the police to
come and, in some cases, as one ex-missionary remembered, the
police would, 'get a bloke and take him out in the bush and bash
him up with a spanner'.[4] Police were enforcers of kartiya law but they
could also be independent providers of its punishment. According
to Michael Gill 'the police became not only the law-enforcers but
also the arbiters of justice…able effectively to administer a sentence
and a punishment of their own' (1997, p. 21). There are currently
young men living in the region who remember police taking them
into custody from Wirrimanu, and stopping off along the road that

led into Halls Creek. There they would be taken out of the vehicle and given a belting before going into town. This happened as recently as in the early 1990s.[5] Sometimes, there have been disturbances in Halls Creek involving violence and alcohol, resulting in a large number of arrests. Such was the case in early 1996, and when these incidents occur the Puntu memory of previous police-behaviour surfaces.[6] Deep anger and frustration emerges.

In 1991 Commissioner Johnston (RCIADIC) commented:

> It is my opinion that far too much police intervention in the lives of Aboriginal people throughout Australia has been arbitrary, discriminatory, racist and violent. There is absolutely no doubt in my mind that the antipathy which so many Aboriginal people have towards police is based not just on historical conduct but upon the contemporary experience of contact with many police officers. (Johnson 1991, p. 195)

At the same time, it needs to be added, there are some police that Puntu trust.[7] These are generally police who have treated them with respect and shown an interest in their lives. Apart from these exceptions, Puntu of this region have now experienced more than sixty years of regular police activity, where certain forms of behaviour have been 'defined as deviant, subject to intense surveillance and recorded and processed by criminal justice agencies' (Tomsen 1996, p. 191).

It can be argued that those occasions where police and others involved in the criminal justice system have earned Puntu respect are few (Cunneen 2001, p. 59). History would suggest that powerful kartiya males have consistently enacted surveillance and control over desert men for many years, and violence has formed part of that surveillance and control (Tomsen 1996, p. 191). To what extent this process has influenced the construction of desert masculinity, and how much 'criminal behaviour' is a consequence of resistance, frustration or powerlessness is difficult to know. It is a topic to which I return in the following chapter. What is evident is that those who come under the intervention of the criminal justice system are severely disadvantaged before they are detained. Being Aboriginal, living in an isolated part of Western Australia, and with few economic, political or legal resources, Puntu have little power and few choices they can exercise when faced by the criminal justice system.

Men, and also women, who are charged or arrested will rarely see a lawyer until just prior to court. At this hectic and rushed moment the details and context of the charge are often discussed for the first time. Often the Aboriginal Legal Service (ALS) solicitor will arrive on the same plane as the magistrate, whether the court is sitting in Halls Creek or Wirrimanu, to face a long list of court appearances.[8] The closest ALS office is Kununurra, and a field officer works out of Halls Creek. There is no ALS representative based in the Kutjungka region. Puntu generally do not speak English as a first language and interpreters are rarely made available, especially for magistrates' courts. Court sessions are conducted in English where the use of language is technical and can assume a sophisticated knowledge of kartiya law. There are no support mechanisms or legal personnel in the desert region to remind Puntu of approaching court appearances, their legal significance or what plea should be entered. There is no public transport to enable people to travel the necessary 280 kilometres into Halls Creek, where most of the courts are held.[9] Sometimes, men can be expected to attend courts in Kununurra or Broome, one-way trips of some 550 kilometres and 900 kilometres. Attending court can become problematic for those charged, and also for families or those who might want to attend or speak for them. There is no financial or other allowance to assist people to return home if the court adjourns the hearing or a not guilty judgment is found. Not surprisingly, men can find it easier to allow bench and outstanding warrants to be served on them, for police to take them into custody and court then to proceed. If men are given fines their financial options in paying such fines are extremely limited. Most have very limited incomes and rely on Community Development Employment Programme (CDEP) or Centrelink payments.[10] They are often faced with the choice of paying a fine, and then going hungry for some weeks, or not paying the fine and going to prison where they will be fed. Food prices in the Kimberley can be more than 50 per cent higher than in Perth (North Australia Nutrition

Group, 2003). Sometimes, arrest and imprisonment offers the best of some very limited choices.

In recent years, some researchers have suggested that young Aboriginal males are seeking through detention an alternative 'rite of passage', that is, a rite quite different from, or an alternative to, the process of male ceremonial Law (Beresford & Omaji 1996). In this understanding, young men are seeking through prison a rite of passage into adulthood. There is some evidence for this position. Men are separated (by police), instructed (in prison) and then re-incorporated (back into society). The process can be understood as providing the moral and social transformation that rites of passage are understood to offer: separation, instruction and incorporation (van Gennep 1997, p. 10; Teather 1999, p, 13). Some young men, according to older desert men, want older men to acknowledge them. The attitude, 'I've been to prison' can, for some, be an attempt to seek the approval of others. Their effort to use prison to make them appear 'tough' is one way they hope to obtain respect as an adult. That these men might keep returning to prison suggests, however, that as a rite of passage it is very incomplete and limited. This is not to deny that, in some cases, men use the prison experience to their advantage. These men may believe they become tougher and stronger men for the experience.

Similar to the above approach is the theory that, 'going to prison may be an enjoyable experience' (Biles 1983, p. 18). When David Biles investigated the experience of prison by Groote Eylandters in 1983 he concluded, 'criminal justice services, in particular the use of imprisonment on the mainland, reinforces and rewards the criminal behaviour of some' (1983, p. 17). However, there are several assumptions in this statement. It can assume that what constitutes 'criminal behaviour' and 'imprisonment' are understood and experienced similarly by kartiya and Puntu men. That desert men have described prison as a 'holiday camp', 'boys' home' and 'hostel' needs to be carefully understood.

Other researchers have proposed that detention for young Aboriginal males is not a rite of passage, 'but rather another venue for the construction of identity, as are schools, leisure groups and more general (and "loose") peer interactions' (Ogilvie & Van Zyl 2001, p. 3). In this theory, detention provides access to resources and experiences that are not generally available in communities. This approach offers a more autonomous view of incarceration, while admitting that any choice about imprisonment 'is the product of a marginalised environment that severely limits the possibilities for choice' (2001, p. 6). The example I have mentioned previously, regarding the payment of court fines, provides support for this approach. Men can use detention to suit their own needs, while it can also express their resistance and agency.

Detention can also be understood as an expression of kanyirninpa. This approach, based on Puntu experiences of prison, attempts to understand further 'the complex web of causes of Aboriginal offending, but also to appreciate the overlay that such causal studies have on the lived experiences of Aboriginal people' (Chappell & Wilson 2000, p. 206). There are elements within the holding experience that can attract men to prison, influence them while they are there and also lead them away from prison. This approach to detention does not exclude the many and various elements, already discussed, that lead to the very high rates of imprisonment of Aboriginal males in Western Australia. It offers an additional approach, through a largely phenomenological understanding of men's experience of prison, and supports the views proposed by Ogilvie and Van Zyl (2001, p. 3). Men make choices around prison but these choices, however risky and unhealthy, need to be understood within a contemporary cultural context.

There are various hand signs that desert people continue to use for communication. One of them indicates that a young man 'has gone into Law', that is, into ceremonial initiation. As the left hand is held out with palm facing downwards the right hand moves under the left, also held with palm downwards. The movement of the right hand sliding under the left represents that a young man has entered a place where he will remain hidden, held and 'locked up' for some period of time. As Puntu say: 'he has gone in'. This same hand sign can also be used to indicate that someone has gone into prison.

While there are some similarities between prison and men's ceremonial 'business', I am not arguing that prison forms an alternative 'rite of initiation'. It is possible that some desert men may use it as a means to promote aspects of their masculinity, such as appearing to be tough. However, within the Western Desert and beyond the Kutjungka region, men's Law continues on a regular basis, and is still considered the most important means by which a marnti (boy) becomes a wati (man). This does not mean that there are not similarities between prison and the Law. There are some, and they are important. They reveal some of the ways in which desert men encounter the prison experience.

Prison, like Law, curtails the freedom and independence of those who are held within it. When Myers referred to Pintupi young men who described the seclusion of Law as 'prison', he understood them to mean that it referred to the place where they were held with greatly restricted autonomy (Myers 1986, p. 238). In both the Law and prison young men are constrained by older men. However, the Law, according to Myers was the key place where kanyirninpa was enacted. Older men mediated the tjukurrpa (ancestral dreaming) through holding the young. The similarity between Law and prison is not simply that freedom is restricted, but in the way in which freedom is restricted. In both cases the autonomy of the younger is constrained by the authority of the older. Young men are constrained in order that they may become more knowledgeable and morally better men. In prison, as in Law, a young person might chafe at such restrictions to his autonomy. However, he might also see there are benefits to 'imprisonment' in the light of the nurturance, teaching and protection that is provided him.

Prison is largely a male domain. There are relatively few female prisoners or prison officers. Women and children are largely excluded and, if they are allowed to visit, it is at very specific times and only at the margins of the prison. Prison can be a place of risk and danger as men have died while in custody. But it is also a carefully protected place, controlled by men whom the prisoners call 'boss'. These, usually older, men can be seen as providing a type of holding relationship with those in prison. The officers keep a close eye on the prisoners as they feed, teach and direct them. While prisoners will distinguish the officers they prefer over others, prison officers are generally considered to be looking after and caring for them. Some men even develop strong and affectionate relationships with particular officers.

The following conversation occurred with three young men who had spent time in prison. Two are around 19 years old, and the third is older, married with children, around 26 years old. They share different kinship relationships and are good friends. They are discussing their experiences of sniffing petrol in the context of being in Broome prison:

> R: So what made you stop [petrol sniffing]?
> A: Broome.
> R: Broome?
> A: I went to Broome and the screw talked.
> R: Who did?
> A: Screw.
> R: Oh, at the prison, the screw told you what?
> A: About no sniffing.
> R: And you listened to him, he was a good screw was he or what?
> A: Mr (name)…
> B: Same as me.
> R: What's that?
> B: Screw.
> R: Yeah, what did he do?
> B: Told me to keep away from sniffing and stealing vehicle.
> R: Same bloke or different bloke?
> B: Different.
> R: You listened to him or what…?
> B: I didn't want to go back in…
> C: Same bloke Mr (name) told me.
> R: And he said, 'give up this petrol'?
> C: Yeah.
> R: And you didn't want to go back in or?
> B: Boss told me, 'ah make some baby outside'.

Earlier I mentioned how some young men can, at particular times, choose to modify their behaviour in the light of advice and encouragement from older men. When a holding relationship exists the younger person is likely to be attentive to that person and the experience can prove transformative. In prison, wardens have authority and some of them are given more respect than others. Their advice can influence men at those times when separation from family and friends can cause them to feel vulnerable, and they want to consider their futures. It is also worth noting that what appears a rather direct and crude statement by the officer, 'make some baby outside', was remembered some years later. As in Brendan Ross' painting and story in Chapter 4, this young man became aware that petrol sniffing was preventing his desire to have a wife and child. His decision to 'change his life' disclosed an important turning point in thinking and behaviour. In this context, a prisoner's experience resonated with that of his friends. Wardens, older males and 'bosses', can be — and have been — catalysts for transformative moments in young prisoners' lives.

As in the experience of Law young men can experience in prison the challenge of being tested. Another young man, presently around 25 years old, related the story of when he had been in prison. Shortly before his release he heard that some of the wardens had taken a bet that he would return. One had bet he would be back in two weeks, another a month. Six months later, the young man was back in Broome accompanying a group of children who were on excursion from one of the desert schools. He went to the prison, saw the superintendent and asked if he could have the money. After six months being out of prison, he figured he had won the bet. This young man lost his father when he was quite young. He spent a period of time in juvenile detention centres. He could speak English well and had developed sufficient confidence to be able to talk up to kartiyas and joke with them. In this context he was aware, as he could be in Law, that older men were watching and testing him. It was a challenge he enjoyed facing but, in this case, the challenge remained incomplete until he had returned to see the officers who had bet against him.

A young woman in her twenties, married with children, has watched a number of her male relations move in and out of prison over the years. One of her uncles was in prison for a long period of time, and other relations have been detained with shorter and often alcohol-related offences. Her husband has never been in prison, but she feels particularly sensitive about those male members of her own family who have. She commented about men liking prison:

> Well some of them, I know it's crazy, but some of them they say they like the friendship with other men, they like being with them, going out to sports and things. They like the food, cause they probably don't get support from other members of the family when they're outside.

Her observations were supported by a number of men who have been in prison. When asked about the benefits of prison, men regularly said they enjoyed the provision of regular meals, a bed, exercise, learning and entertainment. The provision of meals was often mentioned. While the provision of food is an essential ingredient of kanyirninpa, this is not to suggest that prison can be simply described as a nurturing, holding environment. However, that food is mentioned, and given some priority, is significant. Not only are Puntu restricted by low income, and the severely inflated costs of food in their community stores, but most Puntu do not eat three meals a day. That the prison provides young men with regular meals contrasts with what they regularly access when they are at home.

One young man, 27 years old, said, with some pride, that he came out of prison several kilograms heavier. While incarcerated he had been away from grog, had regular exercise and meals. For him, prison had been a very healthy experience. This man is not married and has been in prison a couple of times. He liked to go to town where he could drink, but town had become a place where he found himself under the close attention of police. He resented the fact that police in the past had picked him up for 'street drinking' where they 'lock you up for nothing'. However, 'jail's all right', he said, 'prison not bad, play band on the weekend, talk to family up there all the time'. While he said he didn't want to go back to prison he named the benefits of being there. Food was one. As a footballer he enjoyed the provision of sport, and as a musician he enjoyed the provision of a weekend band. However, it was getting to know other Aboriginal men, his 'family', that he found particularly enjoyable. It provided a benefit that he could continue to experience beyond the life of the prison sentence.

Some years ago this young man was present at Wirrimanu for a funeral. A prisoner had come from Broome for the service, and two prison officers had accompanied him. After the funeral there was some general talk between the officers and some of the men they had known in prison. This young man turned to one of the officers and said, 'Boss, why don't you bring that work truck out here? You could pick up all the men and we could work around the place.' His question and suggestion revealed a number of things. He enjoyed those times in prison when, with a group of men, he was taken by a prison officer and worked around the town of Broome. While clearly obvious in their prison 'greens', the prisoners did not experience shame or embarrassment. They liked working around town with other men, seeing relatives and members of their families, and in the company of a 'boss' who watched over and looked after them.

There is a particular male sociality in prison. This is not to deny that some men can find remand or the confinement of prison very lonely and painful but, as I have mentioned in the previous chapter on playing football, young men enjoy the company of other men. Walking around together, or working together, mirrors similar occasions outside prison where young men move and travel around with their 'mates'. Prison provides the opportunity to meet additional members of one's walytja and make new friends. The young man, just mentioned, described the benefits of this:

R: You mean all families there inside with you?
A: Yuwayi.
R: And that's good, is it?
A: Good to know everyone, you know, from round Kimberleys, from down south, all around.
R: So you meet new people?
A: Yuwayi. And when they come out I say hello. You might see one day he be in Halls Creek or Fitzroy or Derby or Broome.

R: So it's like a mate then is he?
A: Yep, it's like a mate.
R: Not like a yalpurru though?
A: No.

He rejects the notion that those who enter prison together are yalpurru, the name given for those who enter ceremonial initiation together. Prison, despite some of its similarities with the Law, does not suggest such a close and significant sharing of experience. However, he does suggest that prison can help expand and develop one's social networks when one moves away from prison. As he travels through the Kimberley, which he does on regular occasions, the social networks he developed in prison prove very beneficial.

The influence of older men over younger men's behaviour, as described earlier, can also explain how some men enter prison and not others. There are some families where none of the male members of the family have ever been in prison or in a police lock-up. They are relatively few. There are other families where only some have been to prison, and there are some families where younger brothers appear consistently to have followed older brothers into prison. One man, now in his early thirties, has spent several years in prison. During that time he had extensive experience watching fellow desert men move in and out of different Western Australian prisons. He believed that some were influenced by the behaviour of older brothers; they wanted to follow in their footsteps. Young men know that many of their fathers, uncles, older brothers and relatives have spent time in prison. Some were famous and highly respected Law men arrested in old and new Balgo. Young men have heard stories about prison, they have regularly spoken on the phone to men in prison or visited them when they happened to be in Broome. Generally — and there are exceptions — men are not greatly fearful or intimidated by the possibility of going to prison. As in the example of petrol sniffing, they know that those who are older, and who have had shared this experience, have returned safely to their families.

The presence of older male company within the prison can also be important. Young prisoners look to older prisoners to watch over and look after them, especially if they are transferred to a southern Western Australian prison, where there will be less likelihood of having close relations among other prisoners. Older prisoners can use their influence to protect and care for younger prisoners, or they can use it to hurt or harm them. One man, a father of adult sons, described how he had spent some months in prison shortly after his youngest son had been released. He found it a distressing experience being separated from his wife and family. But he also noted, with some feeling, that some of the older prisoners teased younger prisoners. It made them look 'cheeky', he said, a relationship that older men should not take with younger men.[11] Hence, while older men can reinforce a natural and supporting hierarchy among Aboriginal prisoners, some can also use that power against the welfare of those who are younger.

The benefits that men identify within the prison experience — benefits of nurturance in particular — do not apply to all men, at all times or ages. While some men cope well with prison, others cope less well; some find prison relaxing, others find it 'worrying'. While younger men appear to find prison less problematic than older men, a critical factor appears to be the relationship a prisoner enjoys with a wife, girlfriend or family outside the prison at that time. It is the nature of this relationship that can significantly determine whether prison will be a stressful or painful experience or, as some have described it, a pleasant 'holiday camp'. While prison provides sport, videos and other forms of entertainment, it can also be a place of great loneliness and anxiety. It serves to remind men, especially at night when there are fewer activities to distract them, of the cost of separation from those closest to them. Some men become particularly vulnerable when they hear rumours and stories about their wives or girlfriends.

One father described his feeling when his son returned from prison as 'mirritjanu'. His son had come home, 'from the dead'.[12] He and his family were happy in having their son back home but his use of the word 'mirri' indicated the extreme dangers he perceived his son could face when in prison. Puntu are aware that in prison, as in the Law, Aboriginal men have died. No one is safe from sorcery, especially if an offence has been committed and older men, family and maparn are not present to protect them. However small the actual risk of death, separation from walytja places young men at a perceived risk. It is a risk that becomes more evident as Puntu become older, and they experience the powers of sorcery and its ability to be used against prisoners as a means of payback. While no one from this region has officially died in prison or police custody, they have witnessed and know others who have. Those who sit 'outside', whether the Law or prison, can feel worried and powerless over those who are young and held within the possible dangers of such confinement.

Men can experience great stress in prison. I have been told stories of Aboriginal men who self-mutilated or hanged themselves. Some men can feel particularly vulnerable at 'sorry time' when they cannot attend the ceremonies for another's death. One man felt so strongly when his father's brother died that he told the wardens he was going to commit suicide that night: 'I wanted to make them see how much it meant to me.' The deceased belonged to a family that lived a long away from his mother's family, and this young man had only come to know them as he got older. His own father had died when he was young and this 'father', the one who died, had provided a 'father' experience he had missed when growing up.[13] His expression of sorrow, and his threat to commit suicide in prison, was made public for the prison officers to hear and for his walytja as well. The ceremonies around sorry business are main occasions, apart from the Law, when Puntu strongly and publicly celebrate the enduring importance and centrality of relationships within walytja. When a prisoner is not able to express his relationship and sorrow to the family of the deceased he can seek other, more risky ways, to publicly demonstrate the depth and significance of his feelings.[14]

As men get older and enter into marital relationships and have children, prison can reinforce the pain of separation from wives and family. While single, a young man might approach prison in the light of its benefits, such as paying off a fine, but the situation can suddenly reverse when he has a partner. When asked how he would feel if he was sent to prison for not paying a fine, the young man,

previously mentioned for this threatened suicide attempt, and now
in a relationship with a woman, said:

A: So I would have to think about it, I would have to think
   about her as well.
R: And if you didn't have a wife?
A: I'd have no problem with it.

He knows from experience that he can cope with prison. However, once he enters a relationship that might be severely affected
by imprisonment he begins to worry. At another time he recounted
the story of another man, not from the desert, who ended up
committing suicide in prison prior to his release:

A: Like I know somebody who did it while I was in there, over
   woman thing.
R: You heard stories about it or…?
A: *He* heard stories about it.
R: That woman?
A: The woman was outside and trying to have a baby and that
   fella was in there for two years and he knew he couldn't
   come out because that woman had a kid for him already.
   And he went in for something they did, maybe domestic
   violence, and so he goes in two years and…ready to come
   out, two more weeks to come out and he…he just did it,
   next morning.
R: He didn't talk about it?
A: Nah, that night he was all right; played basketball with us,
   just like any other night.
R: So what do you think caused it?
A: Fear of getting out.
R: Fear of getting out?
A: Yeah, fear of getting out and seeing it.

This prisoner had heard rumours about his wife and that she
was pregnant. He was afraid to come out of prison and see her with
another man's baby. He did not want to leave the prison. While
this example and behaviour may appear extreme, the physical and
extensive geographical separation of men from their families can
cause great anxiety. Work, training courses, sport and recreation
provide distraction and help men not to think too much about their

families. However they can, as they say, 'worry too much'.[15] When men have strong connections with their families, female partners or children the prospect of prison can prove a strong disincentive. Once they are incarcerated they are known to worry about their family, feel jealous about their partners and miss their children.

Men can also use prison as a way of hurting their wives or girlfriends. One man, around 32 years of age, has a wife but no children. He has been imprisoned on a number of occasions. I asked him how he felt about the possibility of returning to prison, as he had previously mentioned that there were some benefits in being incarcerated:

> R: So you don't mind going back again?
> A: (click)[16]
> R: Would six months be all right…or twelve months?
> A: Anything…long as it's a holiday camp.
> R: What about five years?
> A: Anything.
> R: Wouldn't miss family?
> A: I don't care.
> R: You wouldn't care too much?
> A: Cause I got no kid for my own, see.

This man is growing up two young children who belong to his wife's extended walytja, but he does not feel for them in the same way if they were his own children. His apparent indifference to imprisonment appeared to cover up his frustration that he could not have his own children. He is able to use prison as a means of punishing his wife. He went on to say:

> A: Yeah, but if I get one more hard time from my missus, that's it.
> R: You'll go and cause trouble?
> A: Yep.
> R: You'll get locked up?
> A: Yep.
> R: And that's okay?
> A: That's okay.
> R: Cause you want to get away or what?
> A: Yes, stay away.

In this context he is able to use a forced separation as a means of coping with his own frustrations, but also as a way to direct anger at his wife. It is even possible that his wife will be blamed for causing him to be imprisoned. A few days after hearing this man talk about prison, I listened to a woman of similar age in another community tell me that a man can 'do something silly and then [he] goes off to prison'. This, she argued, was the result of the wife 'locking up their husband'. Her argument was that some women 'get jealous' and 'tell the men what to do'. This leads to frustration by the men and the need to find a way to get away from their wives. Clearly, she presented a very different perspective as to the causes that might lead men to end up in prison. While he stressed prison as an option he could choose in order to get away from his wife, she believed that sometimes wives pressure their husbands into taking such options. Both views stressed men's agency. Each person saw that there were times when men could use the option of prison as a way of dealing with a tension within their married relationships. A little more than a fortnight later, after the interview just mentioned, the man appeared in court in Halls Creek and was imprisoned for some months. It is quite likely that, after our discussion and in the time prior to court, he was examining his limited options in relation to imprisonment.

Men have learned that, in the context of imprisonment, and within their specific and restricted legal resources, they can exercise some options. The paradox, as with petrol sniffing and football, is that such choices can incur both healthy and unhealthy outcomes. Prison offers men some benefits as it separates them from walytja. The benefits of nurturance: food, bed, male company, sport, learning and entertainment are clearly appreciated. Men can leave prison physically and mentally healthier. They are provided with regular meals, rest and exercise. For some, the break from alcohol can also prove beneficial, although many smoke heavily in prison, depending on their finances. On the other hand, the distress that prison can cause, to men and families, further marginalises men as it reinforces their alienation from their communities, wives and their children. They are absent for important ceremonies and are not involved in key celebrations, events or decisions. Prison separates men from their responsibilities within family and communities.

In some cases men move within a predictable cycle of prison-release-arrest-prison. One man, who has spent several years in prison and observed a number of incarcerated desert men, commented: 'Some of them come out, see nothing there so they go Halls Creek, do something silly there, like get back to jail'. There are occasions when a man does break out of this cycle. I have mentioned the time when a young man heard the wardens make a bet about his return. That he was able to use the experience to motivate himself not to return to prison arose, at least in part, from what the wardens communicated to him. Like the old men in the Law they provided him with a challenge. His response did not guarantee that he would never return to prison, but he believed that he had some autonomy and power over the situation. Some young men rarely experience the potency of such autonomy. They may not have the confidence, as this young man did, to speak English and talk up. They may not have relationships with families, wives or children that cause them to experience the painful cost of separation when in prison. They may define their prison experience in the light of the recognition they see is given to others when they come out of prison. They may not have older men in their lives to offer them the possibility of an alternative to prison, when they are ready and looking for it.

For some, prison offers aspects of the holding experience that was promised them when they were first initiated. The provision of various forms of nurturance, the supporting company of men who are walytja, and the authority of older men provide a context that enables men to know that prison is not the same, shaming, fearful place that it can be for many others. Men can feel protected by older men as they experience the care of older staff. That men experience being held within the prison system discloses possibilities for personal transformation. Prison can challenge, test and encourage. In particular, prison reminds men of the supporting relationships of walytja, wives and children. It can provoke men to leave prison, and consider their role in establishing a family and beginning to hold others. In these experiences men will work hard to avoid incarceration.

Nonetheless, prison can also provide a 'space' where desert men experience some of the holding qualities that are important for them. This space contains an element of 'voluntarism' (Ogilvie & Van Zyl 2001, p. 6). However, the context of such choice arises out of a specific marginalised experience for all desert men who interact with the criminal justice system. As most men in prison (and juvenile detention) can name the precise date of their release, they can also name the order and date of release for each of their fellow 'countrymen'. Daily, and as they wait to be released, they remind themselves, and others, of the cost of separation from those closest in relationship to them.

Prison, football and petrol sniffing affect the lives of all families who live in this desert region. Worry for those in prison, concern over arguments arising from football and anxiety over those who sniff are commonly and publicly expressed Puntu emotions. These emotions indicate the strong bonds that continue to exist within desert society, but they are also expressions of concern by older people for the future and welfare of their young. The suicides by three young men from the Kutjungka region within an eighteen-month period — accompanied by a number of attempted suicides — have only heightened their concerns.

It may seem that the social forces and interactions that lead to petrol sniffing and prison lie outside the influence of older desert people. However, this is not totally true. The relationship young men have with their parents and older relations, older men with partners, or younger men with older brothers or friends, all these can and do influence the context in which young men make choices.

Many of the parents of the young men today, especially those who live at Wirrimanu, grew up in the dormitory system. They did not experience the full potential of being held by their parents and grandparents, especially when critical rites of passage urged significant changes to membership and behaviour within the wider Puntu body. Despite this, and despite the many other changes that have impacted on their lives in the past decades, Puntu continue to place high priority over the ways in which the young are to be socialised and marnti are to become wati. Not only do older men hold younger at their time of initiation, but younger men continue to seek old and new ways of experiencing kanyirninpa until such time that they are able and confident to hold those younger than themselves.

The paradox of petrol sniffing, football and prison is that each of them provides risks to men's health while also contributing to their physical, emotional and social well-being. Petrol sniffing invites brain damage, among other health dangers, damage that may be serious and irreversible. Its social context encourages criminal behaviour, violence and disruption to families and communities. Football can attract men away from their other responsibilities to family, work, land and their communities. Prison separates men from their families, disrupts important relationships and increases the risk of self-harm.

At the same time petrol sniffing provides a transitional space for very young men. They explore a range of experiential and behavioural activities with the support of peers. This can provide them with greater confidence to face the Law and the responsibilities of becoming adult men. Football provides male company with exercise, where skill and competition are prized. It enables young men to travel and meet others. It offers sporting behaviour that is publicly endorsed by members of one's walytja, as it enables men to engage the world of kartiyas. Prison can be a place of nurturance, where men can make new friends, extend their family network, learn new skills and can have a break away from pressures and conflicts within relationships and communities.

As men move within the paradoxes of health that lie within each of these male activities, the often hidden element of kanyirninpa is disclosed. Petrol sniffing does not hold these young men; in fact petrol sniffers suspend the possibility of such for much of their sniffing experience. If they are offered a holding experience away from petrol, young men have been known to put sniffing aside for that opportunity. Petrol is generally a short-term journey and largely cannot compete against the promise of being held by other men. Football offers a longer type of journey where older men coach and which reflects some of the patterns of holding relationships. Prison offers occasional, sometimes repeated, journeys. Men may use it as a way of bridging adolescence into adulthood. Some may use it as a weapon to hurt those closest to them. However, within prison, men may also experience key aspects of the holding experience where nurturance with authority is provided and older men take responsibility for them. So while petrol sniffing, football and prison pose certain dangers for men, they also disclose some of the deeper and more lasting values that continue to sustain desert men and their search for health.

In the following chapter I want to link the key themes of the past chapters to that of the Puntu male and social yarnangu (body). This body has experienced petrol sniffing, football and prison within a history of colonial and mission experience, and the problematic dynamics of sustaining kanyirninpa. It has become a traumatised and wounded body, exhibiting many similarities to a much larger Indigenous male and social body, within Australia and elsewhere.

8

The Wounded Male Body

You can't do much with the adults, you just have
to concentrate on the children.

(Berndt C & R 1972, p. 132)

In the previous chapters I have explored the results of an ethnographic study of men's health where a group of desert men (and women) have provided a narrative and distinctive focus on the social construction of men's lives, health and well-being. In particular, I have described an understanding of kanyirninpa that provides a lens to view Aboriginal men's health, an insight into personal and social well-being that has been influenced by colonial and mission history. I have also explored some of the ways (and risks) in which kanyirninpa continues to be experienced and explored by young men in contemporary desert life.

In this chapter I want to draw together the key themes of the preceding chapters linking them with wider discourses around Indigenous health, both within Australia and beyond. Hence, I will return to some of the key issues around desert understandings of palya and wellness and their consequences for male kanyirninpa, embodiment and health. I will explore different constructions of the male Puntu body: embodiment (the pleated body), the dormitory and prison system (the separated body), trauma (the traumatised body) and experiences of trauma (the intergenerational and intragenerational body). This will lead to the conclusion of this book (the wounded and resilient body).

When a desert person approaches a maparn and requests their help as in 'palyalarni', 'make me well', they are not simply asking to be treated for bodily pain or suffering. If they were seeking pain relief the maparn would direct them to the local clinic to obtain Panadol. Seeking the experience of palya, as a culturally embodied way of being healthy, describes the desire for personal well-being within a social and cosmic context. As I discussed in Chapter 3, a desert person is healthy or palya when their body (yarnangu) is in a right relationship with their inner spirit (kurrun) and with others (walytja). The cosmic meanings of the tjukurrpa (dreaming), expressed within and upon ngurra (land), sustain and valorise that experience. Being 'cold' and 'dry' provides significant body indicators that disclose the balance or discrepancy of relation between the physical body, an inner spiritual reality and an outer, social (and spiritual) world. This sensitivity to the ecology of the body reveals deeper and often hidden relationships between the inner and outer person, between persons, and between persons and cosmic realities. The palya of the Western Desert shows similarities with the miyupimaatisiiun of the Cree of northern Canada, where being 'healthy' 'is less deter-mined by bodily functions than by the practices of daily living and by the balance of human relationships' (Adelson 2000, p. 15).

When Probyn used Deleuze's image of the pleat as a way of resolving epistemologies that separate the 'inner' from the 'outer' body, she was also proposing a more dynamic relationship between the body and self (1991, p. 119). This understanding of 'pleating', as developed earlier, described the inner and outer male body as doubled up and refolded. In this desert context, I have applied it to an understanding of palya, which one desert man described as 'inside, outside, everywhere'. For Puntu, living healthy and palya expresses 'the body and self [that] are intricately folded within each other' (Teather 1999, p. 9). The desert yarnangu can be understood as embodied and gendered, living palya within a network and intertwining of social and cosmic relationships.

As I mentioned in the Introduction to this book, my engagement with the desert male body has been based on many and various encounters with Aboriginal men, including times of ceremony, sorry business, hunting, football, prison and petrol sniffing. I have engaged the desert body as another male body, coming from a very different culturally embodied experience. I first met a 'separated' body of young men in 1973, and older groups of 'ceremonial' bodies, 'sporting bodies', 'imprisoned' bodies, 'wounded' and 'resilient' bodies in the 1990s and 2000s. These were men that offered friendship and relationship, but they were also (em)bodies of sickness, suffering and death. Hence, in seeking to entertain this male body as 'pleated', 'separated', 'sporting', 'imprisoned' or 'traumatised', I am aware I am describing a body, different from my own, that various forces of power, masculinity and race have attempted to define, shape and reconstruct over recent decades.

When in 2001 Central Desert Aboriginal women identified the 'four key principles underpinning all matters regarding the "growing up" of their children', they were describing the health of their children where 'growing up' involved 'holding everything, keeping everything together': walytja (family), ngurra (land) and tjukurrpa (dreaming) (Warrki Jarrinjaku 2002, p. 15). I have suggested a broader and more dynamic understanding of their use of the fourth principle, holding (kanyini). I have proposed that kanyirninpa achieves more than keeping the other 'key principles' together; it actually locates and enacts the unity of walytja, ngurra and tjukurrpa for people's health (see Kanyirninpa model, p. 21). When older people take the younger into ceremonies, the confluence of relationships that people share are reinforced and further increased through the disclosure of cosmic meanings upon and within the land. These important meanings are inscribed on and through the physical Puntu body. The holding that is enacted provides a social and ideological referent for Puntu life, as it celebrates and establishes a Puntu embodiment of being palya that is physical, spiritual and social.

As a result of this primary and gendered holding experience the health (and ill health) of Puntu men needs to be understood from within a particular cultural perspective. This is not to deny the gendered experience of health that applies to Puntu women arising from their holding experiences, but it is to distinguish aspects of the

Puntu male experience of health that differ from those of kartiya men. This can prove both challenging and problematic within contemporary health discourses, where much of the literature around gender issues and health have been focused on the female gendered body, challenging the hegemonic position of unreflected male dominance such that, 'for medical sociologists, gender has meant women — first, patients and nurses, and then doctors' (Lorber 1997, p. ix).[1] This hegemonic position has been understood to apply specifically to 'white, middle-class men's bodies', that is non-Aboriginal male bodies (1997, p. 2). Rarely, has research allowed for the particular and distinctive ways in which male bodies are socially constructed in non-Western cultures, as in Aboriginal societies. These ways offer their own critical perspectives on the construction of gendered (and kartiya) bodies, and the relation of those constructions to contemporary health issues and discourses.

The caveat that I am applying to the following descriptions of the male Puntu body is twofold. I do not wish to apply to Aboriginal men similar assumptions or descriptions about the construction of masculinities that apply to men of Western societies. This is not to deny serious issues that exist within both masculine communities where violence, abuse and various forms of domination over women occur (Robertson 1999; Gordon et al, 2002). However, it is to emphasise that one cannot assume that underlying explanations, or apparent similarities, reflect similar hegemonic masculinities. Secondly, there is a danger in applying a feminist critique that does not allow for the particular relationships that exist, and have developed, between men and women in Aboriginal societies (Mohanty 1995, p. 295). Again, this is not to deny that Aboriginal women have expressed serious concerns about domestic violence and other forms of abuse in their communities. However, it is to acknowledge that their perspective is critical if forms of structural oppression are accurately to be identified (1995, p. 262).[2] These twin cautions do not imply that I am suggesting a return to an ancient, pre-colonial construct of masculinity within desert communities; nor do they deny contemporary and important social and justice issues around expressions of masculinity. It is to emphasise that, as a kartiya male, I need to attend carefully to the ways in which Puntu men and women reveal to me the various constructions of their male social body, and how those constructions align with their understandings and values of what it means to be healthy and palya.

One way to look at the construction of the male Puntu body over recent decades is to examine the transmission of kanyirninpa over past generations and the context and consequences of that transmission. I have already mentioned that the *Bringing Them Home* report gave relatively little attention to the children who had grown up in missions such as Balgo. Its attention was primarily on those children who were removed and taken away for the purposes of assimilation. However, in several important ways the experiences of those who lived in the Balgo dormitories, and many who attended other mission or settlement dormitories, were different from the majority described in the report. At Balgo Mission the parents and families of the children were always visible, despite the presence of social and symbolic 'fences'. Hence, the boys, for example, were segregated from their parents, grandparents, sisters and younger siblings but there were always the possibilities of some contact and communication. Also, unlike many others who were taken away, the children at Balgo Mission were returned to the care of their parents when the dormitories closed in April 1973. However, this particular method of separation and socialising produced its own train of consequences. While children could see their families and have some contact with them, many have grown up with a sense of loss. They now believe that their parents were unable to pass onto them important elements of their culture. This loss was premised on the kartiya belief and practice that kartiya child-rearing practices were superior.[3]

The belief in the superiority of kartiya child-rearing practices was not just confined to Australia. In Canada, Aboriginal children were separated at similar rates as they were in Australia, and between 1920–60 Aboriginal children were being removed from their parents at a rate 20 times that of non-Aboriginal children (Armitage 1995, p. 205). The Canadian residential schools, where children were physically and socially separated from their families for the purposes of education, have been criticised in recent years for the 'psychological and social havoc they created' (Morrison & Wilson 1986).

Christine Choo recorded the experiences of women who grew up at Beagle Bay and Drysdale River (later Kalumburu) missions. She noted:

> One of the most significant effects of dormitory life on the mission girls was the loss of contact with the older members of their families and the community. Generations of Aboriginal women who lived on Beagle Bay Mission have spoken about their deep sense of loss, and their attempts as children to maintain contact with the older people in order to obtain information about the old ways. (Choo 2001, p. 164)

Virginia Huffer has described the dormitory system on Morningon Island through the experiences of Elsie Roughsey where 'the adults who were products of the dormitory system had two disparate types of parental models' (Huffer 1980, p. 55). They spent the early years of their life with their parents and were then taken into a dormitory system that imposed different, sometimes opposing, values from those they had previously experienced.

Rarely did kartiyas protest at this enforced separation or note the likely consequences for Puntu social and emotional health (Berndt C 1962, p. 83). In 1957, William Grayden and other members of a Western Australian Parliamentary Select Committee visited Mt Margaret, Cosmo Newbery and Warburton missions.[4] Their views were clear:

> On this question [of separation of Aboriginal children from their parents] it should be pointed out that it is the considered view of all authorities that the bond of affection between a native woman and child is at least as great as between a white woman and her child. Indeed certain factors militate to make the bond, if anything stronger. (Grayden 1957, p. 32)[5]

They raised ethical issues of consent and duress, explaining that separated children 'would be perplexed to the extreme and would be without a single stabilising influence on which to orient themselves to the new way of life' (1957, p. 32).

Anna Haebich has pointed out that Grayden quoted sections of the United Nations Declaration of Human Rights 1947 when he addressed the Western Australian Parliament in 1956 (Haebich 2000). She noted that John Bowlby's seminal work on the ill-effects of 'maternal deprivation' had only been published by the World Health Organisation a few years before Grayden's address (Bowlby 1952). Parliamentarians and government officials would have had some familiarity with Bowlby's research that was introduced by the following reflection:

> Among the most significant developments in psychiatry during the past quarter of a century has been the steady growth of evidence that the quality of the parental care which a child receives in his [sic] earliest years is of vital importance for his [sic] future mental health. (Bowlby 1952, p. 11)

While Bowlby's research was based on children who were institutionalised in Britain, it is not surprising that in Australia there was 'a curious resistance to accepting' his theory (1952, p. 46). The separation of Aboriginal children from their families, and the reconstruction of their lives according to kartiya values, was based on racialised and rationalised child-rearing beliefs and practices common to Western countries like Australia, Canada and America at that time.

Apart from the form and manner of institutionalised separation of children from their families, the dormitory system assumed a number of kartiya child-rearing and parenting values. The differences between Aboriginal and non-Aboriginal models of child rearing, and the social values that underpin them, have been recently detailed in comparative work performed by Walytja Tjutangku Palyapayi Aboriginal Association in Central Australia. Walytja has listed and contrasted important and current differences between Aboriginal and non-Aboriginal child-rearing practices in *Pipirri Wiimaku ('for the little kids')* (Walytja 2001, p. 8).[6] These practices express key, foundational differences between two cultures where each one attempts to socialise its own children from birth. Hence, examples of feeding, crying, listening, disciplining and teaching reveal specific and important cultural values around relationship, nurturance and authority.

When we examine the dormitory experience through the perspective of kanyirninpa it is clear that the separation of children from their parents provided an alternative and different experience of being held. Children, often as young as five, lived in dormitories with large numbers of others of the same gender, a much larger and more foreign social group than they experienced previously. And, within the Catholic church, as at Balgo Mission, they were usually looked after by an older person of the same gender who was a kartiya and usually not married (that is, celibate). They learned new skills, numeracy and literacy. They came to understand more of the kartiya world and its values. However, they found themselves radically cut off from their parents, and a world of meaning that the desert and cultural enactment of holding supported. When Judith Herman, psychiatrist and clinical researcher, described experiences that, 'destroy the victim's fundamental assumptions about the safety of the world, the positive value of the self, and the meaningful order of creation' she could have been describing some of the consequences of separation and the dormitory system (Herman 1992, p. 33). She was, in fact, describing trauma.

Early in this book I raised the concept of trauma as an early motivating construct for the work I did with the men in the Kutjungka region. I described how some Aboriginal leaders, researchers and others in the past decade have used trauma to interpret a wide range of present and past Aboriginal experience. However, as I mentioned then, I intentionally put theories of trauma aside, preferring to hear how desert men understood what it meant to live healthy, palya and well. I have traced the desert understanding of kanyirninpa into contemporary settings of male praxis. From petrol sniffing to alcohol, from football to prison, I have explored a number of ways in which men currently experience, shape and construct their lives. I now return to the construct of trauma to explore its applicability to what I have learned and, in particular, its relation to this key desert value of kanyirninpa.

The male praxis of kanyirninpa provided key and foundational values for men that embodied adult male identity. A young man experienced security and safety when held in the company of older men. Their knowledge and authority protected him against the danger of cosmic forces that were released particularly during times of ceremony, but were present at other times. As a young man he felt pride in becoming a wati (initiated man) and being able to sit among the assembled group of other wati. His new status afforded him the esteem and respect of his family and others. The Law, ceremonies and the company of men provided him with security in his new adult and social world. He was able to travel as a wati and explore new experiences of autonomy and discover new relationships. Kanyirninpa offered him structure and meaning within a social world that linked him with a physical landscape and earlier generations of men. When these generations of men were separated, young and older men faced the 'betrayal of important relationships' (1992, p. 55).[7] As kartiyas attempted to exercise power and control over such relationships, some older Puntu men found it difficult to perform their roles in relation to younger men, and according to the moral imperatives of the tjukurrpa. Others, younger men, found they were not receiving from older men what had been promised. These, I will suggest, can be named as particular forms and expressions of trauma that were transcribed upon and within the male Puntu body.

Theorists are not in general agreement about the definitions of and differences between stress, trauma and post traumatic stress disorder (PTSD) (Shalev 1986, p. 77). Stress can be understood as either challenging or threatening (hence healthy or dangerous), and PTSD can be explained as a normal or abnormal response to an extraordinary event. What is problematic within such discourses is that within the wide range of extraordinary human suffering, ranging from wars to local disasters, psychopathology as a response, even in the most extreme situations, cannot be predicted. Most people recover from such events and live normal and healthy lives. Some theorists have argued that people respond to extraordinary stressful events in adaptive and normal ways, whereas others argue that responses are maladaptive and not normal. PTSD can then be understood as a normal response that does not resolve the trauma, or as an abnormal response with its own associated symptomatology. In this chapter, while acknowledging that much has been researched about stress and PTSD, I will focus specifically on the concept of trauma and its applicability to Aboriginal experience and within the context of kanyirninpa. I accept Herman's description of traumatic events as those that 'overwhelm the ordinary systems of care that give people a sense of control, connection and meaning' (Herman 1992, p. 33). I also accept that trauma can be understood as affecting a group, as well as an individual, and that there may be trauma at a social level where a group may attempt to respond through custom and particular rituals (de Vries 1996, p. 398). Within cultures, people have developed different ways to protect themselves against extreme suffering and loss, and they have done so by the particular use of social and medical practices. I will explore some of these in the concluding chapter.

There are a number of difficulties in simply applying the theoretical construct of trauma to Aboriginal experience and developing a nosology of Aboriginal trauma related illnesses. Not only are the possibilities of Aboriginal trauma various and wide, but they also can differ in degrees of severity, according to how people experienced them in remote, rural and urban settings. There can be differences according to age and gender, by different communities as well as by individuals. Any conflation can essentialise Aboriginal trauma, suggesting it is equivalent to social change and is manifested as a particular postcolonial or mission syndrome, such as 'battered wife', 'rape' or 'concentration camp' syndromes. Aboriginal experiences of trauma can be proposed as essentially different from non-Aboriginal experiences. As in the discourses around the trauma of refugees and asylum seekers, Aboriginal experience can become stereotyped, with an emphasis on the pathological and dysfunctional within individuals. Solutions can be proposed which reflect a particular Western biomedical approach to trauma, where a therapeutic model can ignore cultural perspectives critical to the meanings as well as the healings of traumatic experience.[8] It can also ignore the resilience factors that people bring from within their own personal and cultural resources. While an ancient understanding of trauma located its presence on the outer human body, there would appear to be a danger in more recent traumatology that critical aspects, linking the physical with the social, are ignored. Trauma can become reified, a psychic and disembodied, private experience.

Despite the dangers inherent in taking a trauma approach to Aboriginal experience, I will now return to the concept of trauma that motivated this research. I will propose two explanatory models of trauma that link the fracturing of social relationships with men's health. In so doing I am not suggesting a deterministic view of trauma, but one that helps explain how critical issues of experience have been inscribed on the male Aboriginal yarnangu. This can be, what Arthur Kleinman described, as trauma 'interwoven with moral-somatic processes that bring social memory into the body and that project the individuality of persons into social space' (Kleinman 1995, p. 188). Trauma, in this understanding, is located neither in mental processes nor manifested in physical ill-health, but in the key relationships that kanyirninpa discloses. The social relationships that bind walytja, ngurra and tjukurrpa have been wounded and the social Puntu body has embodied these fractures as particular forms of trauma. The two explanatory models of trauma I am about to describe are intergenerational trauma and intragenerational trauma. To understand them more fully in a broader context than the Western Desert, I will draw again on Aboriginal experiences of imprisonment and of suicide.

Within this book I have attempted to show that kanyirninpa is embodied and that it is constituted by physical as well as social meanings. Puntu express a detailed body praxis where their relationships within holding are demonstrated through the various ways of being cared for, fed and nurtured. The outward signs of physical care and attention reveal inner meanings of interpersonal connectedness and shared belief. Similarly, when there is lack of care and social relatedness, when kanyirninpa is experienced as absent, this can be articulated in pain or suffering within the social and embodied self. This pain or suffering can be described as a form of trauma that has been deeply inscribed upon the social body. An overwhelming force has been applied against 'the ordinary systems of care that provided people a sense of control, connection and meaning' (Herman 1992, p. 33).

In the following quotation from Pat Dodson a particular form of trauma is identified, intergenerational trauma. It can be identified at those moments within the social body when the transmission of male identity across generations is prevented or frustrated.[9] Here, Dodson is reflecting on the current status of young Aboriginal men:

> The senior men are important, they are the people who can bring you through the path onto the big road…If you don't go there then you're just milling around with another group of young fellas like yourself. You have got no idea how to get over there. You're on one side of the river…You have a sense in your being that there is something that you've got to go to, or you should be part of, or you should be more knowledgeable about…but you're not getting that and so you have this sense of being cut off.

The image of the river illustrates the gulf that can be experienced between generations of men, where both groups experience being 'cut off' from one another and where a holding relationship is not possible. The young do not know how to cross the river and join the company of senior men. The older men are cut off from those they are supposed to hold. While the senior men possess critically important knowledge, they are not able to pass it on to the younger men. It is critical knowledge because it promises to sustain and ensure the future of desert society, as it also promises to sustain and empower younger men. Trauma, as illustrated by this metaphor, does not describe the possible dangers of 'crossing the river' or the difficulty of 'finding a bridge' in order to cross. Trauma lies in the awareness and experience by younger and older men that what is critically important in their relationship and for the larger social body cannot be realised.

This particular form of trauma, intergenerational trauma, where the transmission of male identity across the generations is prevented or frustrated, has several origins. The dormitory system separated boys from a very early age from their fathers, uncles and grandfathers and, in some instances, missionaries used the same system to prevent the ceremonies that linked older and younger men (McCoy 2007c).

Often, the most painful and remembered aspect of the dormitory experience was being separated from family. A desert man, now more than fifty years old, remembers:

> I supposed to be learning from my father when I was ten…or nine…or eight…during the ceremonies they had in the camp with women folks and all. Well the man that do their dancing, well you'll see the one little fella behind…that was when women do their dancing…same time…well I missed out that one.

His example is instructive. He did not describe stories or songs that his father might have taught him. Instead, his example expressed an embodied form of learning that was dependent on him being in the company of his father. The dancing upon the land, the use of his body and the company of others, men and women, provided a context for discovering his identity. Desert men have been emphatic in their talking with me that what is important for them is the handing down of cultural knowledge from one generation of men to the next. While the content of this knowledge is obviously important, equally important, they have stressed, is the context by which this knowledge is obtained. Adult male identity develops within the ambit of male kanyirninpa, as in the example just mentioned, and as a man gets older by his participation in ceremonies (tjukurrpa) that move across the land (ngurra) and involve a multiplicity of ever-developing relationships and responsibilities (walytja). Men have spent much of their lives acquiring and embodying this knowledge. A young man grows into adulthood through the knowledge and praxis of other men, and as an embodied experience within the Law.

The provision of rations was also used to restrict men's hunting practices and put pressure on men to adopt a sedentary life or engage in wage labour. As men faced the separation of their children into dormitories they were pressured to work either at the mission or on pastoral stations away from their families (Berndt R & C 1970, p. 66). The control that kartiya men exercised over their lives included power over the movement and activity of family members, as well as men's social and religious activities. Some men resisted this control. The killing of sheep that began at Tjaluwan in 1939 continued and 20 years later the missionaries were still complaining that their sheep were being killed (McGuire 1959; Worms 1970, p. 371).

In the previous chapter I discussed imprisonment within the context of men's experiences in the Western Desert. Here, I seek to examine imprisonment as one of the more significant ways in which kartiya men have sought to control and dominate Aboriginal men. It has particularly served to separate younger men from their families and from the company of older men. Imprisonment can be described as a form of intergenerational trauma that has been effected upon the Aboriginal social body. Over many years it has served to separate and disrupt key social relationships within the Puntu male social body.

The over-representation of Aboriginal male juveniles and adults in prison represents the Aboriginal male body as a highly 'imprisoned' body. At 30 June 2001, Aboriginal youth in Australia, aged 10 to 17 years, were seventeen times over-represented in Australian detention facilities compared with non-Aboriginal youths (Cahill & Marshall 2002, p. 14).[10] Those who were 18 years and older were eleven times over-represented. The proportion of Aboriginal prisoners to others in prison has increased over past decades. In Western Australia, for example, the proportion of adult Aboriginal male prisoners increased from 9 per cent in 1949 to 37 per cent in 1981 (Lincoln & Wilson 2000, p. 28). The numbers of Aboriginal prisoners in all jurisdictions increased from 1809 in 1988 to 3750 in 1998, an increase of 6.9 per cent, 1.7 times that of the non-Aboriginal prisoner population (Carcach et al. 1999, p. 2). In 1998, 95 per cent of all Aboriginal prisoners in Australia were male (1999, p. 2). In his report to the Royal Commission into Aboriginal Deaths in Custody (RCIADIC), Dodson indicated that 15 per cent of Aboriginal males over the age of 16 in Western Australia were imprisoned during 1983–4 (1991, p. 295). That such a large number of Aboriginal men spent time in prison indicated not only the health status of this social body, but also the relation of that body to a largely non-imprisoned, kartiya and male body.

Beresford and Omaji have linked imprisonment with the forced removal, and subsequent institutionalisation, of children. They have argued that people were denied 'the models of parenting and family life essential to the later task of raising their own children', causing damaging effects 'upon their ability to construct and maintain family life' (Beresford & Omaji 1996, p. 35). Cunneen has described this as, 'the intergenerational transmission of social disadvantage', naming additional research that showed that those who had been taken away from their family as children were twice as likely to have been arrested in the previous five years (Cunneen 2001, p. 43). During 2002–03 when the Western Australian Department of Justice initiated the Kimberley Regional Justice Project (to find out what people in the Kimberley thought about the justice system), their emphasis focused on the 'troubles' of imprisonment, not the causes that generated such a high representation by Aboriginal men (Department of Justice 2003). Hence, there was emphasis on alcohol, fines, legal aid, court orders and so on. The historicity and masculinity factors involved in imprisonment were not explored.

The explanations that are offered around Aboriginal imprisonment rarely focus on relevant gender issues or implications, such as child separation, family parenting and generational authority. Nor do they explore the ways in which the attempted construction, and decon-struction, of Aboriginal masculinities by kartiyas have influenced such a high rate of male imprisonment. This is not to suggest a simple 'male role' explanation for imprisonment, but the need to identify key underlying issues that have led to such a high rate of male Aboriginal imprisonment (Ogilvie 1996).[11]

When Banjo, whose Aboriginal name is unknown, allegedly killed Joseph Condren and Timothy O'Sullivan in 1922 at old Billiluna station, the four separate police parties that set out to find him were as much concerned to apprehend the killer of kartiya men, as the guns he had taken with him. In the early twentieth century pastoralists did not trust their Aboriginal stockmen with guns for fear of what they might do with such knowledge and power (Willey 1971, p. 78; Reynolds 1987, p. 15; Buchanan 1997, p. 87). Kartiya men, especially those who travelled the more remote areas of the Kimberley in the early part of the twentieth century, often went armed. And, it must be said, the relationship that they developed with Aboriginal men was very different to the one they established with Aboriginal women (Willey 1971; McGrath 1987; Ross 1989). Often, they sought to establish their control and dominance over Aboriginal men by the use of coercion ('a belt over the ear'), withholding communication ('a white man was not expected to speak to a black at all') and the support of the police ('unless you happened to be an Aboriginal') (Willey 1971, pp. 52, 60, 78).

Imprisonment has served as an important attempt at social control by kartiya men over Aboriginal men. As discussed in the previous chapter, many desert men have used their prison experience to their advantage and according to the limited choices it has offered them. One of those 'limited choices' has been Puntu power over the attitudes and behaviour of police, who have been described as 'the most consistent point of Aboriginal contact with colonial power' (Johnston 1991, Volume 2, p. 10). Not only were police the instrument used by states and territories to achieve pacification in the early years of colonisation, but they have also consistently been used since then in various ways to subdue, protect and control Aboriginal behaviour (1991, p. 23).[12] In remote areas especially, and over past decades, police have often been able to act unchecked and unaccountable in their behaviour towards Aboriginal men, even at times distributing their own forms of summary punishment. The RCIADIC stated:

> The policeman was the right hand man of the authorities, the enforcer of the policies of control and supervision, often the taker of children, the rounder up of those accused of violating the rights of settlers. Much police work was done on the fringes of non-Aboriginal settlement where the traditions of violence and rough practices were strongest. (1991, Volume 1, p. 10)

Imprisonment has become not just a gendered institution, but a masculinised one where a culture of imprisonment has been based on the particular and historical subjection of Aboriginal men. Sim offers the distinction between 'men as prisoners' and 'prisoners as men', as a means of shifting the focus from the prison to the men within them (Sim 1994, p. 101). In this case, his distinction might be re-phrased 'prisoners as Aboriginal men' (Thurston 1996, p. 140). Nine out of ten prisoners in the Kimberley prison system are Aboriginal and 95 per cent are male (Carcach et al. 1999, p. 4; Department of Justice 2003, p. 1).

Imprisonment has not usually been described as a form of intergenerational trauma but it can be understood as a way in which the Puntu male social body has been subjected to intense surveillance and control, pressured to become subservient. Prison has removed many men from their families and communities and from their ceremonial and kinship responsibilities. It has subjected men to the control and domination of kartiya men. Connell has described the hierarchy of masculinities as 'a source of violence, since force is used in defining and maintaining the hierarchy' (Connell 2000, p. 217). Often this violence has been understood in the context of violence against gay men, or the ways in which young men are conditioned to participate in combat and violent sports. Hegemonic masculinities have imposed a particular form of social order on men through manifestations of social control. This can be seen in the context of imprisonment, where kartiya society has confronted and attempted to pacify Aboriginal men over many decades in a public and social context. As men have been separated from older men, particular forms of generational holding that involved the transmission of important cultural knowledge has been prevented, limited or frustrated. This has not happened to all men, nor in the same ways within different communities or families. However, trauma whose social genesis is historical, and which disrupts the social relationships between generations, can be named as a form of intergenerational trauma upon and within the Puntu male social body.

There is also intragenerational wounding and trauma. When discussing petrol sniffing I mentioned some of the comments that

Puntu have heard around those who sniff petrol such as, 'I might as well be on my own', 'my mother doesn't like me any more... my father doesn't like me any more'. These, and similar expressions by young Aboriginal men, have been disclosed by other research (Brady 1992; Martin 1993). They indicate a strong emphasis on individuation within Aboriginal society that also places value on interrelatedness. David Martin explored in great detail this 'rhetoric of personal distinctiveness and autonomy' among the Wik people of Cape York (Queensland) and quoted some of the statements he heard, as (in English), 'nobody boss for me', 'you can't tell me what to do' (Martin 1993, pp. 12, 17). Maggie Brady, in her work on petrol sniffing, quoted the sniffer who said, 'it's my own body, you can't stop me' (1992, p. 77). Gary Robinson heard among the Tiwi, 'Go on! Make me die then! My mother gone! My father gone! Make me die then! I got one guts to die' (1995, p. 327)!

These, and similar statements by young Aboriginal men, come highly emotionally charged. They are defiant and can threaten violence, but they also call attention to an experience of pain, understood within a cultural context. Pain in this understanding 'combines the physical, affective and cultural dimensions of human suffering in a seamless web of lived experience (Williams & Bendelow 1998, p. 168). While they support Myer's description of the 'reluctance to permit others to impose authority over oneself', they can also reveal the serious risks a person adopts in taking such a position (Myers 1986, p. 22). Do they indicate, as Martin suggested, 'a trend towards increasing individuation and the sundering of the control of the means of social reproduction' (Martin 1993, p. iv)? Are they, as Robinson, proposed, a 'sometimes despairing assertion(s) of autonomy' (Robinson 1995, p. 327)? Or, as Brady suggested with some chronic petrol sniffers, do they reveal 'a form of suicidal behaviour, perhaps the ultimate expression of control over the body' (Brady 1992, p. 77)? Perhaps all statements reveal an important truth: for some young Aboriginal men individuation can be accompanied by a socially perceived, and personally experienced, painful separation from others. In these cases of extreme isolation suicide becomes not the ultimate expression of control over one's body but the embodiment of social and painful disconnection from others. This experience, I suggest, can be described as intra-generational trauma.

Martin proposed that within Wik society there existed a dialectical tension between personal autonomy and social relatedness, a theory very similar to that of Myers and which I discussed in Chapter 1: Kanyirninpa and 'Holding' (see Kanyirninpa model, p. 21) (Martin 1993, p. 11). Martin added that balance in social life 'was always inherently unstable, oscillating between the poles of autonomy on the one hand and connectedness on the other' (1993, p. 38). He used Bourdieu's concept of the 'habitus' to describe forms of social practice that derive from deeper and underlying cognitive and motivating structures (1993, p. 18).

Clearly, an individual's right to autonomy is deeply embedded as a value within many and different Aboriginal groups. However, in the desert, when some young people uttered the statements I have just mentioned, they were interpreted by families as extreme statements, as 'cries for help'. Adults then worked, to use Martin's image, to draw people away from the extreme polarity of autonomy. They did this by invoking the nurture of holding. Not all parents acted in this way, nor did all parents appear as concerned to intervene as did others. However, it would seem that some adults perceived a clear danger with extreme forms of autonomous behaviour, and the accompanying emotions that the young people were displaying. While wanting to recognise the right of a young person to his autonomy, they were offering back to that person what they believed was a more basic value, 'a sense of control, connection and meaning' (Herman 1992, p. 33).

Both Robinson and Colin Tatz have used Emanuel Marx's distinction between coercive and appealing violence, to explain the cultural contexts in which violence can be understood among Aboriginal people (Robinson 1995; Tatz 2001).[13] Robinson suggested that for the Tiwi appealing violence 'has always been part of the pattern of conflict in traditional societies', while Tatz described appealing violence as one explanation of Aboriginal suicide, being 'an appeal for support and assistance' (Robinson 1995, p. 328; Tatz 2001, p. 122). Appealing violence offers a perspective on the social context and public acceptability of some forms of violence, as does self-wounding within the context of ritual sorry business. However, it would not seem to offer a sufficient explanation for those suicides where restraint from others is not possible, nor harmony with others achievable.

While suicide has been the leading cause of death for 15–19 year-old Australian males, it has also become a most serious issue for many Aboriginal communities. For the period 1999–2003, 'intentional self-harm' was the leading external cause of death for Indigenous males. The suicide rate was more than twice that for non-Indigenous males (ABS 2005, p. 159). Within the period 1986–2005 in Western Australia the rate of male suicides nearly doubled that of non-Indigenous males (39.6 vs. 20.2 per 100,000) (Miller et al., in press). The Indigenous group most at risk, and with the highest age-specific death rates, has been the 15–24 year age group, four times for all males within the same Australian age group (ABS 2001b, p. 75). When Hunter examined suicide in the Kimberley in the 1980s, he became aware of the increasing deaths of young Aboriginal men due to external causes. These 'external causes' included motor vehicle accidents, other accidents, homicide and suicide (Hunter 1988, p. 266; 1995, p. 194). He identified three key factors in these suicides: alcohol, precipitating events and warnings and linkages between the suicides (1988, p. 266). In eight out of the twelve males whose suicides he investigated, 'a significant loss or threatened disruption of important interpersonal attachment has preceded the suicide' (1988, p. 268).

In 1999 the results of research into suicide in Indigenous communities in North Queensland were published (Hunter et al. 1999). Their study focused on three communities that had experienced a large number of suicides in the 1990s. From their data the researchers constructed a 'typical' case for the Far North Queensland region:

> It is a young Aboriginal male who has had a relative who has recently died from suicide. He is unemployed, or if employed, works part time on a CDEP project mainly involving manual labour. He has a history of heavy binge drinking and is

intoxicated at the time of his death. He has either threatened or attempted to harm himself in the past. In the days or hours before the suicide some sort of interpersonal conflict occurred, either with members of his family or with his partner, either of apparent significance or what, to an outsider, might seem trifling. The hanging, using material at hand such as rope or an electrical cord, takes place either in or close to his home, in a place visible to members of his family and possibly also to passers-by. (1999, p. 70)

This research linked the vulnerability of young adult Aboriginal men to behavioural characteristics and developmental experiences. Heavy use of alcohol was associated with the former but, in addition, young men were 'within the first generation across large sections of Aboriginal Australia to have grown to maturity since the convulsive social changes of the 1970s' (1999, p. 76). As I have indicated elsewhere in this book, the 'convulsive social changes', while significant in the 1970s, were catalysed by significant social changes effected in prior decades.

Suicide has also been a concern for Native American communities who also have experienced a generally higher rate of suicide than non-Native populations, but with considerable regional and tribal differences (Young 1994, p. 189). Kirmayer et al. have quoted age-standardised rates of suicide for aboriginal youth in Canada being 3–6 times that of the general population (Kirmayer et al. 2003, p. 16). Recent analysis of world trends of suicide has shown the unequal distribution of youth suicide rates across nations, but an increase of such rates in Western countries (Kelleher & Chambers 2003, p. 172). Male rates have generally been higher than female but they also have varied considerably throughout the world (2003, p. 172). In Australia the suicide rate for males aged 15–24 has more than trebled since the 1950s (Eckersley 1993, p. S17). Kelleher and Chambers quote from Eckersley, to try to explain the rise in youth suicide in 'developed' countries where, he suggested, the movement towards postmodernism,

> fails to meet the most fundamental requirements of any culture: to provide a sense of belonging and purpose, and so a sense of

meaning and self-worth, and a moral framework to guide our conduct. (cited in Kelleher & Chambers 2003, p. 174)

They point out that the consistent rise in youth suicide in Western countries 'has coincided with a period of social deregulation, whereby the traditional social institutions such as the church, the state, and the family have become less influential' (2003, p. 174). Colin Pritchard's review of interdisciplinary research around the prevention of suicide names seven positive and encouraging messages, the sixth being: 'the importance and centrality of relationships to sufferers: with their immediate family and community, and with the professional' (Pritchard 1995, p. 174).

Despite their variability across gender, cultures and nationalities, research studies on suicide have stressed the significance of the relationships that individuals share with others in their societies. It is the quality and strength of these relationships that helps to explain the possible effects on individuals when social structures cease to support a person's sense of meaning and value. Without discounting the importance of individual factors within suicide these studies, such as Durkheim's 'egoistic' suicide, have suggested that suicide behaviour can reflect the effect of change to the values, structures and relationships that have provided cohesion and meaning within a particular society (1995, p. 24).[14]

Robinson has looked at the phenomenon of male suicide within contemporary Tiwi life. He has interpreted such actions within a psychodynamic framework where the violence expressed in mourning becomes self-redirected, as the individual becomes frustrated in his efforts to achieve differentiation as a man. There are no longer the social structures that traditionally supported a young man through to adulthood (Robinson, 1990).

Change to Tiwi culture, as with other Aboriginal groups, has affected the performance of traditional rituals by which boys were offered a passage to 'die' and then rise as 'men'. An increase in male premature deaths has resulted in a number of young men in many communities growing up without the presence of fathers, and other significant older males. Without discounting the 'complex relationships' that must be taken into account when interpreting suicide, or that such an act might be 'a desperate attempt at communication', I would argue that the examples Robinson offers reveal something further. Older men are needed if younger men are to experience belonging and relatedness (1990, p. 176). The self-differentiation a young man seeks in becoming an adult is assisted by, and within the company of, older men. However, there are some young men today who cannot access that relationship of male kanyirninpa and, to adapt Martin's image, find themselves at the very precipice of autonomy, far removed from the support of family and the protection and care of relatedness.

This is not to argue that a lack of holding leads to suicide. To suggest this would be to reify holding, and not allow for the different ways in which young men respond to holding experiences and the suicides of others. There are too many differences within and between families to suggest such a simple, causal link. However, when a young person experiences they are not being held — either as the result of highly autonomous behaviour or they discover there is no one to hold them — they can experience great vulnerability, especially when their separation is exacerbated by the threat or the actual loss of a close personal relationship. The oscillating between autonomy and relatedness can lead, especially without the support of the interpersonal structure, care and authority that holding provides, to a personal awareness of extreme isolation from others. Petrol, marijuana and alcohol can heighten and accentuate that awareness. Hunter has described this so eloquently: 'like the bottle, the alcohol-exalted self is acutely fragile, and unstable. Its shattered shards are painful and perilous and cut deep' (Hunter 1990, p. 276). Petrol sniffers can feel further marginalised by their stigmatisation within the social body. Suicide and suicide ideation expose this painful, sometimes angry and violent, intragenerational trauma that lies deeply inscribed within and upon the Puntu social and male body (McCoy 2007b).

Both intergenerational and intragenerational traumas, as I have described them, are traumas of wounded social relationships. They are not traumas of psychological dysfunction or pathology but social woundings that have been inscribed on the social body, and which Puntu encounter and negotiate. These particular traumas are premised on the withholding of an embodied male and palya experience that links the generations of men, and provides health to all in desert society. Not all men, however, have experienced these traumas or in the same ways. Some men have been particularly resilient.

To conclude, I will now highlight the key issues within this book and their possible implications for the health and well-being of desert men. The Aboriginal male body can be understood as both wounded and resilient. The male praxis of kanyirninpa discloses the nature and context of this wound but also its possible healing.

Conclusion

Wounded and Resilient

*Health is the spiritual, emotional, physical health
of people connected very much to their sense of
belonging to a place and belonging to people and
belonging to specific groups of people.*

*The older man teach the young boy how to look
after himself so that he takes that on to his family
and it goes on, generations by generations.*

When in 2003 the ABC released the film *Lonely Boy Richard*, the
story of 35-year-old Richard Wanambi from Yirrkala in Arnhem
Land, they could have been recounting the story of many desert
or other Aboriginal men (Graham et al. 2003). Richard left school
at 14, began drinking alcohol, and it was not long before he was
first arrested. At the time of the documentary he was about to be
sentenced to twelve years in prison. While the film focused on his
drinking, the offence (sexual assault), and the effect of his behaviour
on his family, it revealed a number of the themes that have surfaced
within this book: young men seek to follow the example of their
fathers and older men ('I'm just following in his footsteps'), the
importance of autonomy ('I've got my own choice') and the risks
associated with being 'alone' ('when we are drinking we are not
thinking about the Law').

Early in the film Richard described himself as 'lonely boy'. He
was 'lonely' in that he had followed the example set by his father,

who drank by himself. He had also become lonely in his separation from walytja (family), ngurra (land) and tjukurrpa (dreaming). His father had subsequently died, and his life had become one of great risk. While imprisonment removed him, and in some ways protected him from violence he might enact or receive, it further accentuated his loneliness and isolation from traditional country, family and the social practices of his Yolgnu people.

Like Richard Wanambi, it is not uncommon for young desert men to leave school at 14. Around that age, or even earlier, initiative, autonomy and the offer of a peer group experience can lead some into petrol sniffing and social behaviour that has already been described. Some may end up in juvenile detention. Later, they might put aside petrol for alcohol. This, in turn, provides its own set of health dangers: car accidents, assaults, domestic violence, self-harm and even suicide. While most young men will not spend one third of their life in prison, as Richard Wanambi will have when he is finally released, they all face a similar risk: the separation from the holding praxis of older men and the deeper implications of that separation.

The desire of young men to be held in the company of older men arises from an ancient past, where the rituals around male initiation have been powerful moments for desert society, not just for individuals and their families. The transformation and reproduction of the adult physical and social yarnangu (body) could only be effected through the cosmic meanings that the tjukurrpa (ancestral dreaming) transcribed upon men as they travelled the land and performed ceremony. Young men eagerly sought that journey into adulthood, a journey that began when they were young marlurlu (initiates), separated from the holding care of their mothers and other women.

The social context of kanyirninpa provides a geographical and social space where older men provide knowledge, protection and nurturance to those who are younger. Through that process, and under the authority of older men, a young man begins to understand his place within desert society, and discovers a confidence and ability that he can 'step out', hold and grow up others. This process of transformation requires time and learning, an evolving commitment to social relationships and the right to exercise autonomy. The poles of relatedness and autonomy provide a range of acceptable behaviours allowing him to learn, travel and explore (see Kanyirninpa model, p. 21). These poles also serve to caution and remind him. If he moves too far towards the extremes of autonomy, family members will draw him back to his responsibilities to walytja; if he becomes too dependent or reliant upon others, he will be urged to settle and establish a family where he can have children and begin to hold them. Antonovsky might have described this as an example of salutogenesis, where there is a continuum of health experience rather than a static condition (Antonovsky 1980, p. 37). Kanyirninpa provides a social context for young men to become adult through the company of other men. This is not simply a male praxis but a sociality that provides and reinforces key Puntu values around the dynamic social inter-relatedness of land, family and the ancestral dreaming.

Experiences of loneliness and separation, I have suggested, can arise when young desert men find themselves cut off from significant others. A more serious and potentially damaging experience can also develop from the awareness that particular social and masculine relationships cannot be realised. The trauma that has been transcribed on the Puntu yarnangu can be seen in the effects of colonisation on transgenerational processes and intragenerational relationships whereby older men and younger men find themselves separated. To use Dodson's image, they discover that they are cut off from one another and the relationship they need with each other to sustain them. This wound to the male social body seriously affects the ability of older desert men to exercise kanyirninpa, and for younger men to experience it. This can expose a profoundly destructive crisis in a young man's life, symbolised in two extreme forms of social isolation, imprisonment and suicide. In both of these extremes, where Aboriginal young men are greatly over-represented, some of the consequences of colonisation and resultant wounding of the male social body can be seen. A number of the expressions of this wounding have been described in detail during the course of this book.

The example of Richard Wanambi, as of many other Aboriginal men, is a reminder that in seeking to follow older men (in his case, his father) many young men experience separation. They discover that they are cut off from the power and relationship of older men who can provide them with authority, protection and care. Some of these significant older men have died, are drinking in town or are incarcerated in prison. Others have moved away from their children and families to live elsewhere. In the desert region, similar to many other Aboriginal communities and regions, nearly 60 per cent of the population are under 25 years of age (compared with 14 per cent who are older than 45 years). There are not many older men (or women) available or able to hold and look after those who are younger. Senior has referred this as 'the burden of care' for adults in Aboriginal communities (Senior 2003, p. 198).

Within the Kutjungka desert region most men now aged 45 to 60 spent some years in the mission dormitory separated from their fathers and older male relations. Their fathers' and grand-fathers' generation arrived at Balgo Mission when missionaries' attention and priorities were on children and young mothers. The authority of older men (and women), their knowledge and wisdom were not highly valued. Sometimes, restrictions and pressure were applied to prevent or minimise the performance of ceremonies, kinship responsibilities and promised marriages. As a consequence, key social relationships that linked generations and provided health within them were seriously affected. Older men were particularly marginalised as they were prevented from, and frustrated in, exercising their responsibilities to their families and to the younger men.

Central to the experience of well-being in desert society is being palya, where the inner and outer 'pleated body', yarnangu, can be described as living in relationship. Being cold and dry can reveal an ecology of this yarnangu within a social network of physical, social and spiritual realities. The social value of kanyirninpa is deeply embodied. It describes a praxis that mothers demonstrate from the time of birth when they hold and care for their young. This holding discloses nurturance and the values of teaching, guiding and protecting. A significant shift from female to male holding occurs when a marnti becomes a wati, the time of a young male's first stage of initiation. Here, a young male teenager comes under the holding power and possibilities of older men and begins a journey of incorporation into adult society, the male and adult yarnangu.

There are serious issues facing men's health and the experience of palya today. There has been a deep rending of the desert social fabric and the Puntu yarnangu has experienced trauma. In addition to the power of ancient ways to cause sickness and death, as in sorcery and transgression of the Law, men face the likelihood of premature death (compared with kartiya men) caused by a range of illnesses including cardiovascular disease, cancer and diabetes. A large number of men smoke tobacco, an increasing number smoke marijuana. Young men face additional risks of death and injury due to motor vehicle accidents, violence and self-inflicted harm. The lack of culturally appropriate clinic-based health resources, the predominance of unsealed roads, and the availability of alcohol also add to the health risks for young men living in very remote desert areas.

However, it would neither be sufficient nor valid to conclude this exploration of men's health by focusing only on the wounding of the male Puntu yarnangu, serious and critical as it is. There are signs that the Puntu body continues to be resilient and self-protective, to resist the domination and control of kartiyas, and to promote values that Puntu believe are important. Such values often lie hidden from the gaze, understanding and appreciation of kartiyas. Further, there is evidence that Puntu men promote and encourage certain expressions of male behaviour and relatedness that sustain important meanings and values. However, not only do these meanings and values challenge hegemonic expressions of masculinity within kartiya society, but they can be placed under great stress as Puntu endeavour to embody them.

It is important to restate that not all desert men have experienced colonisation in the same way, nor have all families responded in similar ways. Not all young men take up petrol sniffing. Football attracts most young men, but not all. Prison, also, does not involve all men. Some may be repeat offenders, others may be imprisoned occasionally, and there is a smaller number that has never been arrested or spent time in prison. There are men, young and old, who have been particularly strong and resilient, exhibiting and developing strong protective factors around their health and that of their families.

Protective factors have been defined as those that reduce the likelihood of behaviour that leads to self-harm, whereas resilience factors have been defined as the 'ability to tolerate, to adapt to, or to overcome life crises' (Beauvais & Oetting 1999, p. 103). It has been suggested that protective factors provide a 'trajectory' or life path that avoids some risks, whereas resilience provides resources when crises occur: 'protective factors save you from disaster; resilience lets you bounce back' (1999, p. 103).

Protective factors were identified in the longitudinal study of the development of 505 individuals from the Pacific island of Kauai who were born in 1955 and their lives followed up thirty years later (Werner & Smith, 1992). This study examined the long-term effects of childhood adversity on adult lives (adversity shown by factors such as perinatal stress, poverty, parental discord and psychopathology). The researchers were interested in identifying the protective factors that led to adult health. While, it should be noted, there are obvious differences between the people of Kauai and those of the Western Desert (Kauai is an island economy based on agriculture, with a mixed immigrant background), the results of the Kauai revealed significant protective factors. The study showed that loss or separation from a caregiver in childhood was expressed in coping problems in adulthood (1992, p. 196). It also showed that young people most at risk were strengthened by relationships with older others. These relationships 'provide[d] them with the secure basis for the development of trust, autonomy, and initiative' (1992, p. 209). The Kauai research demonstrated that interpersonal and intergenerational relationships provided protection and resilience against considerable social and environmental odds that placed adult health at great risk. In the context of the research conducted for this book, kanyirninpa can be understood as a similar value that encourages protection and resilience. Holding encourages Puntu to form supporting relationships across generations. It can also strengthen those relationships within generations that, over recent decades, have been seriously wounded.

Despite the obstacles and serious difficulties associated with experiencing kanyirninpa, young men continue to seek its expression. As a value it continues to be practised and enacted between generations on a regular and everyday level. For some, the offering of a holding experience can draw them away from sniffing into an adult male and social world. Football can attract men into a male arena of sociality, skill and enjoyment that enables them to travel and develop relationships within the company and support of older men. Desert men have experienced imprisonment for decades and they make choices within its constraints and possibilities. While having limited power around police behaviour, legal representation, court processes and sentencing options, some men use imprisonment for the benefits it provides. Both protective and resilient factors operate vigorously within desert society, but they exist within a history of constraint and pressure due to kartiya power, influence and values. The role of maparn, a protective factor, and the ritual of sorry business, a resilience factor, amply demonstrate this. They both work to promote Puntu health and well-being, and they engage the energies of men and women. However, like the clinic, they cannot by themselves fully address or heal the wound that has been deeply transcribed upon the Puntu yarnangu.

The importance of maparn can be seen from the time of birth when a person's health is described in terms of being palya. Being sick or unhealthy, the absence of palya, can be embodied in many different ways that require the attention and services of maparn who seek to shift, remove, open up or prevent the many possible sources of illness. Their healing powers restore the sick person to the company of walytja and to significant relationships. Maparn reveal a particular dynamic of nurture and care that a number of male healers bring to those who are suffering, and they disclose a strong desire by men to establish healing within traditionalist memories and understandings. Maparn continue to be an important protective factor for desert people's social and emotional well-being.

The ritual of sorry business provides Puntu with resilience. This ceremony has been mentioned, often associated with Law, as an example of Puntu agency where kartiya values and influence are secondary. The gendered space of sorry business allows Puntu the public outpouring of grief with the reception of support and comfort. Amongst the Tiwi similar rituals have been described as 'collective mourning rituals [that] express in symbolic actions the major psychotherapeutic, integrative processes of Tiwi life' (Robinson 1990, p. 165). In the desert, the use of mawuntu (white ochre) over faces, heads and upper body torsos expresses a deeper social connection of values and ancestral beliefs. Men and women gather as gendered bodies, expressing their grief through shared crying, embracing and sometimes self-wounding. Despite the experience of death, loss and separation, the public ritual of sorry business strengthens extended kinship relationships and in so doing valorises a broad, social inter-relatedness.

Maparn and sorry business express some of the ways in which desert society maintains and reinforces important values around well-being. They are also, significantly, two aspects of desert cultural life where kartiyas are largely absent and uninvolved. However, kartiyas can act to obstruct, modify or restrict these social expressions. Hence, a serious and cautionary note needs to be added. Kartiyas, through their power, pressure and the imposition of their own values, can restrict the possibilities and potentialities that maparn and sorry business offer desert society in terms of protection and resilience. Despite the efforts of Puntu to sustain and maintain the health of their social body, their yarnangu has become a contested site where the wound of colonisation continues to be visible and Puntu health suffers.

When maparn claim they cannot deal with more recent sicknesses, such as cancer or diabetes, their ability to protect Puntu society from certain diseases, or assist them when they are sick, becomes seriously limited. To the extent that Puntu identify some types of illnesses with kartiyas and the consequences of first contact, maparn can only offer little in terms of diagnosis or healing. The protection that maparn offer may, in such cases, lie more in terms of supporting and validating a coherent body of Puntu health beliefs against those represented by clinic care. As I have discussed, desert people strongly maintain their own health belief system, despite the presence of serious diseases and a Western model of health care that has been provided for decades. Consequently, it can be argued, where the clinic has assumed hegemony over Puntu health, and failed to understand or value the care represented by the activities of the maparn, Puntu health beliefs and practices have been undermined. Their physical, social and emotional health also has suffered.

This is not to deny the importance of Western medical health care but to stress that it is inadequate to address Puntu well-being by itself. The work and activity of maparn disclose not only a concern and involvement by desert men in issues of health but also a singularly important way by which desert people understand what it means to be well and sick. In seeking to improve Puntu health, Western medical health care cannot ignore, dismiss or marginalise the importance and meaning that desert people place on being palya, especially the relational, social and cosmic aspects involved in it.

As with the limits by which maparn can protect Puntu health, there are also limits to the resilience the ritual of sorry business can provide. The commitment and agency by which Puntu enact sorry business can confront kartiya staff and their own cultural response to death. When a desert person dies, Puntu are likely to stop work and suspend other activities. They will often travel, in the company of others, to perform sorry business where that person died or where the closest relatives of the deceased live. They can stay away from their home community for days or even longer. If they travel home they may return for the funeral some weeks, even months, later. In many cases, those who are most closely related to the deceased move out of their homes, and adopt severe dietary taboos and other social and physical embodiments of grief. This can continue for several weeks. Not only is this likely to create tensions with those kartiya staff who place greater stress on the importance and continuity of work, employment and education, but they can then place stress on Puntu to limit or restrict their use of these rituals.

While kartiya and Puntu share the universal experience of death there are important cultural differences. Most kartiyas do not experience the regularity of death and funerals that desert people do, and only occasionally are they in a position to receive care or attention from Puntu as an experience of grief. Puntu manifestations of grief are socially expressive and demonstrative, and Puntu can find kartiyas' response to grief impersonal, lacking in emotion and resolved too quickly. As in the example of maparn, sorry business also discloses important differences between Puntu and kartiya belief systems, values and practices. Consequently, pressure can be applied by kartiyas on Puntu to change, modify or let go of their traditionalist ways of behaving and believing.

In the protection of maparn, and the resilience of sorry business, Puntu express and sustain important cultural and social values around their health. These values reinforce the importance of intragenerational and intergenerational relationships for social and emotional well-being. Maparn protect those relationships from serious harm, and the ritual of sorry business offers resilience against the loss and pain of separation when such relationships are severed. While Western medical health care can offer valuable resources, such as diagnosis, medication, counselling and psychiatric support, these resources remain severely inadequate where they do not engage with Puntu health beliefs and the social and relational dimensions that Puntu experience in health, sickness, grief and loss.

Clearly, the trauma that has been transcribed upon the male yarnangu has deeply affected men's mental and social well-being. However, despite threats over decades to its various forms of expression, Puntu have identified kanyirninpa as one response to that trauma. They have continued to use kanyirninpa to strengthen those interpersonal and intergenerational relationships that were discovered to be so important in the research at Kauai for adult well-being. The creative and persistent use of kanyirninpa has enabled Puntu to hold generations together, and members of families within generations, despite the forces that have worked to separate them.

I have quoted many examples whereby older men have taken responsibility to watch over and care for younger men, not just in times of Law but on other occasions, which have strengthened male relationships, within and across generations, as they have provided important contexts for the transmission of male and desert values. It is not surprising that men should seek their own space in the provision of clinic care, the arena of football, within the classroom, or upon the land as they travel and hunt. These gendered and geographical spaces reinforce and strengthen a male sociality across generations, and a shared responsibility towards the social reproduction of desert society. I have offered examples where desert people have responded to hold and care for children in times of crisis. Petrol sniffers have been invited to join older male company, families have invited children to stay with them when a parent has died, or an adult has accepted responsibility to care for children whose parents were drinking in town. These are examples of an active kanyirninpa where adult and male Puntu have responded to young people in the context of separation and loss.

Similarly, there are examples outside the desert region where Aboriginal men have identified the serious health needs of other men and have proposed solutions (Lowe & Spry 2002, pp. 60, 75; Wenitong 2002, p. 54; Brown 2004, pp. 116–25; Working Party 2004, pp. 16–33). They, like the maparn men of the Western Desert, continue to seek the well-being of the male yarnangu in culturally appropriate and strengthening ways. Their proposals, such as increasing the number of male health providers, establishing men's health groups and male health centres (with specific programs), and reinforcing relationships (e.g. uncle/nephew or young fathers with older fathers), act to improve men's health by linking and strengthening male relationships within and across generations. The presence of elders and older males, their wisdom, skills and experience, serves to promote stronger, healthier men in relationship with other men (and with women and children). Through the holding power and presence of older men the needs of young men can be given appropriate attention and support.

In conclusion, I am aware that I am not offering any simple or easy solutions to the improvement of Aboriginal men's health. However, as I have suggested earlier, the Puntu yarnangu remains a contested site where the power of kartiyas to affect and wound

Aboriginal health continues to remain considerable. While Puntu have shown a remarkable resilience in maintaining values that link health with social relatedness, kartiyas have demonstrated a considerable resistance to these values. Biomedical health care has been shown for some decades to be inadequate in dealing with many of the social, gendered and relational aspects of health. In the desert, health care continues to exist as a site of contestation where conflicting values around health meet. There is an unfortunate irony that the particular provisions and enactment of health care by kartiyas to Puntu can serve to undermine desert people's health. Biomedical health care does not stress the social and relational dimensions of health that palya emphasises, and clinic health care rarely seeks a common ground of diagnosis or healing with Puntu models of health and sickness. This not to suggest that less Western medical care is needed in this region. However, it is to suggest that both traditionalist ways, and clinic ways, of providing health care are ill-equipped by themselves to deal adequately with contemporary issues of Puntu health. What desert people understand by health and being palya challenges a number of the assumptions and limitations of kartiya biomedical health care. It is difficult to see that Puntu health will improve until such health care acknowledges its dominance, and then engages and collaborates with Puntu models of health and sickness. Only then will Puntu find some meaning, power and control over its provision and a greater relevancy to their current experiences of wellness and illness (McCoy 2006).

I began this book recounting the time when a group of Puntu provided a narrative about the importance of sustaining kanyirninpa within the difficulties and dangers of their changing world. Since that time Puntu have continued to reveal in ceremonies, stories, paintings and ordinary daily events the values around health that sustain and energise their lives. At the centre of these values is experiencing palya, living alive and well within a range of social and cosmic relationships. Their use of kanyirninpa, adapted and rejuvenated over generations, has contributed to them being palya. It is likely that Puntu will continue to exercise it as an important element of their health into the future.

Appendix
Relationship terms and kinship designations

Aboriginal desert society is divided into moieties and generation levels. Marriage ideally occurs between people of the same generation level marrying into the opposite moiety. In addition, the kinship system classifies people into genealogical moieties that are significant for the conduct of important ceremonies (Hansen 1979; Myers 1986; Valiquette 1993; Koning 1997).

The desert kinship system comprises eight subsections or 'skins'. Each person is born into a subsection, determined by the mother's and father's subsection. This subsection determines a wide range of social relationships and behaviours with all other Aboriginal people who share a section or sub-section kinship system. Apart from actual blood relations others will be classified as one's brothers, sisters, mothers, fathers and so on. There is also an equivalence of siblings where a person can have several fathers (your father and your father's brother) and several mothers (your mother and your mother's sisters). As a result one can have many brothers and sisters, the children of one's 'fathers' and 'mothers'. In cases where the mother or father has not married according to preferred kinship relationships children can be described as having 'two ways'. They possess two 'skin' designations, one taken from the father, as though he had married correctly, and one from the mother, as though she had. When kartiyas come into the Kutjungka desert region they are usually assigned a skin.

The eight sections of the kinship system are: (male subsections begin with 'Tj' and female with 'N'; '=' brother/sister)

Tjakamarra = Nakamarra
Tjapaltjarri = Napaltjarri
Tjampitjin = Nampitjin
Tjapangarti = Napangarti
Tjupurrula = Napurrula
Tjungurrayi = Nungurrayi
Tjangala = Nangala
Tjapanangka = Napanangka

In ritual ceremonies, such as those involving initiation and sorry business, men and women move within two distinct generational moieties. The Tjakamarra, Tjapaltjarri, Tjampitjin and Tjapangarti men move and act separately from the Tjupurrula, Tjungurrayi, Tjangala and Tjapanangka men. The equivalent sibling groups of women also act separately. Each group of men and women includes one's siblings and cousins and those of second ascending or descending generations, such as grandparents and grandchildren. The opposite group consists of one's fathers/mothers, uncles/aunties, nephews/nieces and one's children. These generational moieties express the roles and behaviours of tilitja and yirrkapiri at these ceremony times. They stress the importance of generational, endogamous moieties that result in close, supporting relationships within each moiety.

Notes

Introduction

1. When someone dies the name of that person, or words that sound similar, become kumunytjayi. This means that they are not said aloud and other words are used instead. See Glossary.

Chapter 1

1. Myers takes the phrase 'dominant symbol' from Victor Turner (1967, p. 28).

2. It is possible that when Folds argued that the missionaries held the people at Haasts Bluff by feeding them he was referring more to an example of ngampurrmaninpa (where an ongoing relationship of sharing was expected) rather than of kanyirninpa. However, when ngampurrmaninpa is expressed towards the young then the relationship can be described as kanyirninpa. This distinction is further developed later in this chapter.

3. For a different view, see Richard Trudgen 2000 who places greater emphasis on the destructive consequences caused by the impact of the dominant culture on Aboriginal people.

4. In 1999, Kururrungku Catholic School received a national award for literacy, in 2000 a WA state award for literacy, and in 2002 a national award for numeracy.

5. The CEO intervened to stop this practice in 2002 due to insurance and related liability issues.

Chapter 2

1. Within the last decade there has also been a number of published commentaries on art from the Kutjungka region, distributed through Warlayirti Artists.

2. In recent years there has also been published *A World of Relationships* by Sylvie Poirier (University of Toronto Press, 2005) and two significant works with a focus on women within a desert and cultural context: *Piercing the Ground* by Christine Watson (Fremantle Arts Centre Press, 2003) and *Holding Yawulyu* by Zohl de Ishtar (Spinifex Press, 2005). All of these arose out of research conducted in the region.

3. Some people have suggested that the word Balgo meant 'dirty wind', an interpretation supported by McGuire and others. See Elizabeth Jordan (1983), Susan McCulloch (1999). There seems little evidence for this interpretation. Br Frank (Franz) Nissl suggested that the name derived from a water source near 'Balgo Hill' (1976). Mark Moora has suggested that 'Balgo' referred to palkurr, the native rice grass that grew on the low-lying hills around the Mission (*Xerochloa laniflora*). When the priest asked the name of the 'hills' Puntu thought he was referring to the grass growing on them. The small seeds were ground, made into edible paste and cooked (pers. comm. 1993). Another explanation, and more likely, is that 'parlku' referred to a rockhole near the old mission site, along the tingari dreaming track.

4. Because words do not usually end in a consonant, the euphonic '–pa' is often added e.g. luurnpa, tjukurrpa.

5. There are three different sites that are often referred to as 'Billiluna'. The first, Kilingkarra, was near present-day Malarn Community. It was here that two kartiya stockmen, Joseph Condren and Timothy O'Sullivan, were killed in 1922. The station moved north to Lake Stretch and, after a flood, to its present site. Mindibungu was named after an old man whose country was around McGuire's Gap. The origin of the word Billiluna is not clear.

6. Some words, e.g. Yaka Yaka, are often reduplicated in Kukatja to 'soften' the meaning. See Valiquette 1993 (p. 449).

7. This report recommended that four desert communities south of Wirrimanu be established: Yaka Yaka, Lamarnparnta, Walkali and Piparr. Yaka Yaka was the only community where people returned to live on a permanent basis (Cane 1989).

8. Caution needs to be exercised when comparing the different Census figures of 2001 and 2006. Evidence points to an underestimation of Kimberley data in general (Atkinson et al. 1999, p. 31). There are also issues of desert people's mobility, particularly in the month of August and the quality of data collected. See ABS, 2001a (pp. 80–1) and ABS, 2001b (p. 8).

9. Kukatja belongs to the Western Desert language group of Aboriginal languages with Pintupi, Luritja, Pitjantjatjara and others; Walmajarri,

Ngarti and Jaru belong to the Ngumbin group and Warlpiri to the Ngarrkic group (Institute for Aboriginal Development, 2002).

10. Bliluna station was registered to Joseph Condren on 4 May 1920 and became known as the Billiluna Pastoral Company Limited. It went into voluntary liquidation on 16 December 1925 (Johnson 1956). Condren had previously worked at Sturt Creek Station.

11. What Gordon Briscoe describes as 'the great health panic' came to a head in the Kimberley in the 1930s. For a background on leprosy in WA and the Kimberley see Briscoe 2003 (pp. 152, 173).

12. Sometimes the names of these missionaries are spelt differently e.g. Hugel or Huegel, Krallman or Krallmann, Schungel or Schuengel.

13. Paddy Meranjian was also known as Paddy Paddy or Jingle Jangle.

14. The phrase 'No Man's Land' came from TGH Strehlow and a paper he delivered, 'Nomads in no-man's-land', at the University of Adelaide in 1960. Strehlow had been in contact with Worms.

15. Christmas 1939 has been remembered in a Kukatja song as the first time people heard the Christian message, 'Tjaluwan nyangula Jesus yurrkangka', 'at Tjaluwan we saw Jesus lying in a manger'.

16. Sometimes spelt as Doomendora, Dumendora or Dumend Dora.

17. Audrey Bolger suggests that some Wangkatjungka people who lived around the Canning Stock Route became vulnerable when members of their families were wiped out in raids by pastoralists and police in the 1930s and 1940s (Bolger 1986, 1987).

18. See Andrew Marcus 1990 (p. 74). McGuire was quoted as saying: 'Some people say I run the mission like a dictator…this is wrong, but Balgo has an authoritative type of government. Discipline is sound and the natives are contented. There is no juvenile delinquency' (cited in Johnson, LC 1965).

19. 'Ten girls are in the dormitory, but there are 25 children altogether permanently living at the Mission. Another 10 to 15 are still with their parents leading a nomadic life' (Bleischwitz 1951, p. 27).

20. Allie Evans came to Balgo in 1951 and lived in the girls' dormitory with 28 girls (Byrne 1989, p. 96). Caroline Gye (a pseudonym for Ida Mann) described the mission and dormitory in her visit there in 1953 (Gye 1962, p. 93).

21. There were forty-seven boys in the dormitory, aged between 5 and 15. Initially, only the younger boys and girls returned to their families; they would come to the dormitories in the morning to shower and change their clothes for school and then, after school, change before returning home. Personal records 1973.

22. When the boy (marlurlu) is being prepared for initiation a special hair-belt is put around his waist.
23. See *Macquarie dictionary* for 'cheeky'. It notes the Aboriginal English use of the word as 'unpredictable' and 'dangerous'. Poisonous snakes, for example, can be described as 'cheeky'.
24. The Berndts observed 'changes in some quite crucial aspects of initiation' where 'boys are (or have been) sent by the missionary to be circumcised in Broome or Derby so that the actual physical operation is no longer a prerogative of the religious leaders'. They appear to have avoided any public criticism of the missionaries (Berndt, R 1972, pp. 199, 204).
25. The term 'rice Christians' was applied to those who asked to be baptised as a consequence of being fed or looked after by missionaries.

Chapter 3

1. I am assuming here a range of understandings and discourses around the concept 'health' e.g. the World Health Organisation's (1948) definition as 'a state of complete physical, mental and social well-being and not merely the absence of disease or infirmity'.
2. Apart from the word 'maparn' (or mabarn), similar words are used in other places e.g. 'ngangkari' in central Australia and 'marrnggitji' in Arnhem Land. Puntu also use English words like 'featherfoot' and 'witchcraft', suggesting the influence of the English language and interpretations of maparn activity by kartiyas. In the Kutjungka region Puntu use the word 'maparn' to refer both to those who provide this healing, but also the power that exists, in both their own bodies and in the land, to effect healing or sickness.
3. See MCHS service reports, Kimberley Public Health Unit (KPHU) Bulletin, Matthew Ritson, 2000.
4. Well Men's Checks was a Tristate STD/HIV Project designed to promote Aboriginal men's health. This particular project in the Kutjungka region ceased for some time after a nurse was assaulted in one of the communities.
5. The Well Men's Checks only covered 64 men, average age of 24 years.
6. Aboriginal people in the Kimberley are smoking more than others; the average per capita consumption of alcohol in the Kimberley has been almost 1.8 times the level consumed within WA as a whole; cannabis use is also increasing. See David Atkinson et al. 1999.

7. The underweight group tended to be young petrol sniffers and the overweight group older men.

8. The rate of Aboriginal people with diabetes is at least twice that of kartiyas in WA, except in the East Kimberley where the rate for males is significantly higher than in the West Kimberley (Atkinson et al. 1999, p. 36).

9. In the Well Men's Checks of 2002, 79 per cent admitted to drinking alcohol, reflecting similar high alcohol consumption patterns in other parts of the Kimberley. Some indicated that they didn't drink alcohol and these were mainly younger men. Rarely did a young man both sniff petrol and also drink alcohol. See Atkinson et al. 1999 (p. 39).

10. These two men are not to be confused with the two young kartiya jackaroos, James Annetts and Simon Amos, who died in late 1986, south of Yaka Yaka, when their vehicle broke down.

11. Halls Creek (WA) is 280 kilometres and Yuendumu (NT) is 550 kilometres from Wirrimanu.

12. While members of Christian churches will pray for the sick, Catholics will pray and use holy oil. In this region, most Catholic Puntu believe in, and support the work of, maparn.

13. As explained in the Introduction I am not in this book exploring Christian practice. However, I acknowledge that an important part of that practice can include, for some Christians, a focus on healing.

14. See Elkin 1980 (p. 123), who allows for female maparn but with less prominence. Similarly, Bell 1982 (p. 220).

15. Palya, like kanyirninpa, is polysematic. Here I am using the word that Puntu prefer to use in translating the English word 'health'. It is arguable that Kukatja speakers have come to accommodate their use of the word palya with the English use of the word 'good', especially in the context of describing health.

16. Kurrun refers to one's inner spirit or life essence and comes from the tjukurrpa. Desert beliefs regarding the kurrun are extensive and include its ability to move within the person but also outside. Its relation to a person's experience of health is such that, 'when any part of the body is in pain, the person's spirit is also suffering' (Peile 1997, pp. 92, 95).

17. Note in this earlier work the different uses of the word palya (then written as balya) to describe the various states of one's heart, skin, stomach or spirit (Wiminydji & Peile 1978, p. 506).

18. 'The beautiful and the good are based on the same, namely, the "form"' (Peile 1997, p. 25).

19. Bindon comments on Peile's different uses of some words such as 'dry' and suggests, 'health…would more likely to imply a balance of all the

conditions necessary for health rather than a surfeit of any of them' (Peile 1997, p. 144).

20. Two examples of use of the word 'lalka' in the Kukatja dictionary show the negative aspects of 'dryness' for health: 'no lalka, mimipayi' ('[a person who is] not healthy [lit. dry] is sick all the time') and, 'lalkarringu marnmarlparna' ('I have become dry and am in pain'). In the former example the person is sick by not being 'dry' and in the latter the person is in pain because they are 'dry', they haven't any blood.

21. See comments about the Eskimos/Inuit, Algonkian and Athapaskan Indians, Young 1994 (p. 11).

22. Durack 1960 (p. 105).

23. A murrungkurr is a little person who can leave things that can make people sick.

24. Elkin and Tonkinson refer to the assistance of 'spirits and familiars' (Elkin 1980, p. 23; Tonkinson 1982, p. 232).

25. Neither Peile nor Valiquette mention 'lids' which suggests that the term may be of more recent origin. Professor Bob Tonkinson has suggested the use of a similar word, leti, amongst the Martu people (pers. comm. 17 July 2006).

26. When kids bang tin or iron, 'lids' can rise up from the ground and enter another person as if the noise is 'like they're waking them up'. They can smell a person and are more prevalent and dangerous at ceremonial time, although the wearing of red ochre on one's body (pilytji) can protect a person. The lid cannot smell them. A lid can generate a headache, vomiting, eye problems or urinary problems. It can 'eat all the blood on a person's inside'. The person can get a headache and feel hot. They sleep all day. When they are removed they come mixed with blood and mud.

27. People will negotiate this 'space' by waiting or sitting outside, but they are forced eventually inside if they want the attention of those working in the clinic.

28. Deleuze maintained that Foucault 'found great theoretical inspiration in Heidegger and Merleau-Ponty for the theme that haunted him: the fold, or doubling' (1995, p. 110).

29. Italics are Deleuze's.

30. Men, and women, have strong views about the separation of men and women's business. Privacy can entail both personal and gender boundaries.

31. Wenitong's emphasis.

Chapter 4

1. Here, I am not commenting whether or how younger women might experience being held by older women, but older women have informed me that it does occur.

2. The authors explore etymological links between Indigenous words that are used for man, body and person. They propose that, unlike Indo-European languages, the shift between the words for 'man' and 'person' (which occurs in many languages in the world) is driven in the Australian desert by the cultural significance of initiation.

3. The term yalpurru is also used to identify those who share the same birthday, reflecting a more recent modification in the use of the term. Both uses reflect similar emphases where 'new life' begins at birth and at initiation. See yalpuru in Myers 1986 (p. 223) and yarlburu in Tonkinson 1978 (p. 68).

4. These words are not found in Peile or Valiquette, at least with these meanings. Tjamparti, 'promised bride' (1993, p. 270), is used today to refer to those who perform the initiation. Pilali (not in dictionary) is the name that is used by the person initiated to describe the family of the one who has been initiated, and also the brothers and sisters of the one who performs the initiation. See Valiquette, commenting on Peile's work where 'ceremonial, relationship and avoidance terms are under-represented' (1994, p. 31). Myers refers to pilayarli, where 'an initiate's "fathers" and "mother's brothers" all become pilayarli with his circumciser' (1986, p. 233). See Glossary for both terms.

5. Between 1957–72 non-infant deaths due to external causes were 4–7 per cent of male deaths; from 1982–6 it increased to 23 per cent of male deaths. The sharp increase began in the 1970s.

6. In Chapter 1 see the distinction between kanyirninpa and ngampurrmaninpa: I understand the father is meaning here ngampurrmaninpa.

7. This is not to suggest that after his initiation a young man no longer has anything to do with his mother, sisters or other women. However, after his initiation there is a significant shift in the expression of his relationship with them.

8. For example, Puntu remember how McGuire actively intervened to prevent Law while Hevern provided vehicles so people could attend 'their business'.

9. Brendan Ross Tjangala died as the result of a car accident in January 2007.

10. Kukatja has no equivalent word to the English 'adolescence'. While desert societies referred to the various stages of religious knowledge a man might acquire in his life, once a man was initiated he was a wati.

He was no longer a boy or to be treated as such (Berndt, R & C 1985, p. 177).

11. When a prisoner is released he is given any money owing him from work he has done while incarcerated, plus a bus ticket back to Halls Creek. There is no transport provided from Halls Creek to the Kutjungka region, and often those who are released can take a long time to leave Broome and reach home.

12. Having money and relations in Broome who knew of his release would make it difficult for him not to spend time with them spending his money and drinking.

13. This information was based on an interview with the policeman himself.

Chapter 5

1. I am here making a distinction between young boys and young men; many of those who begin petrol sniffing are in their early teenage years and have not been initiated.

2. See use of the word 'dry' in Chapter 3, Healers and Health, p. 77.

3. 'Larger communities that serve as centres for white administrative activities are particularly prone to also becoming centres of substance abuse' (Langton 1990, p. 213).

4. While Australian Bureau of Statistics (ABS, 2002) figures suggested there were eighty-one men aged between 15–24 resident in the region at the time of the 2001 Census, my own records, confirmed by discussions with others in the communities, show that the figure was probably more than 100, allowing for a further twenty or more to be absent from the region at any one time.

5. 'Learning' in this context means 'teaching'.

6. See Nurcombe, who compared petrol-sniffers with male controls and found 'trends…for the petrol sniffers to be slower at school and to have absent or dead fathers' (1974, p. 68). Morice et al. have noted that 'one of the few consistently reported general characteristics of sniffers has been the absence, actual or relative, of the father' (1981, p. 8).

7. This figure of 30 per cent appears to apply to all young men, whether a person sniffed petrol in the past or didn't.

8. These figures are only approximate but were based on personal observation and confirmed by others. While 'absent' refers here to the current status of a young man and his father living in the same community, in most cases 'absent' describes a situation that has existed for a number of years.

9. While those who took photos knew of my interest in petrol sniffing, I did not ask them to photograph anything in particular. Most of the photos were of other sniffers and walytja. They gave permission for me to use their photos but none are reproduced here.

10. In another group of four young male sniffers, none of them are living with their fathers. One has a deceased father and is living with family relations, two are being brought up by the one grandmother and the fourth is living with his stepfather.

11. The number of young men with kartiya fathers is very few, probably no more than five in the region.

12. The introduction of Avgas, a non-sniffable fuel, into Maningrida (Arnhem Land) and the Pitjanjtatjara Lands in the early 1990s caused a significant reduction in petrol sniffing (Roper & Shaw 1996, p. 6). In 2005, Opal fuel replaced Comgas/Avgas and was gradually introduced into a large number of Aboriginal communities. It is currently available in the Kutjungka desert communities but not at the Rabbit Flat Roadhouse or at all Halls Creek fuel distributors (March 2008).

13. Brady proposes that 'young men and adolescent boys are evidently using petrol sniffing as an attempted solution to major crises of self-image and identity' (1992, p. 95).

14. The 'drunks came and bashed us' (Biven 1999, Appendix C, p. 70).

15. When Hunter visited Wirrimanu in 1987 he noted the word 'warriors' painted on walls around the community: 'clearly, being identified as violent, as 'bad blackfellas', was a greater source of esteem than the void that preceded it' (1993, p. 190).

16. Moving around at night is also considered more dangerous due to the presence and activity of evil spirits such as mamu and kukurrpa. Also, Senior, when describing night life for young people at Ngukurr: '"walkin' about at night" is considered by Ngukurr youth to be one of the defining acts of being a teenager, it flouts parental rules, and creates a group' (2003, p. 193).

17. As mentioned in the previous chapter there are strict rules (and possible sanctions) that govern Puntu behaviour once a Law ceremony has begun with the formal 'taking' of the marlurlu. This applies particularly to women, children and unitiated boys.

18. Such as the three young men, ages 25, 27 and 29 years, who died in South Australia as a result of petrol inhalation and were the subject of a Coronial Inquiry. See Chivell 2002 (p. 1).

19. See Burbank who makes reference to the forces of competing interests upon young male initiates (1988, p. 37).

Chapter 6

1. See Willis 1997 (p. 82). Tjukurrpa stories reveal the actions of those who travel in pairs e.g. wati kutjarra, tjiitji kutjarra and provide an important cultural context for paired activities.
2. Many Aboriginal languages possess a dual number, where the actions of two people can be described, inclusively or exclusively, in relation to a larger group of people.
3. When someone died mourners traditionally moved to another place. 'Opening up' occurred when they believed they could return to that place after summer rains. Sweeping the ground would seem to replace that form of traditional cleansing. See Koning et al. 2000.
4. For example, annual events such as the Yuendumu sports weekend held on the first weekend of August, and the Tiwi Grand Final held in March on Bathurst Island (Northern Territory).
5. I was involved with the Garbutt Magpies Sporting Association between 1979–84 when living in Townsville.
6. The Garbutt Magpies have been registered as The Garbutt National Football Club, Garbutt Magpies and Garbutt All Blacks; Rumbalara have been the Cummera's Invincibles and The All Blacks.
7. In 1990 the average length of stay of students at Clontarf Aboriginal College was 15.1 weeks; in 2000 this had more than doubled to 38.5 weeks. In 1998 there were only 7 Year 12 male students, and 26 in 2002 (Clontarf 2002b, p. 4).
8. The Garbutt Magpies were expelled from the Townsville Football League in 1983; they had won the senior Premiership the year before. The Rumbalara Football Club, then called the All Blacks in 1947, was expelled after one year in the Central Goulburn Valley League. The Club had won the second division premiership the year previously.
9. Between 1991–2000, 77 Aboriginal players were on VFL/AFL lists (Ahmed 2003). In 2004 there were 47 Aboriginal players on AFL lists (Australian Football League, 2004). By 2008 this number had risen to 72, 10 per cent of the competition. 189 Aboriginal players have now played in the AFL (pers. comm., Cameron Sinclair, Australian Football League, 7 March 2008).
10. Avoiding physical confrontation is an important Puntu value and skill. People daily negotiate and maintain a multitude of kinship relationships, each of which assumes respect. Physical confrontation is considered a last resort.
11. Blainey makes no mention of Dawson's records of 1881.

12. The Cummeragunja Mission founder, Daniel Matthews, complained that the men had been playing football for four or five hours, 'a more laborious engagement than any we can give them' (Potter n.d., p. 12).

13. In contrast, Robin Grow described the early games in Melbourne where, 'scoring was low, the game was violent, and the large crowds were passionate' (Grow 1998, p. 5).

14. Peter Skipper describes a game called turlurlu that Walmajarri boys used to play in the desert; it was a game that taught boys how to throw accurately (Walmajarri Storytellers 2002, p. 15).

15. In 2000 five Aboriginal players left their AFL Clubs during the season. 'The problems did not seem to be related to playing football per se, rather football had inadvertently magnified these problems as the individuals had all relocated' (Australian Football League Players Association 2001, p. 3).

16. Transport can also be a problem. Sometimes, players could get a lift to a carnival but after it finished might have to wait days or weeks for a lift back home.

17. While most young men play football there is a small number who do not. However, they will often watch and enjoy the game. They will also accompany other men to sporting carnivals.

Chapter 7

1. There are two juvenile detention Centres in Perth: Banksia Hill and Rangeview. The former is for longer detention, the latter for those on remand and awaiting trial. In February 2003 there were at least 12 desert men in prison; in June 2003 there were 5 male juveniles in detention and 3 on remand. In January 2004 there were more than 20 men and 3 male juveniles in detention.

2. For example, during my last field trip in January 2004, there was only 1 woman from the Kutjungka region in prison. However in July 2007 there were 3.

3. Note: the Queensland rate was 13.5, Northern Territory 10.8. The National Prisoner Census on the night of 30 June 2007 showed that Indigenous persons continued to be 21 times more likely to be in prison than non-Indigenous persons in Western Australia. This was the highest age standardised ratio of Indigenous to non-Indigenous rates of imprisonment in Australia (ABS 2007a). The national average daily Indigenous imprisonment rate in the December quarter 2006 was 2160 per 100,000 adult Indigenous population, an increase of 7 per cent from the December quarter 2005 and an increase of 2 per cent from the previous quarter (ABS 2007b).

4. They refer to times when the Mission Superintendent called the police.

5. There are examples when police have taken juveniles into custody in Halls Creek without informing their parents or walytja, or when interviewing these juveniles they sought the presence of 'a responsible adult' by asking men who had been in town drinking to attend.

6. In 1995 a young man from Balgo died in Halls Creek as the result of a motor vehicle accident and Puntu accused the police of being party to his death. Similar accusations have occurred on other occasions, such as on the death of a young man in the Halls Creek hotel in 1983 and another in a motor vehicle accident in the town in 2003.

7. For example, the policeman in Halls Creek who was asked by a young Aboriginal man to help 'grow him up', as described in Chapter 4.

8. See Natalie Siegel, 2003. She presents a similar experience from the Northern Territory.

9. Occasionally, some magistrate courts are held at Wirrimanu.

10. CDEP began in the mid-1970s as a Federally funded government alternative to unemployment benefits. The CDEP rate in January 2004 was $10.85 per hour (for East Kimberley), which provided $194 per week for a 17/18 hour working week.

11. See footnote 23 in Chapter 2, The Shaping of History, and its explanation of the meaning of the English word 'cheeky'.

12. The Kukatja Dictionary lists the meanings of 'mirri' as: 'very sick person, corpse, an unconscious person or animal, person who is exhausted or drunk, sick, beyond repair (ref. vehicle)'. In recent years the word has generally been used to describe those who are dead (Valiquette 1993, p. 101).

13. See Appendix (p. 226). This is an example where a person can have several 'fathers'.

14. In some cases prisoners can receive permission from the Ministry of Justice to return home for funerals if they come under particular (government) categories of 'immediate family'. In these cases the family of the prisoner subsidises the costs of flying the prisoner and prison officers to the funeral. In recent years, prisoners have been able to fax their apologies for their inability to attend the funeral. This initiative has offered a new, but limited, way for expressing some of the values of sorry business.

15. Here 'too much' means 'extremely'; the anxiety is deeply felt.

16. A 'click' is a sound made with the tongue to show one agrees with what someone has just said.

Chapter 8

1. Similarly Lupton 2003 (p. 26).
2. She adds: 'Male violence must be theorized and interpreted *within* specific societies, both in order to understand it better, as well as in order to effectively organize to change it'. Author's emphasis.
3. There is a growing body of evidence that there are serious inter-generational health implications for Aboriginal and Torres Strait Islander children whose carers experienced separation from their families. See Zubrick et al. 2005. Here, some of the first empirical data has been provided describing generational effects caused by the policies of forced separation.
4. William Grayden was a Western Australian Independent Liberal Politician.
5. See Haebich 2000 (p. 430).
6. 'Waltja' is based in Alice Springs and services the central desert region of some 700,000 square kilometres. 'Waltja Tjutangku Palyapayi' comes from the Luritja language and has been translated as 'doing good work for families'.
7. Herman, also: 'The damage to the survivor's faith and sense of com-munity is particularly severe when the traumatic events themselves involve the betrayal of important relationships' (1992, p. 55).
8. See analysis of 'cultural bereavement' in Eisenbruch 1991 (p. 674).
9. Judy Atkinson identifies Aboriginal trauma differently. She distinguishes between intergenerational and transgenerational trauma: the former referring to what is passed from one generation to the next, the latter referring to what is transmitted across generations (2002, p. 180). See also Robinson 1999 (p. 22).
10. In Western Australia, Aboriginal youth were over-represented sixty-five times, largely due to a decrease in the rate and number of non-Aboriginal youth in detention (Cahill & Marshall 2002, p. 20).
11. See Emma Ogilvie 1966 (p. 219). She argues against using 'rudimen-tary understandings of gender' in explaining criminological theory, 'recognising that there are multiple masculinities'.
12. The Commission used 'subdue' to describe frontier pacification, 'protect' to describe policies intended to 'smooth the dying pillow', and 'control' to express European demands relating to Aboriginal behaviour. These all required the active co-operation and involvement of police.
13. See Emanuel Marx 1976.

14. 'Suicide varies inversely with the degree of integration of the social groups of which the individual forms a part...the more weakened the groups to which he belongs, the less he depends on them, the more he consequently depends only on himself' (Durkheim 2002, p. 167).

References

Adelson, N 2000, *'Being Alive Well': Health and the politics of Cree well-being,* University of Toronto Press, Toronto.

Ahmed, N 2003, 'Memories shared good and bad,' *The Age*, 7 June 2003.

Alroe, M 1981 *True Friends of True Aborigines: The ideology and practice of Roman Catholic missions in the Kimberley*, Dip. Anthropology, University of Sydney.

ANCARD Working Party 1997, *The National Indigenous Australians' Sexual Health Strategy 1996–97 to 1998–99,* Commonwealth Department of Health and Family Services, Canberra.

Antonovsky, A 1980, *Health, Stress, and Coping*, Jossey-Bass, San Francisco.

Armitage, A 1995, *Comparing the Policy of Aboriginal Assimilation: Australia, Canada, and New Zealand*, UBC Press, Vancouver.

Atkinson, D Bridge, C & Gray, D 1999, *Kimberley Regional Aboriginal Health Plan: Aboriginal health in the Kimberley. Current circumstances and future directions*, Kimberley Aboriginal Medical Services Council, Kimberley Health Service, ATSIC Wunan Regional Council, ATSIC Kullari Regional Council, ATSIC Malarabah Regional Council, Aboriginal Affairs Department, Commonwealth Department of Health and Aged Care, and Office of Aboriginal Health, Perth.

Atkinson, J 2002, *Trauma Trails, Recreating Song Lines: The transgenerational effects of trauma in Indigenous Australia*, Spinifex, North Melbourne.

Attwood, B 2000, 'The burden of the past in the present' in M Grattan (ed) *Reconciliation: Essays on Australian reconciliation*, Black Inc., Melbourne.

Australian Bureau of Statistics, 2001a, *Population Distribution: Aboriginal and Torres Strait Islander Australians*, Cat. No: 4705.0, APS, Canberra.

—— 2001b, *The Health and Welfare of Australia's Aboriginal and Torres Strait Islander Peoples*, Cat. No: 4704.0, APS, Canberra.

—— 2002, *Census of Population and Housing: Indigenous profile*, Cat. No: 2002.0, APS, Canberra.

—— 2005, *The Health and Welfare of Australia's Aboriginal and Torres Strait Islander Peoples*, Cat. No: 4704.0, APS, Canberra.

—— 2006, *Census of Population and Housing: Indigenous profile,* Cat. No: 2002.0, APS, Canberra.

—— 2007a, *Prisoners in Australia*, Cat. No: 4517.0, APS, Canberra.

—— 2007b, *Corrective Services*, December 2006, Cat. No: 4512.0, APS, Canberra.

Australian Football League 2004, *The AFL and Indigenous Australia*, AFL House, Docklands, Melbourne.

Australian Institute of Aboriginal and Torres Strait Islander Studies (AIATSIS) 2002, *Guidelines for Ethical Research in Indigenous Studies*, AIATSIS, Canberra.

Australian Institute of Health and Welfare 2000, *Australia's Health 2000: The seventh biennial health report of the Australian Institute of Health and Welfare*, AGPS, Canberra.

Australian Psychological Society 2003, *Guidelines for the Provision of Psychological Services for and the Conduct of Psychological Research with Aboriginal and Torres Strait Islander People of Australia*, May, Melbourne.

Beauvais, F & Oetting, ER 1999, 'Drug use, resilience, and the myth of the golden child' in M Glantz & J Johnson (eds) *Resilience and Development: Positive life adaptations*, Kluwer Academic/Plenum Publishers, New York.

Bell, D 1982, 'Women's changing role in health maintenance in a central Australian community' in J Reid (ed) *Body, Land and Spirit: Health and healing in Aboriginal community*, University of Queensland Press, St Lucia.

Beresford, Q & Omaji, P 1996, *Rites of Passage: Aboriginal youth, crime and justice*, Fremantle Arts Centre Press, South Fremantle.

Berndt, C 1962, 'Mateship or success: an assimilation dilemma', *Oceania*, vol. 33, no. 2, pp. 71–89.

Berndt, C & R 1972, 'Aborigines' in FJ Hunt (ed), *Socialisation in Australia*, Angus & Robertson, Sydney.

—— 1983 (1978), *The Aboriginal Australians: The first pioneers*, second edition, Pitman, Carlton.

Berndt, R 1972, 'The Walmadjeri and Gugadja' in MG Bicchieri (ed), *Hunters and Gatherers Today*, Holt, Rinehart & Winston, New York.

—— 1974, *Australian Aboriginal Religion*, Fascicle Four, Central Australia: Conclusion, E.J. Brill, Leiden.

Berndt, R & C 1960, *Report on Survey of the Balgo Hills Area Southern Kimberleys, Western Australia,* mimeograph, University of Western Australia.

—— 1970, 'Some points of change in Western Australia' in AR Pilling and RA Waterman (eds), *Diprotodon to Detribalization: Studies of change among Australian Aborigines*, Michigan State University Press, East Lansing.

—— 1985 (1964), *The World of the First Australians*, fourth edition (revised), Rigby, Adelaide.

Bibby, P (ed) 1997, *The Telling of Stories: A spiritual journey of Kimberley Aboriginal people*, Catholic Education Office, Broome.

Biles, D 1983, *Groote Eylandt Prisoners: A research report*, Australian Institute of Criminology, Canberra.

Biven, A (compiler) 1999, *Petrol Sniffing and Other Solvents: A community manual*, Aboriginal Drug and Alcohol Council of South Australia, Adelaide.

Blainey, G 1990, *A Game of Our Own: The origins of Australian football*, Information Australia, Melbourne.

Bleischwitz, A 1950, 'Pallottine Mission, Hall's Creek in *Annual Report of the Commissioner of Native Affairs*, year ended 30 June 1950, Department of Indigenous Affairs, Perth.

—— 1951, 'Balgo Mission — Pallottine (Roman Catholic) Order' in *Annual Report of the Commissioner of Native Affairs, year ended 30 June 1951*, Department of Indigenous Affairs, Perth.

—— 1957, *Register of inmates 1958*, ACC 993, AN 418/57, Department of Indigenous Affairs, State Records Office of Western Australia, Perth.

Bleischwitz, A & Huegel, F 1995, (compiled by W H van Veen 27 November 1995), *The Start of the Mission at Halls Creek in the Year 1934*, Pallottine archives, Perth.

Bohemia, J & McGregor, B 1995, *Nyibayarri: Kimberley tracker,* Aboriginal Studies Press, AIATSIS Canberra.

Bolger, A 1986, *Kurungal Women: Socio-economic change amongst women of the Wangkajunga community, Christmas Creek*, unpublished manuscript.

—— 1987, 'Wangkajunga women: stories from the desert', *Aboriginal History*, vol 11, no. 2, pp. 102–15.

Boss, P Edwards, S & Pitman, S (eds) 1995, *Profile of Young Australians: Facts, figures and issues*, Churchill Livingstone, Melbourne.

Bowlby, J 1952, *Maternal Care and Mental Health: A report prepared on behalf of the World Health Organization as a contribution to the United Nations programme for the welfare of homeless children*, World Health Organization, Geneva.

Brady, M 1991a, 'Petrol sniffing among Aborigines: Differing social meanings', *The International Journal of Drug Policy*, vol. 2, no. 4, pp. 28–31.

—— 1991b, *The Health of Young Aborigines*, Australian Institute of Aboriginal and Torres Strait Islander Studies, AIATSIS, Canberra.

—— 1991c, 'Drug and alcohol use among Aboriginal people' in J Reid & P Trompf (eds), *The Health of Aboriginal Australia*, Harcourt Brace Jovanovich, Sydney.

—— 1992, *Heavy Metal*, Aboriginal Studies Press, AIATSIS Canberra.

Brady, M & Morice, R 1982, 'Defiance or despair? Petrol-sniffing in an Aboriginal community' in J Reid (ed), *Body, Land and Spirit*, University of Queensland Press, St Lucia.

Bray, FI 1945, *The Annual Report of the Commissioner of Native Affairs, year ended 30 June 1945*, Department of Indigenous Affairs, Perth.

Briscoe, G 2003, *Counting, Health and Identity: A history of Aboriginal health and demography in Western Australia and Queensland 1900–1940*, Aboriginal Studies Press, AIATSIS, Canberra.

Brown, A 2004, *Building on the Strengths: A review of male health in the Anangu-Pitjantjatjara lands*, Report to Nganampa Health Council, Alice Springs.

Buchanan, G 1997 (1933), *Packhorse and Waterhole: With the first overlanders to the Kimberleys*, Hesperian Press, Victoria Park.

Burbank, V 1988, *Aboriginal Adolescence: Maidenhood in an Australian community*, Rutgers University Press, New Brunswick.

Burns, C Currie, B Clough, A & Wuridjal, R 1995, 'Evaluation of strategies used by a remote Aboriginal community to eliminate petrol sniffing', *The Medical Journal of Australia*, vol. 63, no. 2, pp. 82–6.

Byrne, F 1989, *A Hard Road: Brother Frank Nissl, 1888–1980, a life of service to the Aborigines of the Kimberleys*, Tara House, Nedlands.

Cahill, L & Marshall, P 2002, *Statistics on Juvenile Detention in Australia: 1981–2001*, Technical and Background Paper Series, No. 1, Australian Institute of Criminology, Canberra.

Cairney, S Maruff, P Burns, C & Currie, B 2002, 'The neurobehavioural consequences of petrol (gasoline) sniffing', *Neuroscience and Biobehavioral Reviews*, vol. 26, issue 1, pp. 81–9.

Cane, S 1989, *Return to the Desert*, National Heritage Studies, Hall.

Carcach, C Grant, A & Conroy, R 1999, *Australian Corrections: The imprisonment of Indigenous people*, Trends and Issues in Crime and Criminal Justice, no. 137, Australian Institute of Criminology, Canberra.

Carnegie, DW 1989 (1898), *Spinifex and Sand: A narrative of five years' pioneering and exploration in Western Australia*, Hesperian Press, Victoria Park.

Cawte, J 1974, *Medicine Is the Law: Studies in psychiatric anthropology of Australian tribal societies*, University Press of Hawaii, Honolulu.

—— 1996, *Healers of Arnhem Land*, University of New South Wales Press, Sydney.

Chappell, D & Wilson, B (eds) 2000, *Crime and the Criminal Justice System in Australia: 2000 and beyond*, Butterworths, Sydney.

Chivell, W 2002. *Finding of Inquest*, no. 11/2002, SA State Coroner, Adelaide.

Choo, C 2001, *Mission Girls: Aboriginal women on Catholic missions in the Kimberley, Western Australia, 1900–1950*, University of Western Australia Press, Crawley.

Clement, C 1988, *Pre-settlement Intrusion into the East Kimberley*, East Kimberley Impact Assessment Project, Working Paper no. 24, Centre for Resource and Environmental Studies, ANU, Canberra.

—— 1989, *Historical Notes Relevant to Impact Stories of the East Kimberley*, East Kimberley Impact Assessment Project, Working Paper no. 29, Centre for Resource and Environmental Studies, ANU, Canberra.

Clontarf Football Academy 2002a, *From Little Things Big Things Grow: Statement of purpose*. Clontarf Football Academy, Perth.

—— 2002b *From Little Things Big Things Grow: General report*, Clontarf Football Academy, Perth.

Colmar B 2002, WA *Kimberley Regional Justice Project Market Research*, Colmar Brunton Social Research, West Perth.

Connell, RW 2000, *The Men and the Boys*, Allen & Unwin, St Leonards.

Crugnale, J (ed) 1995, *Footprints Across Our Land: Short stories by senior Western Desert women*, Magabala Books, Broome.

Cunneen, C 2001, 'Assessing the Outcomes of the Royal Commission into Aboriginal deaths in custody', *Health Sociology Review*, vol. 10, no. 2, pp. 53–64.

Cunneen, C & McDonald, D 1997, *Keeping Aboriginal and Torres Strait Islander People out of Custody: An evaluation of the implementation of the recommendations of the Royal Commission in Aboriginal Deaths in Custody*, Office of Public Affairs, ATSIC, Canberra.

d'Abbs, P & MacLean, S 2000, *Petrol Sniffing in Aboriginal Communities: A review of interventions*, Cooperative Research Centre for Aboriginal and Tropical Health, Darwin.

Darkie, M 2000, 'This is my life' in M Grattan (ed) *Reconciliation: Essays on Australian reconciliation*, Black Inc., Melbourne.

Dawson, J 1981 (1881), *Australian Aborigines: The languages and customs of several tribes of Aborigines in the western district of Victoria, Australia*, Australian Institute of Aboriginal Studies, Canberra.

dé Ishtar, Z 2005, *Holding Yawulyu: White culture and black women's law*, Spinifex Press, North Melbourne.

de Largy Healy, J 2001, 'Kinship, travel and migration: Aboriginal country football networks in western Victoria', paper presented at the Australian Anthropological Society Annual Conference, La Trobe University, Melbourne.

Deleuze, G 1995 (1986), (translated and edited by Sean Hand), *Foucault*, University of Minneapolis Press, Minneapolis.

Department of Justice 2003, *Kimberley Regional Justice Report*, Department of Justice, Government of Western Australia, Perth.

Department of Rural Health 2001, *Evaluation of the Healthy Lifestyles Program of the Rumbalara Football Netball Club*, Department of Rural Health, The University of Melbourne, Shepparton.

de Vries, MW 1996, 'Trauma in cultural perspective' in BA van der Kolk, AC McFarlane & L Weisaeth (eds), *Traumatic Stress: The effects of overwhelming experience on mind, body, and society*, The Guilford Press, New York.

Dodson, PL 1991, *Regional Report of Inquiry into Underlying Issues in Western Australia: Royal Commission into Aboriginal Deaths in Custody*, AGPS, Canberra.

DodsonLane 2002, *Kutjungka Region Health Service Delivery*, Dodson Lane, Broome.

Douglas, M 1966, *Purity and Danger: An analysis of the concepts of pollution and taboo*, Ark Paperbacks, London.

Dudgeon, P Garvey, D & Pickett, H 2000, *Working with Indigenous Australians: A handbook for psychologists*, Curtin Research Centre, Perth.

Dudgeon, P & Pickett, H 2000, 'Psychology and reconciliation: Australian perspectives', *Australian Psychologist*, vol. 35, no. 2, pp. 82–7.

Durack, M 1960, *Missions in a Bypassed Land*, Wirrimanu: Kutjungka Catholic Parish archives, unpublished.

—— 1969, *The Rock and the Sand*, Constable, London.

Eckersley, R 1993, 'Failing a generation: the impact of culture on the health and well-being of youth', *Journal of Paediatrics and Child Health*, vol. 29, no. 1, S16–19.

Eisenbruch, M 1991, 'From post-traumatic stress disorder to cultural bereavement: diagnosis of southeast Asian refugees', *Social Science and Medicine*, vol. 33, no. 6, pp. 673–80.

Elkin, AP 1943, *The Australian Aborigines*, second edition, Angus & Robertson, Sydney.

—— 1980 (1945), *Aboriginal Men of High Degree*, second edition, University of Queensland Press, St Lucia.

Evans, N & Wilkins, D 2001, 'The complete person: networking the physical and the social' in J Simpson, D Nash, M Laughren, P Austin & B Alpher (eds), *Forty Years On: Ken Hale and Australian languages*. Pacific Linguistics, Research School of Pacific and Asian Studies, Australian National University, Canberra.

Finalyson, HH 1955 (first published 1935) *The Red Centre: Man and beast in the heart of Australia*, new edition, Angus & Robertson, Sydney.

Finlayson, J 1989, 'Welfare incomes and Aboriginal gender relations' in JC Altman (ed), *Emergent Inequalities in Aboriginal Australia*, Oceania Monograph, no. 38, pp. 95–117.

Finn, P 1963, 'The distant mission of Father Macguire [sic], *The West Australian*, 14 January 1963.

Finnane, M 1997, *Punishment in Australian Society*, Oxford University Press, Melbourne.

Flanagan, M 1988, 'Black magic: different notions of time and space' in R Fitzgerald & K Spillman (eds), *The Greatest Game*, William Heinemann, Richmond.

Folds, R 1987, *Whitefella School*, Allen & Unwin, St Leonards.

—— 2001, *Crossed Purposes: The Pintupi and Australia's Indigenous policy*, UNSW Press, Sydney.

Gill, A 1977, 'Aborigines, settlers and police in the Kimberleys 1887–1905', *Studies in Western Australian History*, no. 1, pp. 1–28.

Gill, M 1967, 'Get off the dole and work: missionary's advice to Aborigines', *The Kalgoorlie Miner,* 22 July 1967.

Glynn, E (writer/director) 2001, *Ngangka<u>r</u>i,* video recording, Ronin Films, Pitjantjatjara Yankunytjatjara Media Production & Australian Film Commission, Alice Springs.

Godwell, D 2000, 'Playing the game: is sport as good for race relations as we'd like to think?', *Australian Aboriginal Studies,* nos. 1 & 2, pp. 12–19.

Gordon, S Hallahan, K & Henry, D 2002, *Putting the Picture Together: Inquiry into Response by Government Agencies to Complaints of Family Violence and Child Abuse in Aboriginal Communities,* Department of Premier and Cabinet, Perth.

Graham, T Haslem, D & Hesp, R (producers and directors) 2003, *Lonely Boy Richard,* video recording, Film Australia, Lindfield.

Grayden, W 1957, *Adam and Atoms,* Frank Daniels, Perth.

Grow, R 1998, 'From gum trees to goalposts, 1858–1876' in R Hess & B Stewart (eds), *More than a Game: An unauthorised history of Australian rules football,* Melbourne University Press, Carlton South.

Guyula, T 1998, 'The Gapuwiyak men's clinic', *Aboriginal and Islander Health Worker Journal,* vol. 22, no. 2, pp. 2–3.

Gye, C 1962, *The Cockney and the Crocodile,* Faber and Faber, London.

Haebich, A 2000, *Broken Circles: Fragmenting Indigenous families 1800–2000,* Fremantle Arts Centre Press, Fremantle.

Hallinan, CJ Bruce, T & Coram, S 1999, 'Up front and beyond the centre line: Australian Aborigines in elite Australian rules football', *International Review for the Sociology of Sport,* vol. 34, no. 4, pp. 369–83.

Hamilton, A 1981, *Nature and Nurture: Aboriginal child-rearing in north-central Arnhem Land,* Australian Institute of Aboriginal Studies, Canberra.

Hansen, KC & LE, 1979, *Pintupi/Luritja Kinship,* Institute for Aboriginal Development, Alice Springs.

Harris, B 1989, *The Proud Champions: Australia's Aboriginal sporting heroes,* Little Hills Press, Crows Nest.

Harris, M 1965, 'Tent town at Balgo mission', *The West Australian,* 13 May 1965, p. 5.

Herman, JL 1992, *Trauma and Recovery,* Pandora, London.

Hill, E 1963 (1940), *The Great Australian Loneliness,* Angus & Robertson, Melbourne.

Hillman, SD Silburn, SP Zubrick, SP & Nguyen, H 2000, *Suicide in Western Australia 1986–1997*, Youth Suicide Advisory Committee, Perth.

Howard, A and Luby, S (producers) 1999, *Desert Healing: A journey towards reconciliation*, video recording, Fraynework Multimedia, Melbourne.

Huffer, V 1980, *The Sweetness of the Fig: Aboriginal women in transition*, New South Wales University Press, Sydney.

Hunter, E 1988, 'On gordian knots and nooses: Aboriginal suicide in the Kimberley', *Australian and New Zealand Journal of Psychiatry*, vol. 22, pp. 264–71.

—— 1990, 'A question of power: contemporary self-mutilation among Aborigines in the Kimberley', *Australian Journal of Social Issues*, vol. 25, no. 4, pp. 261–78.

—— 1993, *Aboriginal Health and History*, Cambridge University Press, Cambridge.

—— 1998 'Considering trauma in an Indigenous context', *Aboriginal and Islander Health Worker Journal*, vol. 22, no. 5, pp. 9–18.

—— 2001, 'An ounce of prevention…: reconsidering prevention in Indigenous mental health', paper presented at The Power of Knowledge, the Resonance of Tradition — Indigenous Studies Conference, AIATSIS and ANU, Canberra.

Hunter, E Reser, J Baird, M & Reser, P 1999, *An Analysis of Suicide in Indigenous Communities of North Queensland: The historical, cultural and symbolic landscape*, Commonwealth Department of Health and Aged Care, Canberra.

Institute for Aboriginal Development 2002, *Central Australian Aboriginal Languages — Current Distribution*, Institute for Aboriginal Development, Alice Springs.

James, M 2004, 'Petrol sniffing on Cape York peninsula: an intervention strategy', paper presented at the Fifteenth International Conference on the Reduction of Drug Related Harm, Melbourne.

Jobst, J 2000, *My Roots, the War and My Vocation*, Hesperian Press, Perth.

Johnson, Inspector 1956, *Pastoral Inspector's Report on Billiluna*, file no. 1772/20, 1 August 1956, Department of Lands and Surveys, Perth.

Johnston, E 1991, *National Report: Royal Commission into Aboriginal Deaths in Custody*, AGPS, Canberra.

Johnston, LC 1965, 'Struggle to pay the debts', *The West Australian*, 9 November 1965.

Jordan, E 1983, *Towards an Alternative Model for Aboriginal Schooling: A case study of a tradition-oriented Aboriginal community*, Macquarie University: School of Education, Sydney.

Kearney, J 1974, 'Our Aboriginal apostolate' in P Willis (compiler), *Kimberley Journal, a Source Book*, 6 May 1974.

Keeffe, K 1992, *From the Centre to the City: Aboriginal education, culture and power*, Aboriginal Studies Press, AIATSIS, Canberra.

Kelleher, MJ & Chambers, D 2003, 'Cross-cultural variation in child and adolescent suicide' in RA King & A Apter (eds), *Suicide in Children and Adolescents*, Cambridge University Press, Cambridge.

Kimberley Public Health Unit n.d. *Report 2000–2001*, Department of Health, Derby.

Kirmayer, L Simpson, C & Cargo, M 2003, 'Healing traditions: culture, community and mental health promotion with Canadian Aboriginal peoples', *Australasian Psychiatry* vol. 11, S15–23.

Kleinman, A 1995, *Writing at the Margin: Discourse between anthropology and medicine*, University of California Press, Berkeley.

Kolig, E 1981, *The Silent Revolution: The effects of modernization on Australian Aboriginal religion*, Institute for the Study of Human Issues, Philadelphia.

Koning, R 1997, *Kukatja Kinship: An introduction*. Kutjungka Catholic Parish, Wirrimanu.

Koning, R, McCoy, B & Church Leaders 2000, *Sorry Business and Funerals*, Kutjungka Catholic Parish, Wirrimanu.

Langton, M et al. 1991, *Too Much Sorry Business: The report of the Aboriginal Issues Unit of the Northern Territory*, Appendix D, Vol. 5, Royal Commission into Aboriginal Deaths in Custody, Australian Government Publishing Service, Canberra, pp. 275–512.

Lincoln, R & Wilson P 2000, 'Aboriginal criminal justice: background and foreground' in D Chappell & P Wilson (eds), *Crime and the Criminal Justice System in Australia: 2000 and beyond*, Butterworths, Sydney.

Long, J 1989, 'Leaving the desert: actors and sufferers in the Aboriginal exodus from the Western Desert', *Aboriginal History*, vol. 13, nos. 1–2, pp. 9–43.

Lorber, J 1997, *Gender and the Social Construction of Illness*, Sage, Thousand Oaks.

Lowe, H & Spry F 1992, *Living Male: Journeys of Aboriginal and Torres Strait Islander males towards better health and well-being*, Northern Territory Male Health Reference Committee, Darwin.

Lulu, F 1999, 'Payalatju Maparnpa — when we started', *Yanginikarrina, Yangingka, Kutjungka, Kayanta, Working Together,* Newsletter of Palyalatju Maparnpa Health and Mercy Community Health, vol. 1, no. 1, p. 1.

Lupton, D 2003, *Medicine as Culture: Illness, disease and the body in western societies,* Sage, London.

McCoy, B 2006, 'Healers, clinics and Aboriginal people: whose health and who benefits?', *Health Issues,* no. 86, pp. 13–16.

—— 2007a, '"If we come together our health will be happy": Aboriginal men seeking ways to better health', *Australian Aboriginal Studies,* no. 2, pp. 75–85.

—— 2007b, 'Suicide and desert men: the power and protection of *kanyirninpa* (holding)', *Australasian Psychiatry,* vol. 15, supplement, pp. 63–7.

—— 2007c, 'They Weren't Separated': Missions, Dormitories and Generational Health, *Health and History,* Special Issue: Aboriginal Health and History, vol. 9, no. 2, pp. 48–69.

McCulloch, S 1999, *Contemporary Aboriginal Art,* Allen & Unwin, St Leonards.

McGrath, A 1987, *'Born in the Cattle': Aborigines in cattle country,* Allen & Unwin, Sydney.

McGregor, W 1992, *Handbook of Kimberley Languages, volume 2: word lists,* Australian Institute of Aboriginal and Torres Strait Studies, Canberra.

—— 1999, 'Kukatja ethno-physiology and medicine, a review article', *Anthropos,* no. 94, pp. 224–8.

McGuire, Fr J 1959, 'What happened at Balgo', *The Record,* Thursday 31 December 1959, p. 9.

Macquarie dictionary: Australia's National Dictionary 2001, revised third edition, The Macquarie Library: Macquarie University, Sydney.

Malins, P Fitzgerald, JL & Threadgold, T 2006, 'Spatial "Folds": the entwining of bodies, risks and city spaces for women injecting drug users in Melbourne's Central Business District', *Gender, Place and Culture,* vol. 13, issue 5, pp. 509–27.

Marcus, A 1990, *Governing Savages,* Allen & Unwin, Sydney.

Martin DF 1993, *Autonomy and Relatedness: An ethnography of Wik people of Aurukun, western Cape York peninsula,* unpublished PhD dissertation, Australian National University, Canberra.

Marx, E 1976, *The Social Context of Violent Behaviour: A social anthropological study in an Israeli immigrant town*, Routledge & Kegan Paul, London.

Maruff, P Burns, CB Currie, BJ & Currie, J 1998, 'Neurological and cognitive abnormalities associated with chronic petrol sniffing', *Brain*, no. 121, pp. 1903–17.

Mauss M 1979 (1950), *Sociology and Psychology: Essays*, translated by B Brewster, Routledge & Kegan Paul, London.

Meggitt, MJ 1984, 'Initiation among the Walbiri' in M Charlesworth, H Morphy, D Bell & K Maddock (eds), *Religion in Aboriginal Australia, an anthology*, University of Queensland Press, St Lucia.

—— 1986 (1962), *Desert People*, Angus & Robertson, North Ryde.

Menon, A, Coppola A, Knox J, Ebringer, A, Kaldor, J & Waddell, R 2001, *Identifying the Gaps in the Management of Sexually Transmitted Infections in Indigenous Communities in Central Australia*, Tristate STD/HIV Project, Alice Springs.

Mercy Community Health Service, October 1998–March 1999, *Service Report*, MCHS, Wirrimanu.

—— April 1999–September 1999, *Service Report*, MCHS, Wirrimanu.

Miller, K Robertson, D & Silburn, SR (in press 2008), *Suicide in Western Australia 1986–2005*, Ministerial Council for Suicide Prevention, Telethon Institute for Child Health Research and Centre for Child Health Research and Curtin University of Technology, Perth.

Mirli Mirli Wangkalaltukurlu, 2001, Kutjungka Catholic Parish Newsletter 9 (29), August 2001, Wirrimanu.

Mohanty, CT 1995 'Under western eyes: feminist scholarship and colonial discourses' in B Ashcroft, G Griffiths & H Tiffin (eds), *The Post-colonial Studies Reader*, Routledge, London.

Morice, R, Swift, H & Brady, M 1981, *Petrol Sniffing among Aboriginal Australians: A resource manual, Western Desert project*, Australian Foundation on Alcoholism and Drug Dependence, Canberra.

Morris, D 1994, *The Human Animal*, BBC Books, London.

Morrison, RB & Wilson, CR (eds) 1986, *Native Peoples: The Canadian experience*, Oxford University Press, Toronto.

Mosey, A 1999–2000, *Dry Spirit: Petrol sniffing interventions in the Kutjungka region, W.A.*, Report for Mercy Community Health Service, Wirrimanu.

Mulan Storytellers [Chungulla, B, Doonday, B, Robertson, I, Billiluna, B, Yagan, M, Tjemma, F, Tax, N, Clancy, E] 1999, *Minya Manpangu Marnu Yapajangka: Stories from our childhood*, translated and compiled by Eirlys Richards, Kimberley Language Resource Centre, Halls Creek.

Myers, FR 1980, 'A broken code: Pintupi political theory and temporary social life', *Mankind*, vol. 12, no. 4, pp. 311–26.

—— 1981, 'What is the business of the Balgo business', paper, Symposium on Contemporary Aboriginal Religious Movements, Australian Institute of Aboriginal Studies, Canberra.

—— 1982, 'Ideology and experience: the cultural basis of politics in Pintupi life' in M Howard (ed), *Aboriginal Power in Australian Society*, University of Queensland Press, St Lucia.

—— 1986, *Pintupi Country, Pintupi Self: Sentiment, place and politics among Western Desert Aborigines*, Smithsonian Institution Press, Washington, and Aboriginal Studies Press, AIATSIS, Canberra.

—— 1998, 'Burning the truck and holding the country: property, time, and the negotiation identity among Pintupi Aborigines' in T Ingold, D Riches & J Woodburn (eds), *Hunters and Gatherers, volume 2, property, power and ideology*, Berg Publishers, New York.

Nailon, B 2000, *Nothing is Wasted in the Household of God: Vincent Pallotti's vision in Australia 1901–2001*, Spectrum, Richmond.

National Health and Medical Research Council 2003, *Values and Ethics: Guidelines for ethical conduct in Aboriginal and Torres Strait Islander health research*, Commonwealth of Australia, Canberra.

National Inquiry into the Separation of Aboriginal and Torres Strait Islander Children from their Families 1997, *Bringing Them Home: Report of the National Inquiry into the Separation of Aboriginal and Torres Strait Islander Children from their Families*, Human Rights and Equal Opportunity Commission, Sydney.

Neville, A O 1935a, Letter to the Honorary Minister Mr Kitson, 1 April 1935, ACC 933, AN 10/35, Department of Indigenous Affairs, State Records Office of Western Australia, Perth.

—— 1935b, Letter to the Right Reverend O Raible, vicar apostolic of the Kimberleys, 6 August 1935, ACC 993, AN 10/35, Department of Indigenous Affairs, State Records Office of Western Australia, Perth.

Ngaanyatjarra Pitjantjatjara Yankunytjatjara Women's Council Aboriginal Corporation 2003, *Ngangkari Work — Anangu Way: Traditional healers of central Australia*, Ngaanyatjarra Pitjantjatjara Yankunytjatjara Women's Council Aboriginal Corporation, Alice Springs.

Nicholls, C 2001, 'Yupinya Nampitjin', *Australian Art Collector* no. 15, pp. 100–3.

Nissl, F 1976, *The Start of a Mission at Halls Creek in the Year 1934*, (compiled by WH van Veen and translated by Franz Hugel), 20 April 1976, Pallottine archives, Perth.

North Australia Nutrition Group 2003, *FoodNorth: Food for health in north Australia*, Population Health, Perth.

Nurcome, B 1974, 'Petrol inhalation in Arnhem Land' in BS Hetzel, M Dobbin, L Lippman & E Eggleston (eds), *Better Health for Aborigines?*, University of Queensland, St Lucia.

O'Brien, Commissioner of Police 1959, Letter to Commissioner of Native Welfare, 21 July 1959, ACC 1733, AN 696/45, Department of Indigenous Affairs: State Records Office of Western Australia, Perth.

O'Donnell, M 1999, *Final Report and Transition Plan for MCHS*, Mercy Community Health Service Framework for Organisational Transition, Wirrimanu (Balgo).

O'Donnell, M & Lock, B 1995, *Report July 1993 to June 1995, Mercy Balgo Health Service*, Mercy Balgo Health Service, Wirrimanu (Balgo).

O'Donoghue, L 2000, 'A journey of healing or a road to nowhere?' in M Grattan (ed), *Reconciliation: Essays on Australian reconciliation*, Black Inc., Melbourne.

Ogilvie, E 1996, 'Masculine obsession: an examination of criminology, criminality and gender', *The Australian and New Zealand Journal of Criminology*, no. 29, pp. 205–26.

Ogilvie, E & Van Zyl, A 2001, *Young Indigenous Males, Custody and the Rites of Passage*, Trends and Issues in Crime and Criminal Justice, no. 204, Australian Institute of Criminology, Canberra.

Palmer, K 1983, 'Owners and managers: ritual cooperation and mutual dependence in the maintenance of rights to land', *Mankind*, vol. 13, no. 6, 517–26.

Pearson, N 1995, 'Aboriginal health: the way forward', *Arena Magazine*, June/July, pp. 20–4.

Peile, AR n.d., *The Botanical Terms and Concepts of an Australian Desert Tribe*, Kutjungka Catholic Parish archives, Wirrimanu.

—— 1981, 'Towards a proper and understanding health-care delivery to the Aborigines, *Nelen Yubu*, no. 10, pp. 28–9.

—— 1997, P Bindon (ed), *Body and Soul: An Aboriginal view*, Hesperian Press, Victoria Park.

Peter, S & Lofts, P (eds) 1997, *Yarrtji: Six women's stories from the Great Sandy Desert*, Aboriginal Studies Press, Canberra.

Petri, H 1968, 'Movements in the Western Desert', paper presented at The VIII International Congress of Anthropological and Ethnological Sciences, Tokyo & Kyoto.

Poirier, S 2005, *A World of Relationships: Itineraries, dreams and events in the Australian Western Desert*, University of Toronto Press, Toronto.

Potter, C 2000, '*Rumba on the Rise': The story of the Rumbalara Football and Netball Club*, VicHealth, Melbourne.

Pritchard, C 1995, *Suicide — The Ultimate Rejection? A psycho-social study*, Open University Press, Buckingham.

Preuss, K & Brown J Napanangka 2006, 'Stopping petrol sniffing in remote Aboriginal Australia: key elements of the Mt Theo program', *Drug and Alcohol Review*, vol. 25, issue 3, pp. 189–93.

Probyn, E 1991, 'This body which is not one: speaking an embodied self', *Hypatia*, vol. 6, no. 3, pp. 111–24.

Raible, O 1935, Re medical treatment of Aborigines, letter to Minister for Aborigines, 7 January 1935, ACC 993, AN 10/35, Department of Indigenous Affairs, State Records Office of Western Australia, Perth.

Randal, B 2003, *Songman: The story of an Aboriginal elder of Uluru*, ABC Books: Sydney.

Rees, C & L 1953, *Spinnifex Walkabout: Hitch-hiking in remote north Australia*, Australasian Publishing Company, Sydney.

Reid, J (ed) 1982, *Body, Land and Spirit: Health and healing in Aboriginal society*, University of Queensland Press, St Lucia.

—— 1983, *Sorcerers and Healing Spirits*, Pergamon Press, Rushcutters Bay.

Reynolds, H 1987, *Frontier*, Allen & Unwin, Sydney.

Ritson, M 2000, *Health Care in Halls Creek 2000: Third World health status, Second World health service, in a First World country*, self-published, Halls Creek.

Robertson, B 1999, *The Aboriginal and Torres Strait Islander Women's Task Force on Violence Report*, Department of Aboriginal and Torres Strait Islander Policy and Development, Brisbane.

Robinson, G 1990, 'Separation, retaliation and suicide: mourning and the conflicts of young Tiwi men, *Oceania*, vol. 60, no. 3, pp. 161–78.

—— 1995, 'Violence, social differentiation and the self', *Oceania*, vol. 65, no. 4, pp. 323–46.

Roper, S & and Shaw, G 1996, '*Moving On': A Report on Petrol Sniffing and the Introduction of AVGAS on the Anangu Pitjantjatjara lands*, Nganampa Health Council, Alice Springs.

Ross, H 1989, *Community Social Impact Assessment: A cumulative study in the Turkey Creek area, Western Australia*, East Kimberley Impact Assessment Project, Working Paper no. 27, ANU, Centre for Resource and Environmental Studies, Canberra.

Ross, H (ed) and Bray, E (translator) 1989, *Impact Stories of the East Kimberley*, East Kimberley Impact Assessment Project, Working Paper no. 28, ANU, Centre for Resource and Environmental Studies, Canberra.

Rowse, T 1998, *White Flour, White Power*, Cambridge University Press, Cambridge.

Roy, P (director/producer) 2001, *Kimberley Cops*, episode 2: 'End of the Road', video recording, ABC, Sydney.

Saltonstall, R 1993, 'Healthy bodies, social bodies: men's and women's concepts and practices of health in everyday life', *Social Science and Medicine*, vol. 16, no. 1, pp. 7–14.

Schungel, J 1995, *The Start of the Mission at Halls Creek in the Year 1934* (compiled by WH van Veen), 8 August 1995, Pallottine archives, Perth.

Senate Community Affairs References Committee 2006, *Beyond Petrol Sniffing: Renewing hope for Indigenous communities*, Senate Community Affairs References Committee Secretariat, Parliament House, Canberra.

Senior, K 2003, *A Gudbala Laif? Health and Wellbeing in a Remote Aboriginal Community: what are the problems and where lies responsibility?*, unpublished PhD dissertation, Australian National University, Canberra.

Shalev, A 1996, 'Stress versus traumatic stress: from acute homeostatic reactions to chronic psychopathology' in B van der Kolk, A McFarlane & L Weisaeth (eds), *Traumatic Stress: The Effects of overwhelming experience on mind, body, and society*, The Guilford Press, New York.

Siegel, N 2003, 'The interaction between petrol sniffers and bush court in Aboriginal communities', paper presented at the Inhalant Use and Disorder Conference, Townsville, 7–8 July 2003.

Sim, J 1994, 'Tougher than the rest? Men in prison' in T Newburn & E Stanko (eds), *Just Boys Doing Business? Men, Masculinities and Crime*, Routledge, London.

Spry, F & Male Health Policy Unit (Territory Health Services) 1999, *Growing up as an Indigenous Male*, report from the 1st National Indigenous Male Health Convention, 4–5 October 1999, Ross River, Central Australia.

Stojanovski, A 1999, 'Mt Theo Story 1999: Tribal elders working with petrol sniffers, Yuendumu', paper presented at the Australasian Conference on Drugs Strategy, Adelaide, 27–29 April 1999.

Swan, P & Raphael, B 1995, *'Ways Forward': National Consultancy Report on Aboriginal and Torres Strait Islander Mental Health*, AGPS, Canberra.

Tatz, C 1987, *Aborigines in Sports*, Flinders University, Bedford Park.

—— 1995, *Obstacle Race*, University of New South Wales, Sydney.

—— 2001, *Aboriginal Suicide is Different: A portrait of life and self-destruction,* Aboriginal Studies Press, AIATSIS Canberra.

Tatz, C & Tatz, P 2000, *Black Gold*, Aboriginal Studies Press, AIATSIS Canberra.

Teather, E (ed) 1999, *Embodied Geographies: Spaces, bodies and rites of passage*, Routledge, London.

Thurston, R 1996, 'Are you sitting comfortably? Men's storytelling, masculinities, prison culture and violence' in M Mac an Ghaill (ed), *Understanding Masculinities: Social relations and cultural arenas*, Open University Press, Buckingham.

Tomsen, S 1996, 'Ruling men? Some comments on masculinity and juvenile justice, *The Australian and New Zealand Journal of Criminology*, no. 29, pp. 191–4.

Tonkinson, M 1982, 'The mabarn and the hospital: the selection of treatment in a remote Aboriginal community' in J Reid (ed), *Body, Land and Spirit: Health and healing in Aboriginal society,* University of Queensland Press, St Lucia.

Tonkinson, R 1978, *The Mardudjara Aborigines: Living the dream in Australia's desert,* Holt, Rinehart and Winston, New York.

Trudgen, R 2000, *Why Warriors Lie Down and Die*, Aboriginal Resource and Development Services, Darwin.

Turner, V 1967, *The Forest of Symbols: Aspects of Ndembu ritual*, Cornell University Press, Ithaca.

—— 1969, *The Ritual Process*, Routledge & Kegan Paul, London.

Valiquette, H 1993, *A Basic Kukatja to English Dictionary*, Luurnpa Catholic School, Wirrimanu.

—— 1994, 'The Kukatja dictionary on disk', *Australian Aboriginal Studies* no. 1, pp. 27–35; AIATSIS, Canberra.

van Gennep, A 1977 (1960), *The Rites of Passage* (translated by M Vizedom & G Caffee), Routledge & Kegan Paul, London.

VicHealth Koori Health Research and Community Development Unit 2000, *We Don't Like Research: But in Koori hands it could make a difference*, VicHealth Koori Health Research and Community Development Unit, Centre for the Study of Health and Society, University of Melbourne, Melbourne.

—— 2001, *Research: Understanding Ethics*, VicHealth Koori Health Research and Community Development Unit, Centre for the Study of Health and Society, University of Melbourne, Melbourne.

Wakerman, J, Tregenza, J & Warchivker, I 1999, *Review of Health Services in the Kutjungka Region of Western Australia*, Centre for Remote Health and Menzies School of Health Research, Alice Springs.

Walmajarri Storytellers 2001, *Out of the Desert: Stories from the Walmajarri exodus*, edited by E Richards, J Hudson and P Lowe, Magabala Books, Broome.

Walytja Tjutangku Palyapayi Aboriginal Corporation 2001, *Pipirri Wiimaku, 'for the little kids': Innovative child care report 2000–2001*, Walytja Tjutangku Palyapayi Aboriginal Corporation, Alice Springs.

Warlayirti Artists 2001, *Eubena Nampitjin*, Warlayirti Artists, Wirrimanu.

Warrki Jarrinjaku Aboriginal Child Rearing Strategy Project Team 2002, *Warrki Jarrinjaku Jintangkamanu Purananjaku, 'Working Together Everyone and Listening': Aboriginal child rearing and associated research. A review of the literatur*e, The Commonwealth Department of Family and Community Services, Canberra.

Watson, C 2003, *Piercing the Ground*, Fremantle Arts Centre Press, Fremantle.

Wenitong, M 2002, *Indigenous Male Health: A report for Indigenous males, their families and communities, and those committed to improving Indigenous male health*, Office of Aboriginal and Torres Strait Islander Health, Commonwealth Department of Health and Ageing, Canberra.

Werner, E & Smith, R 1992, *Overcoming the Odds: High risk children from birth to adulthood*, Cornell University Press, Ithaca.

Williams, S & Bendelow G 1998, *The Lived Body: Sociological themes, embodied issues*, Routledge, London.

Willey, K 1971, *Boss Drover*, Rigby, Adelaide.

Willis, J 1997, *Romance, Ritual and Risk: Pitjantjatjara masculinity in the era of AIDS*, unpublished PhD dissertation (restricted access), University of Queensland, Brisbane.

Wiminydji and Peile, AR 1978, 'A desert Aborigine's view of health and nutrition', *Journal of Anthropological Research,* vol. 34, no. 4, pp. 497–523.

Working Party of Aboriginal and Torres Strait Islander Male Health & Well Being Reference Committee 2004, *A National Framework for Improving the Health and Wellbeing of Aboriginal and Torres Strait Islander Males*, Office for Aboriginal and Torres Strait Islander Health, Department of Health and Ageing, Canberra.

Worms, EA 1960, 'The changing ways of our Aborigines', *Catholic Weekly*, 16 June 1960.

—— 1970, 'Observations on the mission field of the Pallottine fathers in north-west Australia' in AR Pilling & RA Waterman (eds), *Diprotodon to Detribalization: Studies of change among Australian Aborigines*, Michigan State University Press, East Lansing.

Young, TK 1994, *The Health of Native Americans: Toward a biocultural epidemiology*, Oxford University Press, New York.

Zubrick, SR et al. 2005, *The Western Australian Aboriginal Child Health Survey: Forced Separation from Natural Family, Forced Relocation from Traditional Country or Homeland, and Social and Emotional Wellbeing of Aboriginal Children and Young People: Additional Notes*, Curtin University of Technology and Telethon Institute for Child Health Research, Perth.

Zucker, M 2005, *From Patrons to Partners and the Separated Children of the Kimberley: A history of the Catholic church in the Kimberley, WA*, second edition, University of Notre Dame Australia Press, Fremantle.

Index

Page references in *italics* refer to illustrations. Page references followed by *n* refer to notes, which are indexed only when not directly referred to from the text.